May you continue to rise
to this great calling!

Much love

Lynda

Psalm 1: 1-3.

Presented to:

From

Lyndi

Date

Feb 28 2015

IN HIS PRESENCE

Day by Day

LYNDIE McCAULEY

LYNDIE McCAULEY MINISTRIES

IN HIS PRESENCE *Day by Day*

Copyright © 2014 by Lyndie McCauley

www.lyndiemccauleyministries.org

Published by Spirit Led Publishing
P.O. Box 131034, Bryanston, 2021
Jhb, South Africa

spiritledpublications@gmail.com

First Edition © 1999 published by Christian Art Publishers

© All rights reserved. No part of this book may be reproduced in any form without permission in writing from the publisher, except in the case of brief quotations in critical articles or reviews.

Acknowledgement

A special "Thank you" to my friend Sue Rosenrode, who helped me with the re-editing, and Kudzi Chinhara for the design and layout of *Day by Day*

Dedication

I dedicate each treasured moment of *Day by Day* to the most precious woman in my life, my mother Freda Trehair.

Mom, you are the most amazing woman that I have ever known. Through your love, you have taught me so many powerful lessons in life.

Your kindness, generosity, resilience and friendliness encourage me to stretch myself and know that I can do better if I try a little harder.

Watching you overcome the most difficult challenges without one word of complaint, and a smile on your face, has inspired me to greater heights in God.

If there was an award for 'Best Mom', you would be the one to win it. You have passed on to me the jewels of how to be a true Christian mother.

You have always done your utmost to give me the best that you could afford, and for that I am truly grateful.

Thank you for being *you,* and *thank you* for loving me.

January

In His Presence

January 1

And the Lord answered me and said, Write the vision and engrave it so plainly upon tablets that everyone who passes may [be able to] read [it easily and quickly] as he hastens by. For the vision is yet for an appointed time and it hastens to the end (fulfillment); it will not deceive or disappoint it. Though it tarry, wait (earnestly) for it, because it will surely come; it will not be behindhand on its appointed day.
Habakkuk 2:2-3

New Beginnings!

This is an awesome opportunity to experience a brand new year! What is past is past, and the New Begins!
What are your goals, this year, and for the next five years? Are there some things that need change, growth, working out? Take your notepad and begin to write, a three-month plan, a one-year plan and a five-year plan, this is a great way to start!

Turn every area of your life inside out. Perhaps you have left your gifts and talents lying dormant – write down "stir up the gifts"! Examine your family situation, your career, your spiritual walk, your love walk, and your health!

Write it down in simple detail, the goal and the means by which to accomplish it. Make it practical and attainable. Once this is done, apply your faith, and it will come to pass!

I set the vision for my life annually. When the year is done, I look back and see how faithful God has been to help me get to where I should be going.

A determined stretch feels good when it is needed!

Don't delay, start today!

January 2

And it shall come to pass in the last days, God declares, that I will pour out of My Spirit upon all mankind...
Acts 2:17

God Wants To Pour Himself Out On You

These are the last days!

I lived as a dry Christian for many years before being filled with the Holy Spirit.

I lived in such fear of those who would pray for me, as many of them lacked wisdom and left me in a state of confusion, instead of me being filled with the Holy Spirit.

I determined that if it were the Lord's desire for me to be filled, I would receive the Holy Spirit. One night while lying in my bed, I said to the Lord that I would begin to make sounds by faith, and He should fill me!

Needless to say, as I began to make sounds I broke out in tongues, stopped, and spoke again! It wasn't a few minutes later that my telephone rang, with the person on the other side saying that I had just received the infilling of the Holy Spirit! How on EARTH did they know? Obviously, the Holy Spirit got them to call, as He knew that I needed confirmation... Wow!!

Being Spirit-filled is like having a tiger in your tank! It adds power to everything you do: your prayer life, your love walk, your peace and your compassion... I could go on and on!

Don't let fear or embarrassment hinder you from receiving your personal prayer language. Get alone with God and step out in faith and you WILL be filled to overflowing!

Commit your life daily to the Lord and He will fill you to overflowing.
Pray in the Spirit and you will be filled with power from on high.

January 3

But when the Comforter (Counsellor, Helper, Advocate, Intercessor, Strengthener, Standby) comes, Whom I will send to you from the Father, the Spirit of Truth Who comes (proceeds) from the Father, He [Himself] will testify regarding Me.
John 15:26

You Need Help!

The Holy Spirit and Jesus agree on everything that the Father does. There is no disagreement in the Trinity. Whatever the Holy Spirit does, He will testify of the great love of Jesus and the goodness of the Heavenly Father. Whatever Jesus does, He supports and honours the Holy Spirit!

I cherish the way the Lord calls Him our "helper". When Krissy was little girl she always used to say, "Mommy, I want to be your helper." Her willingness to support me was so precious!

The Holy Spirit has been sent by the Father at the request of Jesus, to help you in all areas of your life. You can manage on your own to a degree, but how much more effective will you be when He is involved to lead you, guide you, comfort you, teach and help you!

He is called Holy Spirit – He will not aid you in the area of committing sin, but in everything that God is calling you to do!

He will carry out His assignment in full, and your life will testify of God's wonderful goodness.

Whenever you have something important to do run it past your Helper, and you will make the right choice and have the strength to do it! Call on Him and He will lead you in the perfect will of God.

January 4

A capable, intelligent, and virtuous woman – who is he who can find her? She is far more precious than jewels and her value is far above rubies or pearls.
Proverbs 31:10

What A Woman!

What a powerful scripture about a Godly Woman! In general many people have thought that a woman can never be intelligent and capable? So much for that!

The Lord is in the designer business. He made you special and then threw the used mould away. Some women have such a poor self-esteem, but when they find out who God says they are, their whole life and vision changes.

Without Christ in your life you can only attain to what others think and say about you. With Christ as the centre, you will soar and become all that God is calling you to be!

Daily I see new things being birthed in my life. Outside of the Lord, I would not have recognised or experienced any one of them.

"Her value is far above rubies or pearls.." Now that's true value!

Satan knows the woman's heel is going to bruise his head, so he holds on tight. But it is too late, as Jesus has already paid the price for us to be God's Amazing Women.

Rise to be the woman that The Designer Himself made you to be!

January 5

[Not in your own strength] for it is God Who is all the while effectually at work in you [energising and creating in you the power and desire], both to will and to work for His good pleasure and satisfaction and delight.
Philippians 2:13

God Is Working In You

You spend your life trying to "work" for your own good pleasure, while it is God's good pleasure that you should be working for!

When you work for God's good pleasure your focus is not on doing what pleases you, but on doing what pleases Him. This kind of pleasure is fully satisfying and fulfilling and will last for eternity, and not just for a brief moment.

He will bring true meaning to your life, and the necessary growth and change that you need will happen, as you yield your life to Him.

Allow Him to "work" in you, and through you. Not only for your blessing, but also for the blessing of all of those around you!

While He is working in you, He is doing a good work, and you are changing.

It is God's good pleasure to work His will in your life. When God is in control, life is blessed! All the pressure leaves, and the heavy weight lifts!

Give your life wholly to the Lord. Let Him work in you and through you. Don't be afraid, because He is the great Master-Plan Master.

January 6

For the Lord your God is God of gods and Lord of lords, the great, the mighty, the terrible God, Who is not partial and takes no bribe.
Deuteronomy 10:17-18

What A Mighty God!

He executes justice for the fatherless and the widow, and loves the stranger or temporary resident and gives him food and clothing.

The Lord on High is Mighty! He is our Great King, our Great God. The more time that you spend in His Presence, the more you will feel His heartbeat for those who do not know Him.

He cannot be bribed. He chose to love you before the foundation of the world. You cannot buy, or earn His love. His love is unconditional, and He loved you before the foundation of the earth.

He is God of justice and will deal with you accordingly. What an awesome privilege to know the only true and living God – through His Son, Jesus.

There is none like Him, and NO other God can stand before Him. All you have to do is call upon His name and He is there!

Lift up your hands and open your heart and let the King of Glory come in!

Speak aloud and tell Him you love Him – share your heart with Him. He cares more than you will ever know.

January 7

For the story and message of the cross is sheer absurdity and folly to those who are perishing and on their way to perdition, but to us who are being saved it is the [manifestation of] the power of God.
1 Corinthians 1:18

Message Of Power

We must understand that the miracle of the cross is foolishness to the world.

I have been mocked for my commitment to the Lord! I have been called old fashioned, a puritan and one who has no idea of the 'wild' side.

In my heart I find myself saying: "Lord, help them to understand," and then love overrides their foolishness. I don't try and convince them of anything, but I allow my actions to determine their decisions!

I have learned that your life and not your words, is the strongest testimony that you have. Words speak, but your lifestyle speaks louder!

Before too long these precious people ask me what I think about certain things, and where they should go to visit a church! Their mocking is a sign of their hunger for the truth.

There must be no animosity for those who do not know the power that lies in the cross; they are blinded and cannot see.

This is true of friends and family members. They have lived close to you for many years, and your "born anew" experience is confusing to them. Let them see your fruit. Let Christ live BIG in you and through you, to all those who are watching on the sidelines!

You will be persecuted for the Word's sake, but God is on your side and He will not be mocked.

January 8

For we take thought beforehand and aim to be honest and absolutely above suspicion, not only in the sight of the Lord but also in the sight of men.
2 Corinthians 8:21

You Must Live Right

Our lives are not faultless; otherwise we would be in Heaven. As Christians we need to be aware of our actions, and take consideration before we act. We must do what we can to be living epistles to those around us.

As a baby Christian I was very disappointed with what I saw in Christian circles around me. In fact, some of the folks drove me back to a reformed church. As Christians, they were living empty worldly lives, and much confusion surrounded them.

The first time I met Kenneth Hagin Jnr. I knew that I had met a man of God. All of his actions spoke of a God who loved me, and wanted to bless me. There was no chasm between the God that Pastor Ken spoke about, and his own personal life. As I watched him, I witnessed a gracious and kind man, caring and concerned for those around him, and even for my own personal future. What I witnessed in him drew me closer to Jesus.

Your life is a powerful witness to others, positively or negatively. Be careful how you respond and handle things. If you fly off in the flesh, don't be surprised that others may not believe your Christian witness. Measure your actions and walk in a way that honours God and His Word. I did not say that you should be perfect, but let it be Christ that others see in you, NOT only at church, but in your home too!

You never know who is watching you.

Living for God always brings blessing to the lives of others!

January 9

The heart of her husband trusts in her confidently and relies on and believes in her securely, so that he has no lack of [honest] gain or need of [dishonest] spoil.
Proverbs 31:11

Can You Be Trusted?

What a wealth it is for a husband to know that he can trust his wife, that she is reliable and will keep a confidence. Marriage is a partnership and everything is to be shared. A miracle takes place the moment you enter into the marriage covenant and say "I do". It is where each member honours, trusts, respects and celebrates the other.

When a man finds a woman of this nature, he will succeed in all that he does if he will do it God's way. But if she does not live up to this expectation, he may become deceitful himself.

When the miracle of two flesh becoming one is sealed, the devil begins his work to try and break down the anointing and power that lies in this union. He knows what strength there is in unity, trust and peace. At all costs your marriage covenant is the most important contract you can enter into.

Be faithful to the covenant and make the right choices. It's up to you!

You are in covenant with your spouse. Respect, honour and value that covenant, and you will harvest a lifetime of blessing together.

January 10

For every person will have to bear (be equal to understanding and calmly receive) his own [little] load [of oppressive faults].
Galatians 6:5

Take It On The Jaw!

Each one of us has little faults and failures that need overcoming. Wouldn't it be nice if when we were born again everything changed? At least the spirit is made brand new... but the rest needs fine-tuning! In fact the scripture says that we should die to the flesh daily!

I remember a Pastor sharing one Sunday morning about how the flesh needs to be crucified daily on the altar, but the major problem is that it keeps trying to crawl off!! That's when you know it's alive!!

Over the years I have learnt that it is the "little loads" that spoil everything.

Big things in our lives normally change quite easily as we begin to grow in God. But it's the little things that take time to change; your mouth, attitude, negative thinking, un-forgiveness etc. Most of these are learned behaviour and will take a little more time and patience to unlearn.

What a glorious day it is when you begin to gain the victory over the lusts of the flesh and the souls vain imaginations.

I am a testimony to the power that lies in the Word of God. It works! I have been released from a number of "little foxes" over the years, and God will help you to do it too.

Don't let the little foxes get you down. Exercise a greater commitment for change in your life through patience and self-control, stand firm, and the victory is yours!

January 11

May He grant you out of the rich treasury of His glory to be strengthened and reinforced with mighty power in the inner man by the [Holy] Spirit [Himself indwelling your innermost being and personality].
Ephesians 3:16

Come Up Higher

God wants His children to be strong. He planned and ordained for the Holy Spirit to reinforce you with mighty power from His rich treasury, equipping you for the work you are called to do for Him.

How often I cry out: "Oh Lord help me!" Within minutes I feel the inner man beginning to rise up inside of me, giving me assurance of the Father's support and strength. He has provided for you all the power you could ever need.

Absolutely nothing is too big for you to handle, or too great for you to bear.

As a child of God, you have supernatural help in the Spirit.

Make the effort to be quiet for a while and call upon Him for your needs. After all, it is Almighty God who is on your side!

Trust in the Greater One; draw supernatural ability from Him in your time of need.

January 12

O clap your hands, all you peoples! Shout to God with the voice of triumph and songs of joy!
Psalm 47:1

Shout For Joy!

When the going gets tough there have been times in my life that I wanted to shout at myself, and the circumstances around me.

Instead of shouting at my circumstances and myself, God's Word says that I must do the complete opposite. It says that I must shout to God with a voice of triumph. What a crazy thing to do, but if God says to do it, then you must know it works!

Since I have changed my tactics I have found out that this always works for me, and it will work for you.

Look at your circumstances and look at the Word of God: Which one never fails? Which one will stand forever? Which one will never change?

Once you have established which one is the more powerful and lasting, do a victory shout and tell the devil where to get off! Begin to clap your hands and shout to God, and joy will arise in your heart.

Over and over again there is pressure for you to let go of your confession, but don't do it! Stand firm in the Lord and Praise Him.

He will never let you down. He will never fail you. He will always watch over His Word to perform it. He is on your side!

A shout of praise is a powerful weapon!

January 13

She opens her hand to the poor, yes; she reaches out her filled hands to the needy [whether in body, mind, or spirit].
Proverbs 31:20

Give Something Away

Our hands are filled with abundance to share with others. Everyday is an opportunity to touch the life of another. Going about your daily chores causes you to bump into folks who are lost, hungry and hurting. What are you as children of God going to do about it?

At Church, there are many ministries touching the lives of the destitute and sick. You may be thinking: "What can I do?" You certainly do not have to take on a huge responsibility, but you can start by sharing with the lady behind the counter or giving a sandwich to the hungry. You may be able to help someone else learn to read, and write. You may even be called to pray for those in the hospital who have no family or friends, to pray for them.

You can contribute in some way or another. If you suffer from insecurities, this will be the perfect opportunity to prove God's faithfulness in your life.

You have the ability in the name of Jesus – that is what He promised you. Pray and the Lord will open the doors for you to give, as it is written in Mark 16:15-20.

Don't be afraid to step out in faith and serve the Lord – start now!

January 14

That they all may be one, [just] as You, Father, are in Me and I in You, that they also may be one in Us, so that the world may believe and be convinced that You have sent Me.
Proverbs 31:20

Make Us One

Jesus desires for His body to walk in agreement and unity. He prayed "that they all may be one" just as He and the Heavenly Father are one.

This unity is so powerful that the devil is on a special assignment to keep it from happening. He will use any device, including doctrines, to cause confusion and division. Thank goodness that Jesus prayed for all of us!

What was the reason for this? So that the world would see something! What? That by our oneness they would know that Jesus was sent by the Father.

No wonder the fight for unity and oneness is so great. We must stand strong in the power of the Lord to manifest this unity.

There is enough fighting in the world without the church joining in. We must love, honour and protect one another and let the world see Jesus in us!

Do not allow strife and confusion to have any place in your personal life. Keep it out of your church and walk in love.

January 15

When suddenly there came a sound from heaven like the rushing of a violent tempest blast, and it filled the whole house in which they were sitting.
Acts 2:2

Suddenly!

When we hunger and thirst in the Presence of the Lord to be filled with the anointing and power of the Holy Spirit, He will always answer, and it could come – suddenly!

It may even come as a violent tempest blast!

However, when it comes, it will be God's perfect timing for it!

The Lord loves you to come into His Presence expecting to receive and to be touched by Him. He longs to bless your life with His goodness, to fill you to overflowing, and to confirm all that He has promised you.

If the disciples had not been together in the upper room as Jesus instructed them to, waiting for the blessing of the Lord as He had commanded, they would not have received it.

When you choose to be quick to obey and to do the will of the Father, you will be fully supplied with His infilling, and everyone around you will be blessed.

When you are too absorbed by things around you, draw aside for a few moments into His Presence. A few moments in His Presence will cause something to happen suddenly for you!

January 16

*For I endorse and delight in the Law of God in my inmost self
[with my new nature].*
Romans 7:22

Delight In The Word Of God

It is wonderful to give your life wholly over to the Word of God – to endorse and delight in doing His will and have your life moulded and changed to what He wants for you.

As you grow in God, there will always be a constant battle in your flesh to see who is really in control.

One of my difficulties was giving up smoking. I went to Rhema Bible Training Centre still addicted to the smelly habit! However, God is faithful and when I seriously chose to get rid of it, the Lord helped me and I did!

Thank goodness for the ministry of the Holy Spirit who is there to help, comfort, strengthen, counsel, teach and guide you, but you have to be willing to follow through.

The devil knows your weakness and is always trying to get you to stumble. Thank the Lord, you can be rid of all that old baggage once and for all, the moment you choose to be done with it!

The new life you have received through the shed blood of Jesus will set you free from the old life. Jesus destroyed the work of the evil one.

Delighting in doing the will of the Lord will strengthen and deliver you from all temptations.

January 17

She opens her mouth in skilful and godly Wisdom, and on her tongue is the law of kindness [giving counsel and instruction].
Proverbs 31:26

What Is Coming Out Of Your Mouth?

Women often get into trouble with their mouths. Many friendships have been destroyed by the power of destructive words. Many marriages and children have been destroyed by the power of destructive words.

As women, we can control the words that come out of our mouths. God says that we have the ability to speak with skilful and godly wisdom, and also to have the law of kindness on our tongue. This is going to take an active decision on your part.

When you are about to blurt out something, stop and think of the consequences of what you are about to say. You could be breaking down something, destroying something, and hurting what God is trying to build up or change.

Do you have to say it with such "fire" or could you temper it a little and mix it with a little more love, and not destroy the one you are addressing?

Be wise and careful how you answer.

January 18

But now put away and rid yourselves [completely] of all these things: anger, rage, bad feeling toward others, curses and slander, and foulmouthed abuse and shameful utterances from your lips! Do not lie to one another, for you have stripped off the old [unregenerate] self with its evil practices, And have clothed yourselves with the new [spiritual self], which is [ever in the process of being] renewed and remoulded into [fuller and more perfect knowledge upon] knowledge after the image (the likeness) of Him Who created it.
Colossians 3:8-10

A New Life

The old man has to go! And this is NOT your father in-law! You cannot walk around in the newness of life carrying all that old "stuff" with you. Anger, rage, bad feelings toward others, bad language, and shameful attitudes have no place in your life now!

The life you left behind is full of evil practices. Leave it behind do not try and carry it into your new life. That clothing belongs to someone who died – burn it, bury it, get rid of it!

The image that God has of you is a glorious image, without those blemishes. Work at getting your image into what God has planned. Continue the process of being moulded and renewed by God on a daily basis.

Get rid of the old man and put on the new.

January 19

Jesus answered, If a person [really] loves Me, he will keep My word [obey My teaching]; and My Father will love him, and We will come to him and make Our home (abode, special dwelling place) with him.
John 14:23

Do You Love The Lord?

When we tell the Lord how much we love Him, we need to measure our love by our obedience to God's Word!

Words slip glibly off our lips in times of worship and we walk away forgetting our commitment. A person, who really loves the Lord, will follow His words with an act of obedience.

Jesus made a tremendous promise for our obedience. The Heavenly Father will love us, and they will come and make their home with us! What more could you ever ask for? It would be pretty crazy for us to think that God would bless and agree with a rebellious person.

Loving God takes more than just your words. It's in your actions that your heart is truly made evident to the Father and to others. Saying the words "I love you" does not require much effort and sometimes it is spoken quite glibly, without much sincerity. For a person to prove that they are truly sincere - time, effort, and action are required.

How could you ever sacrifice this amazing promise by simply not obeying the Word of the Father God?

January 20

My heart is fixed, O God, my heart is steadfast and confident! I will sing and make melody.
Psalm 57:7

Come On Sing!

When you know who is in control it is easy to sing! It is easier to sing when your heart is doing well, than when the pressure is on! It takes an active step of faith and a lot of courage to overcome your discouraged attitude, by encouraging your heart to break forth into singing.

The folks thought when Joshua was crazy when he told them to walk around the walls of Jericho in silence and then on the last day to shout as loud as they could. The walls obeyed them and came tumbling down, and there was no doubt as to the victory in their obedience.

There are times that the Lord asks us to do things that we think are unusual. But obeying God brings victory!

Singing tells your heart and your mind that everything is going to turn out just fine. Singing demonstrates your victory in Christ. It lifts your spirit and causes you to rise above the problems. It is something that the devil can do nothing about.

Every opportunity is an opportunity to sing!

Make sure that you never let anyone steal your song! When times are tough, it is then that you sing your longest and your loudest!

January 21

And the eye is not able to say to the hand, I have no need of you, nor again the head to the feet, I have no need of you.
1 Corinthians 12:21

You Need Me And I Need You!

The body is an amazing miracle. Although each part can do so much on it's own, it needs the other parts to function as a whole.

God knew what He was doing when He designed the Body of Christ. Not one of us can accomplish anything of any consequence without the assistance or co-operation of others as far as God's plan is concerned. Together we will build the Kingdom of God!

It would be quite a thing if your hand broke off from the rest of your body and said: "I have had enough of you so I'm on my way, see you later!" Fortunately, your body knows better. When your eyes are weak, your head does not pop them out!

Let's see the value in one another, and bring out the best in one another! When things go wrong in a relationship, don't say, "You go your way and I will go mine." Make a stand that you will work at getting things right, no matter how challenging it may be.

Often the very person you are having the most difficulty with, is the one that is fine-tuning your life. Great lessons on patience or love are learnt this way.

Let's do it God's way and get our attitude sorted out.
Let us build together!

January 22

He who heeds instruction and correction is [not only himself] in the way of life [but also] is a way of life for others. And he who neglects or refuses reproof [not only himself] goes astray [but also] causes to err and is a path toward ruin for others.
Proverbs 10:17

Listen To God When He Instructs You

To live prosperously is to live by God's instruction and correction, embedded in His Word.

If you do this you will be the kind of person that others will look up to, and want to listen to. You will be light, and you will be salty.

Ignoring God's instruction is a sure way to destruction. Even if you do not see the trouble now, it will reap a harvest in your life.

You are going to have folks who will follow your life. Your children will be the first to imitate you. I have told my children not to do certain things, and then they say: "But you do it, Mommy!"

Make your choice and never give in to pressure from those who are angry with you for living according to God's will.

Give God all the room He needs in your life. The result will be life and living more abundantly!

Only a fool would choose the path of destruction. Let your path follow God's wisdom and your life will be blessed.

January 23

That I may make the voice of thanksgiving heard and may tell of all Your wondrous works.
Psalm 26:7

Speak About God's Goodness

We must have a heart of thanksgiving. Not only should we know it, but we should tell it.

Firstly, we need to be thankful for the brand-new life that God has given us, even when we did not deserve it.

Secondly, He loves us in spite of ourselves and has promised His Presence with us for all the days of our lives.

Thirdly (to top it all!), He has not only given us a new life, but one that is abundant!

Opportunities to tell others of God's goodness are abundant: in the mall, at school, playing sport. You may never know the difficulty that others may be going through, but a precious word of encouragement in season, may give them every reason to live another day.

Our lives are an open book for others to read, or rather, we are walking epistles. What do others see in all that you do?

Not only should life be in our walk, but it should be in our talk too. What do others hear in all that you say?

Don't be afraid to share a word of encouragement when you see someone in pain. You may save their life.

January 24

She looks well to how things go in her household, and the bread of idleness (gossip, discontent, and self-pity) she will not eat.
Proverbs 31:27

Stay Occupied

Idle hands get into a lot of trouble!
What a JOY to have a life that is filled with the blessings of the Lord. To manage an organised home, a husband and children needing attention, your boss constantly calling you on the phone, and the neighbour knocking on the door wanting you to help them take their kitten to the vet!! Wow...

As they say, "A woman's day is NEVER done"!

I think of my own mom who worked a full time job for most of her life. She would come home after a full day's work, prepare the family evening meal, help me with my homework and my brother with his upcoming test, while catching up with my dad's daily news and she would be busy knitting me a sweater! How blessed I am to have had her as my example.

Being occupied is not something to complain about, but something to be blessed about! God promises that He will bless the work of your hands. I have always thanked the Lord for that blessing, and seen it manifest over and over again in my life!

When you are idle and have nothing to occupy your mind, you will get into trouble. You will end up having conversations that you will be sorry for down the road, and doing things that bring condemnation in your heart.

It is a blessing to be productive, needed, satisfied and appreciated in this life.

January 25

For God did not give us a spirit of timidity (of cowardice, of craven and cringing and fawning fear), but [He has given us a spirit] of power and of love and of calm and well-balanced mind and discipline and self-control.
2 Timothy 1:7

A Spirit Of Power And Love

When you were born again you did not receive a foreign spirit that does not come from God. You received exactly what God wanted you to have; A spirit of power and of love, a calm and well-balanced mind, and discipline and self-control.

There is no reason why you cannot accomplish and do all the things that God has put in your heart to do for Him.

When you have the urge to cower away from and cringe away in fear, remember whose child you are. When you are in the will of God nothing can stop you from getting where you are supposed to go.

You will need to dig down deep into the things of God and rise up above the weakness of your own strength. You need God's strength now in the name of Jesus.

Stand up straight and put your shoulders back. You are a child of God about to gain the upper hand. If anyone is going to cringe it is not going to be you!

Love never fails, so handle the situation properly, and do not get into an unnecessary fight.

January 26

Blessed (happy, fortunate, and to be envied) are those servants whom the master finds awake and alert and watching when he comes. Truly I say to you, he will gird himself and have them recline at table and will come and serve them!
Luke 12:37

Are You Awake?

You must keep watch for the returning of the Lord. He will come again, and when He does, will He find you busy about His work and doing what He has called you to do?

It is only after you have been serving the Lord for many years that you discover what kind of Christian you really are; Weathering storms, walking in love, reaching out to those who are hurting and giving yourself consistently in worship to the Lord.

While you are busy about the Kingdom of God's business, stay alert and awake, not serving because of works, ritual or habit, but serving because of Who He is and because you love Him.

Your passion is precious to Him!

Stay ready! The attitude of your heart is paramount to the Lord; if you love Him, your foremost desire is to welcome Him.

January 27

*But as for me, I will walk in my integrity; redeem me and
be merciful and gracious to me.*
Psalm 26:11

I Will Not Compromise

A fine line exists between doing what is acceptable and doing what is right. Telling the truth and living honestly go hand in hand.

Today you will be faced with deciding to do what is acceptable, or to do what is right. Not even a little compromise should be present in your choice if you want God's Presence and blessing.

As a young lady I understood what it meant to tell a lie, but as I grew older I discovered that adults had turned lies to colours! A black lie was the worst, a grey lie not so bad, and a white lie was possibly acceptable!

Seriously, lies are lies no matter what colour you choose to make them!

You have to use wisdom in how you answer, but you do not have to lie. One lie always leads to the next. The most difficult thing is to remember to whom you told what!

Integrity is honesty, morality, goodness and truth. These attitudes should govern your life with the help of the Lord. Integrity is being truthful with oneself! "It is doing the right thing, even when no one is watching" - CS Lewis

Honesty is being truthful with others!

Start today and make a quality decision not to allow circumstances and people to rob you from your integrity. The blessings of this decision are far beyond measure.

January 28

Then He laid [His] hands on her, and instantly she was made straight, and she recognised and thanked and praised God.
Luke 13:13

Lay Hands On The Sick

Jesus laid hands on people when they had a need. It is part of our calling as Christians to impart the anointing that resides within us to others.

Laying your hands on someone is a step of faith for their need to be met.

This woman came to Jesus, and she needed healing in her body. As Jesus laid His hands on her she was instantly healed. She realised, without a shadow of doubt Who had healed her. She began to thank and praise God for her miracle.

When folks come to us with sickness in their body, before we do anything we should in faith offer to pray for them, and lay our hands on them. It is not our responsibility to heal them, but the responsibility of the Lord. All we do is obey God and follow the example set by Jesus.

The next time you are in the presence of someone who is ill, offer to pray and lay hands on them. You will receive the blessing, and they will praise God for their healing.

January 29

Do not [earnestly] remember the former things;
neither consider the things of old.
Isaiah 43:18

Leave The Baggage Behind

Cease to dwell on days gone by and to brood over past history. The past is the past. In fact, what you did two minutes ago is now in the past!

To go forward unhindered you are going to have to confront the things from the past that are holding you back. Examine your heart and search them out; determine if they have had an adverse effect on you. If you have not dealt with them, do it now. If you have dealt with them, then forgive yourself and get on with your life.

When God sets you free, you are free indeed. He carries no memories of your forgiven past. It's you who has not forgiven you of your past. Get rid of it! Don't drag this old baggage around, as it will stop you from moving quickly and freely ahead.

Remorse, guilt, regret and shame are some of the tools that Satan uses to keep you in bondage. Jesus nailed these things to the cross when He died for you. Leave them there; otherwise they will cloud your vision and hopes for the future.

Leave the past with all of its failures at the cross!

January 30

What then shall we say to [all] this? If God is for us, who [can be] against us? [Who can be our foe, if God is on our side?].
Romans 8:31

Who Does God Say That I Am?

od places a tremendous value on your life, so what does it matter what others may think or say about you?
When you become confident in your faith that you are truly who God says that you are, then the opinion of man will not weigh you down. Allow yourself to become totally convinced (renew your mind) by God's Word, and you will become dead to the praise and censure of man.

You can set yourself free from seeking man's approval by becoming more aware of what God's Word says about you. Each time you are confronted with negative thoughts about yourself, ask this question: "But who does God say that I am?"

We have become inundated by a standard of "perfection" set by the world through television, advertising, fashion and standards. Don't miss the mark by allowing others to measure your values. You are priceless!

Desiring to grow in skill and knowledge is an excellent thing, but don't let your only desire be to please man. Please God first, and then man will not be able to turn a blind eye on you.

In Christ you are the best that is available.

January 31

Her children rise up and call her blessed (happy, fortunate, and to be envied); and her husband boasts of and praises her, [saying], Many daughters have done virtuously, nobly and well [with the strength of character that is steadfast in goodness], but you excel them all.
Proverbs 31: 28-29

She's The Best!

To be a woman celebrated by her family, is something that most women desire!

Often it is those outside of our homes that get the best of us, when it really is to our families that our best light should shine!

Daily we give out of our lives and share with others, not knowing the distance to which our love and kindness will travel. Even in the office many may say, "She's the best"!

But really it is a greater reward when your family witness and experience the best treasures of your life. Be sure not to give the left overs to the ones who deserve the best!

I have seen it in my own life as I have done all that I know to be a blessing to those around me. Even though my children are grown, I now have little Grand babies that need a loving, caring Granna who is there for them when they need her!

It is from my children that I desire to hear the words, "My mom is the best"!

I am thrilled that I gave my life to Jesus at the age of 19. He has helped me to become the woman I am today because "He is the BEST"!

Now is the time to prepare for excellence as a woman, wife and mother. Let God help you, and in no time you will not recognise yourself.

February

Treasured Moments

February 1

For which of you, wishing to build a farm building, does not first sit down and calculate the cost [to see] whether he has sufficient means to finish it?
Luke 14:28

Count The Cost

Before you actually start a project, first consider the cost of finishing it.

Everything that we do here on earth has a cost. This wisdom can be applied to many areas of our lives.

How to measure?

Find out in God's Word if it is in order with Him to do what is in your heart to do. Examine your circumstances and see if you are able to afford the time, effort and money that it will take to complete the task. Take the project to experts and see if your calculations are correct. If all is in order, and it is the will of God, then go ahead and do it!

It's wise to get whatever support you can when making a big decision. There is protection in wise counsel.

Never be too proud to seek advice from experienced people who have your interests at heart.

February 2

Heal me, O Lord, and I shall be healed; save me, and I shall be saved, for You are my praise.
Jeremiah 17:14

Lord, I Praise You!

The only one that can bless and fulfil your life is the Lord. People run around in all directions trying to get help and answers from anything. As Christians our help comes from the Lord, and none other can satisfy and calm our lives the way that He does.

Jeremiah knew that. He knew that even if the circumstances were bad or his enemies raged against him, nothing could stop or hinder what God was going to do. He would praise the Lord and thank Him for the life of blessing that He had already given him.

It should be that simple for us, as we have all the information we could ever need in written form. The Bible is God's book of life, written to us.

When God does something, nothing can change it and nothing can stop it. When God heals us, we are healed; when God delivers us, we are set free forever!

Your God is able to take your life exactly where He wants it to go!

February 3

For in Him we live and move and have our being...
Acts 17:28

Moving With God

We are all in different levels of maturity and growth in God, but one thing is sure: we all have a lot more growing to do!!

To grow to the next level of maturity will take hunger, desire and obedience on your part!

It is like driving a car up a hill. It takes energy to get that car to the top, and once you are on top you get to cruise for a while. However, be assured there will be another hill still to come! Each level prepares you for the next – you are never going to get to the place where you will stop growing.

While on earth, we continually need to be moving on in God.

As we hit the potholes and speed bumps of mediocrity in our lives, we can feel God starting to move in our hearts. The energy levels begin to increase, and determination rises up inside of us to start climbing the hill again.

Make the decision to always be growing in God, and to ultimately reach full maturity.

You will never become what you ought to be, without the Lord in the centre of your life

February 4

For the Word that God speaks is alive and full of power
[making it active, operative, energising and effective];
it is sharper than any two-edged sword...
Hebrews 4:12

Power To Produce

While attending the Campmeeting in Tulsa and about to be ordained, Brother Hagin stopped in the middle of his message and called me up to the front. I felt a little odd as the whole Tulsa Assembly Centre was seated!

Dad Hagin prophesied over me and said that I would speak as the pen of a ready writer, and that I would work for the Lord and RUN with the Vision that God set before me! Then he commanded me to "run"!! Well, I took off running like a rushing river down the aisle to the back of the Assembly Centre and then turned around and ran back to the front where Dad Hagin was standing, He laid hands on me and I fell to the floor, BLESSED!

I have often thought of what would have happened if I had not run! When God speaks we need to listen, and act immediately. When God says "run" don't question why?

Don't dare let the Word float off into thin air and not produce in your life. When God speaks to you, don't sit on that Word.

The Word of God is alive and full of power and it will energise you! It is sharper than any natural sword, and goes deeper than a surgeon's knife. It is able to divide the spirit and the soul, and it WILL set you free from anything that is hindering your life.

The Word of God will build inside of you, compassion, faith, endurance, peace, joy and the love of God that never fails!

May I encourage you to allow God's powerful Word
to produce good fruit in your life!

February 5

Therefore if any person is [ingrafted] in Christ (the Messiah) he is a new creation (a new creature altogether); the old [previous moral and spiritual condition] has passed away.
Behold, the fresh and new has come!
2 Corinthians 5:17

A Fresh Start

This is a new beginning! You are on a whirlwind with God; you are on a roller coaster ride. It is so much fun to ride out this life with God; there is nothing to compare with it.

God will take you higher than you could ever go in the natural. You will touch His heart and He will touch your life. You need to give Him your all – everything you have belongs to God. He has given you this opportunity in life to live wholeheartedly for Him.

God desires to take you to the next level, but it often means total abandonment to oneself and true surrender to God. God will make something beautiful of your life.

He is willing and able to mould you and give you a hope and a future. You need to take the first step!

When was the last time you did something for the first time?

February 6

Behold, I set before you this day a blessing and a curse – The blessing if you obey the commandments of the Lord your God which I command you this day; And the curse if you will not obey the commandments of the Lord your God, but turn aside from the way which I command you this day to go after other gods, which you have not known.
Deuteronomy 11:26–28

What Will You Choose?

Parents teach and train their children to obey, because they want it to be well with them. A parent's heart is joyous when their children obey them, as it brings protection, prosperity and blessing to their children's lives.

God is your Father and He knows what will bring blessing into your life.

One day in Bible School, a man walked up and gave us a five-carat diamond ring with which to start the ministry. We were thrilled!

That night while attending a conference, the Lord encouraged us to give the ring as seed into the offering, toward our future ministry! It took a lot of courage for us to obey and sow it, as we thought we had the need for the ministry met, through the ring!

But God's ways are higher than our ways, and we obeyed and sowed the ring! That seed made a way for us for many years to come, and we never had a need in the area of finances! We always had more than enough!

I am so grateful that we obeyed the Lord that day. Obeying God will bring boundless blessings to your life.

God's blessing will be visible in your life.

February 7

And the vessel that he was making from clay was spoiled in the hand of the potter; so he made it over, reworking it into another vessel as it seemed good to the potter to make it.
Jeremiah 18:4

Make Me What I Ought To Be

When you are confronted with a difficult situation, allow the Lord to take control and you will get the best results.

There is nothing wrong with starting again if you do not get it right the first time. When you are dealing with real problems and people, you will make a mistake now and then.

You know it is not a sin to make a mistake, as long as you don't keep repeating the same mistake! It's how you come out of it that determines how you pass the test.

Our hearts should be like the clay in the potter's hand, completely pliable. If the potter finds the base a little large, he puts pressure on it until it changes shape. If the belly of the pot is too wide, he pulls it upward, stretching it to capacity until its shape changes. He knows exactly what each pot should be.

Life Coaches will tell you that CHANGE can be painful and the hardest thing to do, but when it is complete it reaps the greatest rewards!

God knows what you need.

Are you willing to allow Him to pull, press and prod you?

Are you ready to become that excellent pot?

Well then, get ready for the changes!
God has got your life in full view!

February 8

And you shall love the Lord your God with all your [mind and] heart and with your entire being and with all your might.
Deuteronomy 6:5

Lifestyle Of Love

God wants your love. He wants you to fall hopelessly in love with Him, to think about Him all day and to meditate on His Word.

When you love God, you will be found feeding the poor and destitute; you will be found laying hands on the sick, walking in love with others, and keeping the unity. You will be found setting the captives free, and helping others to be filled to overflowing with the precious Holy Spirit; you will be serving the Body of Christ, and using all your talents and gifts for the Glory of God.

We need to respond to God's love in us. If He has told you to do something for Him, yield to it and let Him lead you forward!

As in any relationship, where love is found – so too are actions. Christ's love for us sent Him to the cross. Where does your love for Him take you?

When your heart is pure before Him, and the love you have for Him becomes intimate, you can't help but be about the Master's business.

Love is not in word only, but in deed!

February 9

Therefore you should do and give effect to My statutes and keep My ordinances and perform them, and you will dwell in the land in safety
Leviticus 25:18

Don't Delay To Obey

Every time God talks about obedience in the Old Testament, He speaks about blessing. Choose to obey God, and the blessing flows!

God gives you a choice where a "yes" or "no" answer may be required.

Soon after I had been filled with the Holy Ghost, I was offered a bursary to attend the Rhema Bible Training Centre in Tulsa by Pastor Kenneth Hagin Jnr. He was on a ministry trip to South Africa when in the car on the way to the airport, he turned to me and asked me a question, "If I give you a bursary, will you come to Rhema Bible Training Centre? You cannot pray about it, or think about it, I want an answer now, "Yes or No"?

I am so grateful that I said "yes" and obeyed the call of God on my life. I cannot imagine what would have happened to me, had I have said "no"!

Make a stand for God and His will for you life, and don't compromise.

A number of years ago God encouraged me to go downtown with a group of ladies and touch the lives of the hungry, sick and hurting. I found it difficult to see so many precious men and women suffering in such a terrible way. But when God sends you, you will rise to the occasion, and everyone He places in your presence will be touched by His love!

If we simply obey and don't delay, we will eat of the good of the land.

February 10

It is because of the Lord's mercy and loving-kindness that we are not consumed, because His [tender] compassions fail not. They are new every morning; great and abundant is Your stability and faithfulness.
Lamentations 3:22–23

Great Is Thy Faithfulness

Our God is a Mighty God; His Presence is all consuming and awesome, that you have to be born anew by the blood of Jesus, to be able to enter it.

Let us not waste the opportunity of knowing that our God is on our side and that He wants us to live daily in His compassion and faithfulness.

A good mother or father would provide love, kindness and goodness for their children. How much more does the Heavenly Father want to show His love to you, His blood-bought child!

Every morning, as you wake, remember that His mercy is new every morning and for that day. His kindness is overflowing and constant towards you.

Take the opportunity to see and know that you belong to Him, a Mighty God, Who wants to bless your life as you take His love to a world that has no hope outside of Him.

As you worship Him, say "Thank You Lord" for all you have done!

Daily give thanks to the Father for His tender mercy and loving kindness – He is faithful.

February 11

But your shall receive power (ability, efficiency, and might) when the Holy Spirit has come upon you, and you shall be my witnesses in Jerusalem and all Judea and Samaria and to the ends (the very bounds) of the earth.
Acts 1:8

Power To Live Right

When the Holy Spirit came down to earth after Jesus ascended, He brought with Him all kinds of abilities for us to walk in. The most important of these is the power to be a witness for Christ.

This simply means that your life will speak of God's goodness, and of His love, in all that you do. Power to be a witness!

I have often thought about the fact that my life speaks volumes to people that are keeping an eye on me. What does your life speak?

Through the power that the Holy Spirit equips you with, you are able to live a good, acceptable, holy life before God and before others. He is the One who empowers you, to live for Him

When you are a witness in court you are there to give the absolute facts about a situation without any error. It's the same when we witness for Christ, we are revealing in and through our lives, that He is alive!

Do not be discouraged about the state that you are in. Begin now and allow the Holy Spirit to work the will of God in you.

You are a witness!

February 12

And I will give them one heart [a new heart] and I will put a new spirit within them; and I will take the stony [unnaturally hardened] heart out of their flesh, and will give them a heart of flesh [sensitive and responsive to the touch of their God].
Ezekiel 11:19

A Brand-New Heart

The moment you receive Jesus as your Lord and Saviour you become what the Bible calls "a brand new creation". That old life, with all its nasty ways passes away, and you get a brand-new heart and a brand-new life in Jesus Christ.

Now you need to be on your guard because the devil is not happy with this miracle in your life. He will spend much of his time telling you how stupid you are and that you don't need God in your life. He will try to distract and occupy your time with fruitless things. Don't let that happen!

What happened to your heart is real. Make sure that you study your Bible and speak to the Lord every day. Find a good church in which to grow, and give your love and service to the Lord. Develop healthy relationships with other Christians, your family, who are part of the Body of Christ.

I am amazed at how many Christians do not attend church. Don't be one of those!

Get your heart into the things of God. If someone disappoints you, don't blame the whole church. Grow up, and get on with what God wants you to do: attend church and be a blessing, keeping your eyes on Jesus.

Being "born anew" is the *greatest* miracle of all.

February 13

For we are God's [own] handiwork (His workmanship), recreated in Christ Jesus, [born anew] that we may do those good works which God predestined (planned beforehand) for us [taking paths which He prepared ahead of time], that we should walk in them [living the good life which He prearranged and made ready for us to live].
Ephesians 2:10

Determined To Succeed

God has awesome plans for your life! If you are living in only a small percentage of His blessing, then you need a revelation of what Jesus did for you on the cross! His GRACE has provided for your increase and blessing!

I am saddened when people go home to be with the Lord that they have never experienced His wonderful plan, provision and power in their lives. We must sharpen up when it comes to God's plan.

I have wonderful plans for my own children's future. I support them in every way that I can, and offer them whatever is available for them to reach their goal – I do whatever it takes! Just like you, I want my children to have the best in life, to be successful.

God has the same desire for you: to see you succeed, prosper and have victory over the enemy. He is a WONDERFUL Father with only the best plan and desire for you life.

Step out of your boat and TRUST Him! He wants you to walk on the water!

Are you determined to rise up and get what God has planned for your life? Exactly how hungry are you?

February 14

But if not, let it be known to you, O king, that we will not serve your gods or worship the golden image which you have set up!
Daniel 3:18

There Is Only One God

So many things in our lives can become graven images: our home, job, children, car, hobby, sports, and so much more. It is not wrong for us to enjoy the wonderful things that God has given us in this life, but they are to have their rightful place. For example, money must be our servant and not our master!

Often we allow these things to hold our attention, and we begin to worship them. We place them on the centre stage of our lives, and when things begin to fall apart we say: "What have I done?"

The only One that has the right to sit on the centre throne in your life is the Lord. Knowing and understanding His ways helps us to get our priorities in order: relationship with God comes first then your spouse, children, church and job.

When these become imbalanced, everything is out of order. Your children are far more important than your job, and your spouse is far more important than your children. One day when your children marry, you will be left looking at someone you do not know, if you have not drawn them near to your heart!

Let the enemy know that you will not bow down and worship any graven images. You have given your life to the Lord God Almighty and Him only will you serve.

February 15

Fear not, nor be afraid [in the coming violent upheavals]; have I not told it to you from of old and declared it? And you are My witnesses. Is there a God besides Me? There is no [other] Rock; I know not any.
Isaiah 44:8

A Worthy Witness

You are a witness of Christ's power, His resurrection power. He took each one of us that was dying and useless in society and He set us free, delivered us and gave us a wonderful, brand new life!

Many people feel that because they are not on the platform they are unimportant. Well, that's not true. Each one of us is important in God's eyes. Whether you are a greeter in the church or the Pastor, you are valuable and precious to God.

God wants to use you right where you are! If you are waiting till everything falls into place, you may wait a long, long time. Now is the perfect time to serve the Lord, with all your heart. .

1 Peter 5:8 tells us that the devil as a roaring lion, walks about seeking whom he may devour. Don't be the "whom"! Don't give up on the things that God has given to you, for the things of the world.

Protect and guard the beautiful jewels that Jesus has invested in your life and live as a worthy witness of Him.

February 16

Though the fig tree does not blossom and there is no fruit on the vines, [though] the product of the olive fails and the fields yield no food, though the flock is cut off from the fold and there are no cattle in the stalls, Yet I will rejoice in the Lord; I will exult in the [victorious] God of my salvation!
Habakkuk 3:17-18

I Exalt You My Lord!

Habakkuk is saying: "No matter what happens around me and in my life, I will lift up my God, for He is the one who will save me; He is the one in whom I rejoice!"

When it seems that it takes all your faith to get out of bed and face another day, then remember that you are not alone and that God is on your side! You are victorious because you are a child of God.

Habakkuk knew the power of praise to deliver him out of all his difficulties. When he started taking account of his circumstances, everything looked very bleak, but his heart began to rise when he thought about his God.

Stop and see who you are in Christ!

We praise because He is God; not because the circumstances are good or bad, but because we love Him above all else.

With storms to face and victories to enjoy,
no matter the circumstance...
I WILL PRAISE YOUR NAME!

February 17

And if it seems evil to you to serve the Lord, choose for yourselves this day whom you will serve...
Joshua 24:15

Free To Choose

*E*veryday you are faced with choices of what you are going to do with your life.

You have the choice to be depressed, or productive and joyful. What attitude are you going to wear today; whom are you going to serve? This day, choose to go with God.

Don't fear man or be intimidated by what man says and does. Realise who you are in Christ Jesus, and rise above those feelings of failure.

Who would ever think that God would take a shy young lady and use her in full-time ministry?

Who would ever think that God would cause a Rugby player like Pierre Spies, to serve Him and bring life to others!

If you think that you are a nothing, I have news for you, God is NOT looking at your ability, but at your availability. If He could use a donkey, He will use me, and He will use you.

Purpose in your heart to put aside the world's ways and choose to fulfil what God has for your life. It's called the BLESSED life!

If you do the desiring, God will do the producing in your life.

February 18

For God's gifts and His call are irrevocable. [He never withdraws them when once they are given, and He does not change His mind about those to whom He gives His grace or to whom He sends His call.]
Romans 11:29

God Is Calling

There was a time in my life, not too long ago, when I was pastoring that I lost all heart for what I was doing. A number of the male pastors in the church, decided to come against me because I was a woman, and agreed that they would never submit to a woman in ministry.

How utterly sad that gender would hinder one from being obedient to God, and hinder one from receiving from God! I was not acting on my own authority, but on the authority that was given to me by the Senior Pastor.

Fear of man had overwhelmed me and I had succumbed to it. I began to withdraw, as my heart was deeply discouraged. I could not seem to get on top of my discouragement.

There was tremendous pressure on me and I gradually withdrew from all that the Lord had for me to do.

God began reminding me of the open windows of opportunity He had given me when He first called me to do His work, and now He was calling me again. From out of the bottom of my heart, I cried: "Yes, yes, yes God!" I will never say "no" to my God. God told me there and then to take my place.

God removed those who did not witness with my calling. He strengthened me and helped me to make my stand.

You are anointed and appointed by God for a divine calling. Make the decision today to walk in His plans and purposes for your life.

February 19

Truthful lips shall be established forever, but a lying tongue is [credited] but for a moment.
Proverbs 12:19

Speak the Truth

While dealing with people over the years, there have been times when I needed to be brutally honest with them, to help them. Even though it was painful at the time, it yielded to peace as they reflected on what they had heard.

The Holy Spirit is called 'The Spirit Of Truth'! It is his leading and his assignment to bring you to TRUTH in all that you do. God never wants you to be in a place of deception or to believe a lie!

TRUTH is amazing as the Bible promises that when you hear it and receive it, it will make you free! A lie is endless in confusion and never comes to a positive end, as it cannot stand the test of time!

Personally, I would rather hear the truth about a situation than have it ignored. I have challenged myself over the years to tell the truth in all circumstances and to know that there are no small or big lies.

If what you are going to answer and telling it all could be a problem, don't tell it all, just say what needs to be said in truth, and be quiet about the rest, then you won't be responsible for a lie!

It is wrong for you to encourage your children to lie for you by telling folks on the telephone that you are not at home or in the bath, when you are not! Rather say that you will call back later.

Guard your tongue and speak the truth in love – remember, you will reap from what you sow.

February 20

I do not consider, brethren, that I have captured and made it my own [yet]; but one thing I do [it is my one aspiration]: forgetting what lies behind and straining forward to what lies ahead, I press on toward the goal to win the [supreme and Heavenly] prize to which God in Christ Jesus is calling us upward.
Philippians 3:13–14

Press On!

There will always be something in the way that will try and hinder you from moving forward, to the greater things God has for your life. It is at these times that you cannot be moved by circumstance or people, but only by what God has for your life.

Jesus had such occasions in His own life and ministry, yet He kept progressing toward what He was to do. A runner does not simply become a runner! It takes hours of training, and even losing some races, to finally become the champion that will win through the pain.

I have had to do that at times, to press on through past the pain. That possibly is the most victorious that I have been in my entire Christian walk.

This is when patience is very necessary. Things may not change immediately, but slowly and surely, it will begin to turn around.

When your love for Jesus, and your desire to be a blessing in the Kingdom of God overwhelms you, you WILL press on past every bit of opposition, to where you are supposed to be. You will NEVER give in or give up!

Joseph is a great example of running the race and winning the prize. It took over 20 years for the plan of God to be realised in his life, but he pressed on! Talk about patience...

Forget the past and press on for the future!

February 21

He who walks [as a companion] with wise men is wise,
but he who associates with [self-confident] fools is
[a fool himself and] shall smart for it.
Proverbs 13:20

Who Are My Friends?

We need to be wise when it comes to whom we spend our time with. Often we may think that a relationship with a friend is purely innocent, but be careful! Not every friend you meet, is sent to you by God!

Always check with your heart whether you are coping well. If you are not sure, then draw back and take a wise account of what is happening. It would be better for you to stick close to people who love God and are not "self"-motivated, or living with one foot in and one foot out of the Kingdom.

Nobody should have such a hold on your life that they lead you into questionable circumstances. Only your relationship with God should have that kind of place in your life. Cut ties with such people, as a foolish friend will lead you into trouble.

When you give your life in friendship, let it be with someone who will value and appreciate your commitment, someone who will be loyal, dedicated, honest and prepared to go through thick and thin with you.

Friendships always go through challenges, but if they are Godly friendships they will bless your life. Foolish friends will tear you apart and in the end your heart will be broken.

To have a special friend is a gift from God. Love and appreciate them, and never take them for granted.

February 22

A man's mind plans his way, but the Lord directs his steps and makes them sure.
Proverbs 16:9

Divine Destiny In God

God paid a very high price for you. Jesus died so that you are able to have a future in God. He gave you the controls – they are in your hands. You can't blame your parents, your church or the government if you are messing up your future.

It's good for you to go ahead and plan your life when you are submitted and walking in tune with the Lord. He is the one that will lead you in those plans and keep you on the right track.

If you keep close to the Lord you will avoid the very things that will waste your time and energy.

The wrong decision at the wrong time equals disaster.

The wrong decision at the right time equals mistake.

We all make mistakes and have even had some disasters. Learn how to get over them and rise above them. Don't carry old baggage of mistakes and disasters of years gone by. Let them go!

There is a new opportunity for you, every single day. Make it count; do not lose heart, but stay strong in God.

Confess this:

"I am born with a destiny and a purpose. I am valuable and indispensable to God. I make a decision to live in divine destiny in God."

February 23

Beloved, do not be amazed and bewildered at the fiery ordeal which is taking place to test your quality, as though something strange (unusual and alien to you and your position) were befalling you.
1 Peter 4:12

Excellent Quality

If you are going through a tremendous storm at the moment, then rejoice, because you are going to come out great on the other side.

Christians think that they are not going to face one problem or challenge from the moment that they give their lives to Jesus.

That cannot possibly be true, just look at what the disciples went through. We are living in different times but the pressures are similar. You live in a very real world. You will have to be strong, and know who your God is, to be able to live your life successfully in the Lord.

The difference in knowing the Lord is that when the storm comes, you know what to do.

We all face a "fiery ordeal", but we walk through it just like we walk through the valley of the shadow of death. God is on your side fighting with you. The battle will make you stronger, and if it is a war then hold tight and never let go of what you know belongs to you in Jesus.

When the fiery ordeal comes, brace up, and put on your armour. Remember, the battle is the Lord's, but the victory belongs to you.

February 24

Where there is no counsel, purposes are frustrated, but with many counsellors they are accomplished.
Proverbs 15:22

Help Me!

Never let pride keep you from speaking to someone you can trust about your decision, especially if it is a major one. Learning to make wise decisions takes a lifetime. You can avoid mistakes by sharing with someone who is trustworthy, who may have walked the same road before. The hard thing about making a mistake is that you lose a tremendous amount of time getting back on track.

The Word of God is clear about getting help when you are not 100% sure, or do not have 100% confidence in your decision. God encourages us to speak to others and get their counsel.

Over the years I have had to make some major decisions. My biggest mistake came when I did not want to speak to anyone at the time, as I had lost my trust in people.

Be sure to have no shadow of doubt about what you are supposed to do. In other cases, where there are doubts, seek wise men or women in their particular field to advise you.

Don't go to a person who has had three marriages and ask them how to keep your marriage healthy!! Rather, go to a couple that have celebrated their 40th wedding anniversary and get counsel from them.

If you are about to embark on a major change, speak to someone who has successfully passed the test.

February 25

For the [true] love of God is this: that we do His commands [keep His ordinances and are mindful of His precepts and teaching]. And these orders of His are not irksome (burdensome, oppressive, or grievous). For whatever is born of God is victorious over the world; and this is the victory that conquers the world, even our faith.
1 John 5:3-4

I Am An Overcomer!

I never said it, He did! When you act on His commandments and walk in love you will stand out among the crowd and victory will be all over your face.

The world cannot attain the victory that is available to the child of God, because the victory that the child of God obtains is not of this world. It comes from the Father God who has obtained a greater way for us to live through His precious son Jesus.

The world destroys you with its yoke, and its burden is killing. Jesus said that His burden is light and His yoke is easy.

You have been raised up by the power of God into newness of life, as a victorious conqueror over the bondage of the world. Then walk in it?

If you belong to Jesus, then wake up. Take His burden, and if your burden now is heavy, realise that it is not from God and deal with it accordingly.

Refuse to be manipulated by the devil and do not compromise your confident stand in God.

February 26

He who covers and forgives an offence seeks love, but he who repeats or harps on a matter separates even close friends.
Proverbs 17:9

I Will Protect You!

You and I are not perfect. We are striving to be more perfect and we will only be perfect when that which is perfect is come, namely Jesus!

When someone near you stumbles and they ask you for forgiveness and you forgive, cover his or her weakness, and you will have God's blessing in your life. When you expose their weakness and faults, you will break down your relationship and you will reap what you sow.

Some folks require a lot more forgiveness than others do. They may continually be doing something that generates problems, but if their hearts are right you will have to be there for them, supporting them, as they get stronger in the Lord.

Others are simply determined to cause as many problems as they can, and do not care what strife they may generate. These folks are dangerous, so find another friend.

God puts the onus on us and expects us to protect one another from wolves, that would like to devour us at every opportunity.

February 27

Create in me a clean heart, O God, and renew a right, persevering, and steadfast spirit within me.
Psalm 51: 10

Heart Transplant

There is plenty of evil going on in this world and South Africa is no exception.

When crime breaks loose, that is when you need to hold fast and keep your eyes on Jesus. You need to realise that the devil's time is up, and that he is fighting with every ounce of his being to do what he does best - kill, steal and destroy!

This is when you have to guard your heart from whatever challenge you are facing. Only by staying close to God will you be strong enough to deal with everything that comes your way. He will keep your heart in a good place.

To keep your heart pure, you must guard your meditation. Be careful what you read and watch on television; be careful what conversations you participate in! If you don't, you will become hysterical about the circumstances, and then your faith will not work for you.

God has given us the anointing to handle our lives wisely. We must listen to His encouragement and allow Him to lead us into green pastures.

God is building a new nation, with a new heart and purpose. Are you going to be a part of it?

February 28

Charm and grace are deceptive, and beauty is vain [because it is not lasting], but a woman who reverently and worshipfully fears the Lord, she shall be praised!
Proverbs 31:30

Beauty Is Skin Deep

From the world's point of view about a stunning woman, you would have to look like Michelle Pfeiffer and sing like Celine Dion!

God looks for something a little different! He looks for one that will worship and fear His name. When He finds such a woman, she is beautiful naturally and has charm and grace to go with it all.

A woman who loves the Creator is wise and knows that:

Without His wisdom, she cannot get anything properly done.
Without His peace, she is covered in frowns of stress.
Without His love, she cannot cope with daily challenges.
Without His joy, she is a miserable pain.
Without His approval, she is nothing in a nothing world.

A God-fearing woman has beauty that comes from within, it does not fade through sin and strife, but blossoms by the satisfaction of her years.

She has learnt all about grace, kindness, goodness and compassion from her Father. When she speaks, others are taken by her words of love and wisdom.

She will be praised just as God has promised her!

February 29

*Beloved, I pray that you may prosper in every way and
[that your body, may keep well] even as [I know]
your soul keeps well and prospers.*
3 John 1:2

God Wants You To Prosper!

Prosperity does not mean you lying at the pool with a glass of champagne in one hand and a cigar in the other – hopefully not! The world does not know another way to depict prosperity.

True Bible prosperity means to meet any given need at any given time, through the power of God. Touching broken lives, praying for the sick, loving the unlovely and giving to the poor. It is about having enough resources to reach anything at any time.

The Father has blessed my life with prosperity. When I was discouraged and deflated, He spoke a powerful word into my life: "Take your place!" That word of prosperity put me where I am today – on fire and in love with Jesus. What word has the Lord spoken into your heart lately?

The Lord supplied food for me, when the cupboard was bare. When I needed transport he supplied a bright red Cadillac. When I battled to have children, God gave me two beautiful children. God is so good.

It's the Fathers desire for you to prosper above all else.
In your soul – peace, joy, calm, understanding and knowledge
In your body – health, strength, and long life.

Prosperity for abundant life in Jesus belongs to us.

March

Best Foot Forward

March 1

*A happy heart is good medicine and a cheerful mind works healing,
but a broken spirit dries up the bones.*
Proverbs 17:22

Hallelujah!

*G*uard your heart from all sorts of things that would bring discouragement, depression and fear your way. Meditate on the Word of God on a daily basis, and He will lift your spirit and give you something to sing about.

Singing is good relief to a heavy heart, and laughter will cause you to see everything through different eyes. It is important that you are aware of what is going on around you in our world, but when those things begin to drag you down, you are heading for a sick body and a discouraged mind.

I have a natural gift of encouragement, and whenever I am around people I try and encourage them to reach for new heights. I know that when I am around a joyful person I find myself humming and singing a new song to the Lord.

Continue to give thanks to the Lord for all He has done for you, and you will never look back or slip into a pit.

Keep your heart singing in all circumstances. Keep your mind fixed on the Lord. You will work healing in your body and all those around you will be blessed.

March 2

I give you a new commandment: that you should love one another. Just as I have loved you, so you too should love one another. By this shall all [men] know that you are My disciples, if you love one another [if you keep on showing love among yourselves].
John 13:34–35

One Body, One People

God is calling the Body Of Christ together. Jesus only has ONE bride and not many as some would think! We may live in different houses, but we are certainly ONE unit.

As I travel across South Africa preaching and teaching in churches, I sense more and more the heart of the Father, for us to come together in UNITY. It would not take long for us to get the world saved if this happened! Can you imagine how powerful the church would be?

God's Word says that our unity and our love for one another, reveals Jesus and that we ARE His disciples. How sad it is that sometimes the only time the world sees our love is when there is a tragedy.

We must never give up on our desire to come together as the Body Of Christ in unity, as it is in that place, that God COMMANDS His blessing upon us.

We experienced a miracle in South Africa and we came through very difficult circumstances, but it brought us together as NEVER before! Now, we have to see the miracle continue as we seek His face as a Nation, on behalf of the Nation.

Stand up, put your shoulders back, put a smile on your face and reach out and love one another, as God has commanded. We have a miracle in the palm of our hands.

March 3

Look carefully then how you walk! Live purposefully and worthily and accurately, not as the unwise and witless, but as wise (sensible, intelligent people), Making the very most of the time [buying up each opportunity], because the days are evil.
Ephesians 5:15–16

Best Foot Forward

How is your walk? When you have the opportunity to walk in kindness, do you?

Are you carrying peace around with you wherever you go?

All these attitudes are vital to making your character line up with the Word of God and not just relying on the anointing. The anointing will only enhance your life if the fruit is there. What good is it if you have the anointing, but have no love and no kindness?

Are you walking in confusion, are you walking in strife, or are you walking in peace, joy and self-control?

The Word tells you to live purposefully and worthily as a wise, sensible and intelligent person. You will have to make the decision to do just that.

Life is amazing, and we are blessed to be able to enjoy it the way God has planned. Put your best foot forward and don't give God your second-hand attention.

Let your character Glorify God!

March 4

He refreshes and restores my life (my self); He leads me in the paths of righteousness [uprightness and right standing with Him – not for my earning it, but] for His name's sake.
Psalm 23:3

Follow His Lead

*C*haracter is more important than what you achieve. It is carefully moulded and developed over many years of training. It cannot be shaped in a moment; it is what you are becoming on a daily basis.

Your character will affect the decisions you make, the words you speak, the relationships you develop and the actions you take. It takes a lifetime to develop a good name and a moment to break it down to nothing.

After whom are you fashioning your character? Perhaps you had a good example in your parents. If not, then you will have to be careful and take a good look at yourself. Can you see the Godly traits?

Fashion your character after your Father God and Jesus. Take the examples set in God's Word and allow the Holy Spirit to help you to live by them.

Can you say as Paul said: "Imitate me, as I imitate Christ"?

You can develop character with the help of the Holy Spirit and by the power of God.

March 5

Hear counsel, receive instruction, and accept correction that you may be wise in the time to come.
Proverbs 19:20

I Want To Be Wise

Are you prepared for your future? What are you doing to know what direction you should take or when you should take it?

When you are counselled do you hear what is being said? Do you take the instruction and act upon it?

The Lord gives us encouragement when He says that we are to be teachable and pliable in the decisions we make. Sometimes a slight adjustment makes the whole plan not 75% sure but 90% sure, and that is wise. Nothing should ever be in our lives without His input.

Good instruction and correction can come from other avenues too. My mother has helped me make many wise decisions, and so have many of my precious friends. It is not wise to cut yourself off from avenues that are going to help lead you into prosperity.

When you are in doubt, seek wise counsel and then honour the counsel you have received.

God brings people into our lives to strengthen us.

Pay attention to wise counsel and then go forward boldly.

March 6

To the weak (wanting in discernment) I have become weak (wanting in discernment) that I might win the weak and over-scrupulous. I have [in short] become all things to all men, that I might by all means (at all costs and in any and every way) save some [by winning them to faith in Jesus Christ].
1 Corinthians 9:22

Culture Shock

Have you considered that God might put you in an extraordinary situation so that you can bring Christ to different people? The only culture that is right is the Biblical one.

Americans like to drive big cars, but in some countries, if you drive a big car, you're a con or a pimp. Germans like to have schnapps, but in America if you have schnapps some people may think that you are not saved.

When you find yourself being confronted with unusual groupings, you don't have to compromise your Christianity, but you can be the light!

I have had the wonderful opportunity of visiting many nations. Some have been more pleasant than others, but in all of them, one feels the love of God for the precious people.

Even when their culture does not match your own, make up your mind to see the best in all that you experience.

Christianity is NOT a religion, but it is having an intimate relationship with the Father God through Jesus the Son, and the Holy Spirit who is sent to be our Help.

Christianity will cross any boundary and reach across any culture line, because it is founded on LOVE.

We need to see every individual as valuable and precious!

March 7

He who finds a [true] wife finds a good thing
and obtains favour from the Lord.
Proverbs 18:22

I Am The Good!

My understanding of Proverbs 18:22 has changed quite a bit over the years.

Proverbs 18:22 when talking about a "good thing", in the original the word "thing" does not exist! Praise the Lord! The original reads like this, "He who find a (true) wife finds the good and obtains favour from the Lord".

I LOVE the original, because I have always thought... "I really don't like being called a "thing"!

Through the centuries women have been so badly abused and misused. The Word of God teaches us differently about the right way to treat a woman and especially a wife.

God expresses Himself in this Scripture to the fact that a precious wife is one to be honoured, respected, and appreciated. She is a treasure that will make a man, and if wrongly treated, she can break a man too.

A wife is a partner in life. She is one to share responsibilities, help carry the home, manage the children and support and minister to her husband. Together they are an unstoppable team.

Showing respect, honouring and adoring one another, encouraging each other to excel and blossom in their gifts and calling is what it is all about. Marriage is not a competition between two people, but a completion between two people. The "L" stands for Love!

Finding favour with the Lord is something we all desire.

God calls a good (true) wife "favour from the Lord".

Men need to discover this favour and enjoy the blessing
of what they have found.

March 8

These words I speak to you are not incidental additions to your life, homeowner improvements to your standard of living. They are foundational words, words to build a life on. If you work these words into your life, you are like a smart carpenter who built his house on solid rock. Rain poured down and the river flooded, a tornado hit – but nothing moved that house. It was fixed to the rock.

Luke 8:13

Challenged To Change

But if you just use my words in Bible studies and don't work them into your life, you are like a stupid carpenter who built his house on the sandy beach. When a storm rolled in and the waves came up, it collapsed like a house of cards.

It's not going to do you any good running from meeting to meeting just to get your ears tickled by the flavour of the month teachings. The Word you hear has to become the Word you do.

Jesus gives us an example of two types of hearers:

The one who heard and stayed the same.

The one who heard and was changed. Are you changing?

Have you grown in the last few months in the Lord?

The reason why Jesus came into this world was to set the platform so that you could change from the old to the new! Don't spend the rest of your life carrying old baggage around with you.

Changing for the better is part of the Christian walk.

Make a concerted effort and challenge yourself to greater heights.

March 9

*Do not say, I will repay evil; wait [expectantly] for the Lord,
and He will rescue you.*
Proverbs 20:22

I Give It To You, Lord

The last time someone attacked you personally, how did you respond, especially if you were innocent?

If you became bitter and allowed hurt to overcome you, then Satan has the upper hand. You may even have acted and said things that you would regret in the future.

The Father is always on the side of the righteous, and when we leave evil people who do not know what they are doing to themselves, they will eventually destroy everything around them.

Sure, it is difficult to stand by and watch someone try to destroy you. However, when God says He will rescue you, you can be sure of the best protection and deliverance available. Keep away from those who want to suck you into their confusion and strife.

I think of David listening to the yelling of Goliath everyday as he humiliated the Jews! But when you study it, it was defeating Goliath that made David who he became! Without Goliath, there would be no David? An enemy can be the best thing that will ever happen to you, as it will cause you to be raised to where God wants you to be! When David ran at Goliath with his sling, he shouted "I come to you in the name of the Lord of Hosts". David never backed off one bit!! Then he cut Goliath's head off...

Nothing can destroy a child of God when he walks upright and follows the instructions of the Lord.

Let God take control of your unjust circumstances and take note as
He exalts you in the presence of your enemies.

March 10

Do not judge and criticise and condemn others, so that you may not be judged and criticised and condemned yourselves. For just as you judge and criticise and condemn others, you will be judged and criticised and condemned, and in accordance with the measure you [use to] deal out to others, it will be dealt out again to you.
Matthew 7:1-2

Growing Pains

Honesty is easy for some but not as easy for others.

By whatever measure you measure your neighbour, be prepared to receive the same measure in return. Do not for one moment think that you can dish out all kinds of judgment on others, and get away with it; your turn will come!

We need to be truly careful about how we examine the lives of others if we are doing similar things. Your adversary will make sure that your weakness is exposed.

It is so much safer to have mercy and kindness foremost in your heart. In my old nature I could be quite critical of the faults of others, and was amazed when I heard rumours about what others said about me. I have been able to develop the law of kindness on my lips, and now things are really different for me.

How perfect are you? How loyal are you? How kind are you? Look at the weaknesses in your own life before you pick on others.

March 11

Every Scripture is God-breathed (given by His inspiration) and profitable for instruction, for reproof and conviction of sin, for correction of error and discipline in obedience, [and] for training in righteousness (in holy living, in conformity to God's will in thought, purpose, and action).
2 Timothy 3:16

Teach Me, Dear Lord!

Every Scripture in the Bible was planned by God and holds its position today. It was written to give us a clear understanding by which we could live the abundant life in Jesus. Many of the lessons will challenge you, and even discipline and correct you in daily living.

Discipline is hard for the one being disciplined, but the end result is blessing. Sometimes we rebel against discipline because our "self" does not like to be told what to do by anyone other than "self".

The Word tells us clearly that the purpose of Scripture is to teach us truth. It is the mirror against which we have to measure ourselves, to get our roots "firmly and deeply implanted in Him, being continually built up in Him" (Col. 2:4-7).

The Word that God breathes into us will develop us into dynamic people. Ahead of us is a challenging road of wonderful blessings. If we walk the road with God we will have the rich treasure of His Presence. If we try to do it alone we will be comfortless, and our fruit will be in vain.

How staggering to have God's Word written and in our hearts.

March 12

The righteous man walks in his integrity; blessed (happy, fortunate, enviable) are his children after him.
Proverbs 20:7

How Am I Walking?

Who is a righteous man? He is one who practices good ethics, fairness, nobility and justice. He lives a honourable life and can be trusted.

The righteous man lives an uncompromising life governed by the Word of God. He meditates, listens to and obeys the voice of the Lord. He has sown his seeds of righteousness, and his harvest continues to come to him long after he is dead.

The fruit of his life is blessing in abundance. All who have had the opportunity of being touched by his life are enriched and blessed.

The children of a righteous man will be envied by all for the opportunity of them being exposed to the fine example he has set. If they follow his example, they too will be blessed.

The most precious lifestyle that you can live is one that continues to bear fruit long after you have left this earth.

What fruit are you bearing?

Make the changes.

March 13

For You did form my inward parts;
You did knit me together in my mother's womb.
Psalm 139:13

You Are Unique

While in preparation for doing a teaching, I came across some very exciting meanings and synonyms for the word "unique".

Unique: incomparable, matchless, peerless, unequalled, unexampled, unrivalled, the only one of its kind, unusual and remarkable.

Isn't it sad that, despite the individuality God has bestowed upon each of us, we still find ourselves competing as well as expecting others to conform to the "competition"? We should be able to walk into the company of anybody and feel the freedom to be ourselves.

Don't try and be someone else. If you give in to this pressure you will no longer be unique but a poor copy. It is good to admire someone who might be a Godly example, but make sure you don't lose your individuality by cloning everything they do.

God has made you different from any other individual. He was there from the second you were conceived. Walk in that confidence and allow your particular character and personality to shine.

You are one of a kind. Stop trying to be who you are not and begin to enjoy who you are.

March 14

The King's heart is in the hand of the Lord, as are the watercourses;
He turns it whichever way He wills.
Proverbs 21:1

God Is In Control

What are you afraid of?

We need to learn to trust the Lord and have confidence in Him when it comes to our future. No matter what circumstances we are living in, God has got a plan.

All God requires of us is to pray, trust and be obedient, and to know that He has everything under control. He will do what is necessary to bring our lives to a peaceful state.

Being raised as a South African, and having lived through the miraculous changes that have taken place in South Africa has been a breathtaking experience. To see liberty come to millions of people and to know that the heart of God is blessed by our decision, is more than enough for me to know that we are on the winning side.

When we honour and love one another in the fear of the Lord, and when we put our trust in the Almighty God, we shall eat of the good fruit that we sow and our lives will be enriched in His Presence.

God knows what He is doing!

March 15

Keep awake and watch and pray [constantly], that you may not enter into temptation; the spirit indeed is willing, but the flesh is weak.
Mark 14:38

Willing But Weak

Are you having trouble getting your flesh to obey your spirit? Do you really desire to do what is right, but when the crunch comes your flesh gets the better of you? If this is your experience it is a sure sign that you need to spend a little more time in prayer building up your resistance to the flesh.

We make promises to Him and ourselves, but we do not keep them. Remember all the New Year's resolutions, which we made in the past about what we were going to change and did not keep? Wishful thinking will never help us get where we want to go in God.

However, God is tolerant with us, but we keep disappointing ourselves. We know how to get out of our weaknesses, but we do nothing constructive about them.

As we are forever before the Father, we will build strength against temptation.

Temptation will come, so what are you going to do with it? You should turn your back on it and just say "no".

March 16

Who are you to pass judgment on and censure another's household servant? It is before his own master that he stands or falls. And he shall stand and be upheld, for the Master (the Lord) is mighty to support him and make him stand.
Romans 14:4

You Can Get Up Again

While learning to walk, a toddler will continue to fall down. The parents jump up and help him to his feet, encouraging him to try again until he has perfected the walking lesson. Jesus does the same for you. When you fall down, He is there to pick you up. Don't shun His support; appreciate and accept His helping hand.

The devil wants to keep you down. Don't let him! Listen to the Good news. The price has already been paid. If you listen to the bad news, you will continue to make mistakes.

We have all fallen short of the glory of God. Pick yourself up and get your heart and attitude right so that you can be of help to someone else. You don't know what God is busy doing in their lives.

If we confess our sins, He is faithful and just to forgive us our sin and cleanse us from all unrighteousness (see 1 John 1:9).

March 17

It is better to dwell in a corner of the housetop [on the flat oriental roof, exposed to all kinds of weather] than in a house shared with a nagging, quarrelsome, and faultfinding woman.
Proverbs 21:9

What A Challenge!

Well, what can we say about that! Sometimes we ladies forget that we have covered the subject a hundred times, and so we repeat it just one more time, in case nobody got it the first time!

Ladies must do their best NOT to nag their husbands and sound like a dripping tap! In fact, you may see the men disperse when the wife starts to list the order of the day!

What's a wife supposed to do?

Mind you, it seems like the same thing was happening when this Scripture was written. One would think that men would have learned to pay attention when the wife speaks by now.

Ladies, let us make a concerted effort not to repeat an issue more than twice. Don't be quarrelsome. If you shorten the repeats, shock will set in, and the point will be made. Who knows, but the Lord, what results will be evident.

Another scenario would be to allow the men to live on the roof!

Help us Lord to communicate without frustration.

March 18

*Be well balanced (temperate, sober of mind), be vigilant
and cautious at all times; for that enemy of yours, the devil,
roams around like a lion roaring [in fierce hunger],
seeking someone to seize upon and devour.*
1 Peter 5:8

Draw The Line

It's time to get aggressive with your enemy, the devil. Don't let the devil or any individual take control of your life. Stand up and protect yourself and your goods from destruction.

Too often we have allowed ourselves to be bullied. As a result, we have never fulfilled the vision that God has given us.

Whether you like it or not, there is a war going on and you must not let anyone cross over the border into your territory. Draw the line and declare it out of bounds.

Take control of your own life. Rise up and walk in your God-given authority. Most of all, let him who stole, steal no more.

Realise that the devil is seeking whom he may destroy– do not open the door for him to enter. Keep all your protection barriers up and stay strong in the Lord. The devil has his place, and it is under your feet.

The devil is seeking a "whom"; don't you be the whom.

March 19

He who guards his mouth and his tongue keeps himself from troubles.
Proverbs 21:23

Keep Out Of Trouble

When we suffer a personal attack from someone, we feel it is our right to belittle him or her with whatever words that will come out of our mouths at the time.

This is when we are the most vulnerable. The Lord has given us wonderful counsel in that we are in control of what comes out of our mouths. We are not forced to say the things we say.

Put a guard at your mouth and take account of every word that you speak. Idle words are wasteful, but words of wisdom and peace are precious. It is the idle, fruitless words that we are to guard against.

Not one person likes to find himself in trouble. Trouble fills your heart and days with wasted energy. Trouble is described in the thesaurus as: distress, calamity, woe, misfortune, worry and tribulation.

Keep your life from trouble. Before you utter one word, be aware of what is about to proceed from your mouth. Evaluate whether the impact of your words will enhance or bring your life into trouble.

When confusion comes knocking at your door, set a guard before your mouth and take an account of every word that you speak.

March 20

Just think of Him Who endured from sinners such grievous opposition and bitter hostility against Himself [reckon up and consider it all in comparison with your trials], so that you may not grow weary or exhausted, losing heart and relaxing and fainting in your minds. You have not yet struggled and fought agonisingly against sin, nor have you yet resisted and withstood to the point of pouring out your [own] blood.
Hebrews 12:3-4

Hear And Do

After your New Year's resolution you decided to get your body in shape. Did you go to the gym and pay all that money, and never go back there again?

Most discipline is just learning to say "no" when your flesh says "yes" and saying, "yes" when your flesh says "no".

Simple!

How often have you attended church and decided: "That was a good word; I am going to do that" and nothing comes of it? Have you been given good counsel and ignored it?

You need to be disciplined. You might not enjoy it, but the end result makes it worthwhile.

The more you get your "yes" to be "yes" and your "no" to be "no" you will gain the upper hand over your flesh.

We can resist all the things that would distract us from living a life of purity in Christ. You need to do your good intentions.

March 21

Take no part in and have no fellowship with the fruitless deeds and enterprises of darkness, but instead [let your lives be so in contrast as to] expose and reprove and convict them.
Ephesians 5:11

Follow Jesus

You are familiar with the phrase "everybody's doing it". It is usually used when you feel like you need to give an explanation for something you are doing that may be a problem to others!

Unacceptable is purely unacceptable!

Guard yourself against going with the flow of the world. Live by the standard of your own decisions and do not be influenced by another's compromising stance. You are going to have to answer for your own lifestyle. See that your life will bring others closer to the Lord and not cause them to stumble or slip away.

In God's Kingdom it's not majority rules. It is God rules!

You have heard about the "W.W.J.D" bracelets that all the sportsmen are wearing. It stands for "What Would Jesus Do?" When you are pushed to compromise and follow the crowds, ask yourself: "What would I do?" Follow Jesus' example.

Allow Jesus to be the one you fashion your life after.

This will expose the works of darkness and give you the victory in every situation.

March 22

Train up a child in the way he should go [and in keeping with his individual gift or bent], and when he is old he will not depart from it.
Proverbs 22:6

Come, My Child

How hard my mother worked at teaching me what she thought was right for my life. Today, I hear her words echo in my heart, "Lynda, have you done your homework?" Even though I never once had a real desire to do my homework, I know that all the effort I put into my life at an early age, has helped me to become what I am now.

When you think back on the wonderful instruction your mother (if she was wise) gave you, you will find that you are passing the same information on to your own children.

That is why it is very important that you plant the Word of God into their hearts, and when they come to an age of accountability for their own lives, they will make the right choices.

Training someone takes patience, effort and lots of LOVE. Look for the gifting in your child's life, and encourage them to blossom. Do not try to develop them into what you wanted to be. Do not try to live your life through them. Allow them to grow into the special person that God wants them to be, and then your life will be blessed.

Never think that the seeds you are planting will not bear fruit. The Word of God will produce good fruit every time.

March 23

For the body does not consist of one limb or organ but of many. If the foot should say, Because I am not the hand, I do not belong to the body, would it be therefore not [a part] of the body?
1 Corinthians 12:14-15

Find Your Place

Have you figured out where you fit in the Body of Christ? Have you made an effort to become involved in your local church?

We are a team working together to build God's Kingdom; everyone of us has something to do. To be a part of this great team encourages us to do our part as a team member.

Imagine in soccer if the goalie just decided to leave his team and play for the other side. What a disaster! Christ is the one who places you in the team where He wants you to be placed; you cannot place yourself. The hand needs the eye and the eye needs the foot.

Don't desire to have someone else's position. If you do, you will be like a square peg trying to fit into a round hole.

One day you'll stand before your Heavenly Father, and He is going to ask: "My child, did you do what I told you to do?" You will not be able to blame anyone for your disobedience.

Find your place, and knuckle down and be useful in God's Kingdom.

March 24

If you faint in the day of adversity, your strength is small.
Proverbs 24:10

I Will Get Through This

Never look at adversity and think that you are not going to cope. Adversity will show you just how strong you really are.

In fact, the adversity you experience will make you stronger.

When a young man decides to build muscle in his body, he will not accomplish his goal by eating protein powder and thinking about how strong he is getting. He is going to have to sweat a little for a long time before he sees his muscles beginning to show.

He may start with little weights initially, but shortly he will be working out with much heavier weights as his muscle strength increases. If he gives up after the first workout he will never reach his goal, and he will be demoralised.

The Father encourages us to push through the pain and get to the other side. Yes, it is hard to get through; yes, it takes physical, emotional and mental strength, but the prize is huge and you can do it.

Actually, between you and I, adversity has been a blessing to me. I'm a much better person now, and I don't give in under pressure anymore.

This challenge is going to cause you to rise up to the next level – welcome it and go for it.

March 25

Casting all your care on Him, for He cares for you...
1 Peter 5:7

He Cares For Me!

Have you ever thought that God does not really care about you? That's normal, and it is an old trick of the mind and the devil.

You may be facing some dismal circumstances right now, or may be hassled by some small issues. No matter how big or small they might be, God cares so much for you that He has them in mind, and when you give them to Him, He will deal with them so that you can be set free. He longs to touch your life in such a mighty way, but He needs your co-operation.

You are going to have to gain confidence in God's love to learn how to release the pressure in your life to God.

He says, "casting all", not some of it, but all of your cares. If you continue to fret and worry about that situation, then you are either not trusting God to take care of your problems, or you have not handed them over to Him yet.

Don't try and do God's work. If your cares are in His hands you can be sure He will do something about them.

Pray this prayer aloud:
"Father God, I trust You explicitly; I cast the whole of my care once and for all on You. I refuse to be anxious, because You have my life in the palm of your hand... in Jesus' name!"

March 26

Obey your spiritual leaders and submit to them [continually recognising their authority over you], for they are constantly keeping watch over your souls and guarding your spiritual welfare, as men who will have to render an account [of their trust]. [Do your part to] let them do this with gladness and not with sighing and groaning, for that would not be profitable to you [either].
Hebrews 13:17

Good Shepherd, Good Sheep!

Shepherds are anointed to look after the sheep.

To be a shepherd you have to be called by God and have the recognised fruit of a shepherd in your life. You cannot set yourself up as a shepherd. If you do, you will not succeed, as God is the one who places shepherds in the Body as He wills.

Sheep should not be telling shepherds what to do. Could you imagine a little sheep saying: "I have had enough of you, Mr. Shepherd, so I am off to another pasture"?

Shepherds are also not to abuse their sheep, but to nurture, protect and lead them to pasture. Jesus is the Good Shepherd, and your shepherd should be following Him.

Fit into the Body the way that God expects, and stop doing your own thing. Follow God-fearing men and women of God who have the fruit to show for their calling.

Let your Pastor know how much you appreciate him/her.
Do it today!

March 27

*A word fitly spoken and in due season is like apples
of gold in settings of silver.*
Proverbs 25:11

You Speak Gold Apples

How precious is a word in season that encourages the heart. You need to be sensitive to the fact that an encouraging word spoken over someone's life is invaluable. A little "hello" or "you are a blessing" could make the day for someone who feels unloved.

Do your best when you are around people to be aware of their needs. Too often, you have your own needs foremost in your heart, when actually folks around you are in a much worse state.

Recently, I was in a restaurant with a friend, and the waitress serving us was in quite a state. I immediately knew that she was having a rotten day, so I smiled at her and let her feel the warmth of my heart. Before we knew it, she was smiling and bouncing around our table.

At the end of our meal I said: "Thank you for the wonderful service, and God bless you." This was too much for her as tears rolled down her cheeks. Without saying much, our love had touched her heart and had given her strength to continue her day.

You will never know the value of your smile, the warmth of your touch, and the preciousness of a treasured word.

March 28

You will show me the path of life; in Your presence is fullness of joy, at Your right hand are pleasures forevermore.
Psalm 16:11

No High Like The Highest

Talking along God's pathway is the most exciting thing you could ever do. It is a pathway of life. Nothing compares to Him.

People who do not know Jesus have looked at religion and thought: "How boring!" But having a personal relationship with the Lord is so far removed from what they think.

In fact, the closer you grow to the Lord, the more exciting your life becomes, the more joyous your life becomes and the more meaningful your life becomes.

Opening your heart and allowing the Lord to take control is like a shot of adrenaline. To enjoy the tremendous advantage you have, you must stop putting a lid on your walk with Him. Take the lid off and explode into His Presence; His high is the highest high you can ever experience.

People try many things to take their mind off their difficulties, but all they accomplish is an addiction to something that drags them down. Only the one Who made you knows what you need.

The pleasures that God gives you will never leave you with a hangover.

March 29

If your enemy is hungry, give him bread to eat; and if he is thirsty, give him water to drink; For in doing so, you will heap coals of fire upon his head, and the Lord will reward you.
Proverbs 25:21-22

Sort The Enemy Out

o you want to retaliate? Think again! What kind of retaliation gets "God" results?

Over the past 20 years I have used this method against my enemies. Each time I have been unfairly persecuted or ridiculed, I have blessed my enemies.

It is hard to ignore the hurt that people have caused you, especially when they are close to you. Naturally, you would like to attack them and give them a good shot back. But this is not the way that the Lord deals with His enemies. Of course, He handles things in an unusual manner, but His way will work to your benefit.

Let God lead you and show you the way to respond in each situation; a bowl of flowers, a box of chocolates, a card, a telephone call with no argument attached.

If your friend does not want to forgive you, love him anyway.
If your family does not support you, love them anyway.
If your child turns his back on you, love him anyway.
When a stranger rebukes you, love him anyway.
These actions get full marks from the Lord.

If the heart of your enemy does not change, at least you will be smiling.

March 30

*The idols of the nations are silver and gold, the work of men's hands.
[Idols] have mouths, but they speak not; eyes have they,
but they see not; They have ears, but they hear not,
nor is there any breath in their mouths.*
Psalm 135:15-17

Two-Way Communication

No relationship ever stood the test of time where only one person did the communicating.

Often, when being witnesses to people, they will attempt to justify themselves with the age-old excuse that they have their own religion and often pray to God.

This however, is the difference between their "religion" and our "relationship" with God. We not only pray to God, but we hear from God. Hallelujah! Imagine how frightened non-believers would be if one day God spoke back to them.

This is the Good news that we can share with them.

God is great but not too great for us to reach Him!

We can approach Him anytime and speak with Him directly, because Jesus made a way for us to be reconciled to our Father.

He is not a lofty God who does not concern Himself with the small problems in our lives.

He cares for us and is waiting for us to involve Him in our lives.

He is a loving God Who speaks to us, hears us, and sees us. When we move towards Him, He moves towards us.

March 31

But let him who glories glory in this: that he understands and knows Me [personally and practically, directly discerning and recognising My character], that I am the Lord, Who practices loving-kindness, judgment, and righteousness in the earth, for in these things I delight, says the Lord.
Jeremiah 9:24

Do You Really Know The Lord?

God wants you to know Him personally. That is why you come to the altar and receive Him as your Lord, inviting Him into your heart to make the difference in your life.

As you draw closer to Him, you will understand and know His will and His desire in every situation. Not one thing that is revealed in His Word is hidden from you as you spend time in His Presence. In fact, it pleases the heart of God when you come closer to Him.

When do you start? Right now!

Do not waste another moment.

Begin by simply telling Him you love Him and how much you appreciate Him being a part of your life. Sing and lift your hands in worship to Him.

Having an intimate time with the Lord is vital; it will encourage your heart.

The Lord wants is to be a part of your everyday life.

April

My Great Expectation

April 1

And now, Lord, what do I wait for and expect?
My hope and expectation are in You.
Psalm 39:7

My Great Expectation

There are times when you actually do not know what to do next. If you do not have a relationship with the Lord you will probably struggle! But when you do KNOW Him, this is the perfect time to seek direction and clarity from Him.

No matter what happens around you, and no matter what your thoughts may be telling you, your confidence and your hope must be in the Lord. He has great plans for your life which He has prepared for you, if you are willing to follow after Him and serve Him.

Having God as your Father is so exciting as you never know what adventure is around the corner. Each day is filled with new unexpected things and glorious moments.

Like Peter taking that first step out of the boat onto the water, so that he could get to Jesus who had invited him to "come"! Step out of your comfort zone, "your boat", into the exciting life that God has prepared for you! Walking by faith is the only way to go!

There is NEVER a dull moment when you fully give your life to God, and you fully TRUST Him.

Increase your expectation in the Lord. He has something up His sleeve and when it comes, step out and go for it!

April 2

Many, O Lord my God, are the wonderful works, which You have done, and Your thoughts toward us; no one can compare with You. If I should declare and speak of them, they are too many to be numbered.
Psalm 40:5

There Is None Like You

While watching an Oprah Winfrey television broadcast one day, I was encouraged by the idea of starting a "thank you" journal.

This entails daily writing down at least five things for which to be truly grateful.

How often do you take time to thank the Lord for what He has done in your life? It seems as though we spend so much of our time talking about the problems in our lives, that we forget about the many thousands of wonderful blessings we have received.

Getting a new heart when you were "born again" is one of the reasons why you need to give thanks to the Lord! The miracle of your new life, and your old stony heart being replaced by a heart of love is a GREAT reason to give thanks!

I offer you a challenge! Today is the day you begin your "thank you" journal. Purchase a little dairy and make a list of five blessings you experience each day. You will not know yourself after a month, and you will be amazed at the daily victories you experience without even realising it!

Give thanks to God, for He is good and His mercy endures to all generations. Thank Him now!

April 3

My heart overflows with a goodly theme; I address my psalm to a King, My tongue is like the pen of a ready writer.
Psalm 45:1

My Heart Is Full

When your heart is full of the wonderful things that God is doing in your life, you cannot do anything else but lift your head up high, and sing and praise His name.

Singing is the one thing that I do to release the praise and the joy that is in my heart!

Have you ever walked around a shopping mall and found yourself singing along with the various songs you hear? How distressing when it's: "Yesterday, all my troubles seemed so far away, and now it looks as though they are here to stay, oh I believe in yesterday".

Your heart wants to sing! Be sure that what you are singing is a healthy song. When good things are in you in abundance, they will come out of your mouth.

There is a song of worship inside every one of us. By simply opening your mouth and making a melody while adding some words of worship (whether they rhyme or not) is how you glorify the Heavenly Father. It's a simple step of faith.

Let your worship always be pure and simple.

April 4

Whenever, though, they turn to face God as Moses did, God removes the veil and there they are – face to face.
2 Corinthians 3:16

Lift The Veil

Don't hide behind that veil!
Are you shining with the Presence of God?
Are you unveiled as you look at Him, face to face?

There should be nothing hidden between you and God, just openness, truth, honour and grace.

Has a shopping attendant ever asked you why you are so happy? The joy in your heart should reflect on your face for all to see.

Once, Jerry Savelle was walking through a shopping mall and someone was following him wherever he went. Eventually, they approached Jerry and enquired why they could see a bright light covering him, wherever he went!! Jerry was so blessed by this experience, as he was unaware of the "Presence" of the Lord that was evident to others, in his life.

You are a brilliant light in a dark world. Don't try and cover or hide your brightness away, but allow your life to speak volumes of God's love and goodness to others.

You are a bright light in the darkness; so let that light shine.

April 5

For He will give His angels [especial] charge over you, to accompany and defend and preserve you in all your ways [of obedience and service].
Psalm 91:11

I Am Safe

Having a personal "body guard" around today could be rather expensive! The Word of God promises us that God will assign His Angels to us to accompany us, defend and preserve us, in ALL our ways, when we serve Him.

The best news is that this divine protection comes at NO cost to us, but only for us to simply serve the Lord, and believe it!

This scripture has been a massive part of my life for many years, as I have travelled on countless airplanes across the globe, driven on highways and in taxis on my way to meetings and preached in dangerous venues! Nothing has given me more confidence than to KNOW that my Angels are assigned by God to take special care of me!

Not only do I believe this divine protection for myself, but I pray it daily over my children and Grandchildren. Oh what a joy, to know that we have SUPERNATURAL DIVINE PROTECTION in the crazy days in which we live.

While taking a flight to the USA, a lady spotted me on the plane and she ran to me to greet me saying, "I am so glad that you are on my flight, now I know that everything is going to be OK!"

Many of God's Heavenly Host are bored on their assignments these days, as most Christian folk do not believe that they exist! How very sad!

You are not on your own. You have your own divine army to protect you wherever you go.

April 6

But we do [strongly and earnestly] desire for each of you to show the same diligence and sincerity [all the way through] in realising and enjoying the full assurance and development of [your] hope until the end.
Hebrews 6:11

Continue Until The End

When you walk close to God and desire to do His will, you will continue to grow and maintain your zeal and diligence. No matter how much you feel you have already grown, you will discover that you are only beginning to walk by faith and still have lots to learn. In fact, the more that I learn, the more that I realise just how little I really know!

God is looking for someone who will have a teachable spirit and not stagnate; one who will continue to move up to higher places with Him. When you walk with God remember, "It's not how you start, but how you finish that counts".

Of course it's a challenge but in the end you will have grown closer to the Lord and you will be so much stronger. Every step of the journey is part of your beautiful progress in God.

I know a number of folk who started in the ministry with a bang and did amazing things for God, but after a little while when things became a little tough, they lost heart and simply began to fade away into obscurity.

Serving the Lord is NOT a 100-yard dash, but a cross-country marathon. Choose to be stable and consistent through the whole journey, and be sure to stop and smell the roses!

I am thankful that He loves us too much to leave us the way we are.

April 7

And overwhelming astonishment and ecstasy seized them all, and they recognised and praised and thanked God; and they were filled with and controlled by reverential fear and kept saying, We have seen wonderful and strange and incredible and unthinkable things today!
Luke 5:26

Fill Me Lord To Overflowing

You cannot put God in a box and tell Him how to do things. God is God.

There have been times in my life when God has done something beyond my understanding to bless me! I did not expect it or choose it, but He did it for me, in spite of me!

When this happens to you, let your heart be open to this miracle working God who is able to do beyond what you could ever dream or imagine! We love to put God in a box of 'how' we will accept His move! But God will move and do things according to His plan and NOT ours!

Could you imagine being around while God was creating the heavens and the earth? We would surely have seen some wonderful, strange, incredible and unthinkable things! It would certainly have taken our breath away!

Being awe struck by God is not a new experience. Picture Moses and the burning bush or Daniel in the lion's den.

When God shows up, nothing can match His power and His Presence.

April 8

Hear therefore, O Israel and be watchful to do them, that it may be well with you and that you may increase exceedingly, as the Lord, the God of your fathers, has promised you, in a land flowing with milk and honey.
Deuteronomy 6:3

Blessings Of Obedience

God has a plan for your life that you have not yet even begun to dream or imagine!

For you to receive and walk in this plan, you will need to get into agreement with His Word and His will for your life. Anything in opposition to God will not be advantageous to you.

God is no man's debtor. He chooses to bless your life because He wants to bless it, not because you deserve it, or think you can earn it, but because of Jesus and what HE has accomplished on the cross for you!

When God reveals His plan for you, it is through obedience to that plan that the blessing will unfold in your lives! If He reveals to you that you need to walk away from something, it is only because He has something much better for you in mind.

His desire is for you to increase in all you put your hand to, not just by a little, but to be exceedingly blessed!

The land flowing with milk and honey is where the blessing of the Lord is. Even if you are living in a desert He will make that desert bloom for you. He can turn any difficult situation into a great victory.

This promise was given to Israel – how much more blessing is there for the Bride of Christ.

April 9

He shall not be afraid of evil tidings; his heart is firmly fixed, trusting (leaning on and being confident) in the Lord.
Psalm 112:7

Faith Drives Out Fear

The Lord's promise is protection and abundance.

It is a temptation in our day and age to feed our fears, as we lend our ears to one horrific story of violence after another. We are clearly faced with two options; either feed that fear or starve it.

If you feed it you are sure to be among the numbers whose hearts will fail them for fear. If you choose to starve it, you will walk in peace and be a blessing and example to many.

Have you ever thought about the many times that you have escaped a serious accident just because the Lord had delayed you for a moment, to answer a telephone call, or talk to your child.

I have heard so many amazing stories of God's powerful delivering ways. If you are alert, you will drive out fear and walk through victoriously.

By lifting God up as your shield, you will shun the enemy.

We will dwell in safety when we trust confidently in the Lord

April 10

You did not anoint My head with [cheap, ordinary] oil, but she has anointed My feet with [costly, rare] perfume.
Luke 7:46

Worship The Lord

While this woman was washing Jesus' feet with the best that she had to give Him, the disciples wondered why He would allow her to "waste" this very expensive perfume on Him. They were more interested in the cost than the Presence of the One they were accompanying.

It is the same with our own lives today. How often do we not understand Whose Presence we are enjoying? We offer the bare minimum of our service to God. When it comes to giving a gift we scratch the bottom of the barrel for a little something to give. Unfortunately, this is the norm.

What would we do if Jesus offered us the bottom of the barrel, if we needed forgiveness and He dug down deep to see if there was any left for us? If His forgiveness were second or third-hand, would we still love Him with the same measure?

Jesus loves us unconditionally, how much more should we be sure that when we give, we should give of our best. God does not need our second-hand stuff!

Always give your best to God, never think you are doing Him a favour, after all, He gave His best for you in the first place!

April 11

And a woman who had suffered from a flow of blood for twelve years and had spent all her living upon physicians, and could not be healed by anyone, came up behind Him and touched the fringe of His garment, and immediately her flow of blood ceased.
Luke 8:43-44

Touch Him And Be Healed

This story teaches you how important it is to put your trust in the right person for your healing. Physicians are there to help you but your trust must be in the Lord.

This particular woman had suffered with this problem for twelve years and spent everything that she had. She was desperate to get her healing.

At some stage she must have heard about this wonderful Jesus and joining the crowd, she pushed and shoved until finally she stretched with all her might to touch His garment, and the healing power of Jesus came upon her, and she was healed.

How determined are you to get your healing from the Lord? Do you try every route until finally you give up and turn to the Lord?

The moment you discover that you have a need, you should immediately go to the Healer and worship Him and touch His garment.

Jesus in the midst of all those people felt someone touch Him in faith, and He turned around and asked the question, "Who touched me?"

It is Jesus that we need to touch.

April 12

Nevertheless, do not rejoice at this, that the spirits are subject to you, but rejoice that your names are enrolled in heaven.
Luke 10:20

My Name Is Known In Heaven

We are seated together in Heavenly places in Christ Jesus. This fact, is the reason for our extraordinary confidence, we have authority over the devil, and over all foul spirits that try to mess with our lives.

Jesus gave us a simple instruction saying that we should not be happy that the devil is subject to our authority, but rather that our names are written in the Eternal Lambs book of Life.

When the devil messes with your life, recognise him for what and who he is, use your authority in the name of Jesus and immediately send him packing. Don't spend your time entertaining him by talking to him, simply rebuke him, and get him out of the equation!

Jesus won the battle, He obtained the victory for us that we might walk in that victory and glorify the Father. All other things around us are unimportant.

Rejoice. You are on your way to spending eternity with our Heavenly Father.

April 13

For all His ordinances were before me, and I put not away His statutes from me.
Psalm 18:22

Let God Have The Final Say

Have you made any major decisions this week? Making major decisions in your life can be quite daunting, especially if you are bombarded by so many options. Just remember Who knows best! Move on God ideas and not good ideas.

As a new Christian I found myself encountering problems. Some days my zeal for God was amazing, and then on other days I would struggle to be motivated. I wondered about this at times as it made me feel a little inadequate! Thank God for His Word as I had learned NOT to be moved by what I felt but by what God's Word said I should do. This was a wonderful help to me and I began to grow and become more stable in my walk with God.

When you feel a little unsure in yourself, you can go to God's Word and allow it to be your Captain! In a moment, you will be back on track and doing what God says you should do and feeling the way God's Word says you should feel!

Thank goodness God knows better than you or I. God sees potential in your life where you may see nothing much!

Allow your love for the Lord to dominate your every feeling and decision.

April 14

Whatever you have spoken in the darkness shall be heard and listened to in the light, and what you have whispered in [peoples'] ears and behind closed doors will be proclaimed upon the housetops.
Luke 12:3

What Secret?

Read it again. WOW! Paying attention to this wisdom will stop you from getting into trouble with your life! Everyone needs to hold his or her tongue when it is not appropriate to blurt something out! Developing discipline in your life will keep you from a mountain of issues!

It begins with a simple step of choosing not to participate in secret things be it an action, or a conversation.

Nothing that you do in secret remains a secret. Note, your secret will not just be exposed but it will be shouted from the rooftops. In other words, you could find it published in the newspapers or on the television news.

I chose many years ago to do my best at keeping my conversation, and my life, in a good place.. Not even a little bit of compromise would I tolerate! If we want to go as high as God is willing to take us, we will have to be responsible people. If we make a mistake, simple bible steps will help us. Apologise, and be wiser next time.

It's the little foxes that work at breaking down the vine at every opportunity. Rather, keep control of your actions and speech and run away from the appearance of evil, especially when you are on your own. Do what is right.

Sin is pleasurable for a season!

April 15

*A hot-tempered man stirs up strife, but he who is
slow to anger appeases contention.*
Proverbs 15:18

I'm Cool!

To appease means: to calm, soften, pacify, quiet, alleviate. It is so easy to react instead of respond in a contentious situation.

Once when I was driving, I saw a man in a car crash into another car, he then reacted wildly and jumped out of his car to hit the other person. It was obvious that he was a hot-tempered individual.

Today, "road rage" is a serious issue with folk. They carry guns and shoot after one another, just because the one driver did not give way to the other!

What temperature is your temperament? If you are a calm tempered man you will try and quiet a difficult situation down, but a hot-tempered man will stir up strife.

You are always going to be faced with challenging situations that could cause you to react in the wrong manner. If you are not careful, the results could be horrendous.

Listen to the Lord's instruction and develop godly character that is pleasing in His sight. Keep out of trouble. When you want to explode, count to ten or praise the Lord. After a couple of seconds you will have a much better perspective of the situation. Disciplining the flesh takes regular exercise, and this kind of victory is a milestone in character building.

Watch for the next opportunity and give Satan the brush-off.

April 16

But seek (aim at and strive after) first of all His kingdom and His righteousness (His way of doing and being right), and then all these things taken together will be given you besides.
Matthew 6:33

What Are You Seeking?

Stop running after things!

I know that it is nice to buy a new dress and get a lovely piece of jewelry or a car, but these are only material things and should never control our lives.

Our love and affection should firstly always be on the Lord and our drive must be to get closer to Him. He promises that if we desire His presence above all else, He will bless us anyway.

Jesus said that we must not allow "things" to get too much of our attention. We are to be absorbed with His presence and to live a life that is satisfied in Him. We are encouraged by His promise that He is the one that will add the necessary things that we need in our lives.

I can testify that this is true in my life. God has been faithful and takes good care of me. Whenever He wants to, He sends a special blessing my way, it reminds me that He is my Lord and as I seek Him, He will take care of all of the 'things' that I need.

Stay hungry and engrossed with seeking the Kingdom.

April 17

Blessed (happy, fortunate, to be envied) is he who considers the weak and the poor; the Lord will deliver him in the time of evil and trouble. The Lord will protect him and keep him alive; he shall be called blessed in the land; and You will not deliver him to the will of His enemies.
Psalm 41:1-2

Consider The Poor

We must reach out to the poor. We, as children of God, cannot stand by and ignore the fact that there are many precious people in need. Jesus came for the sick, the hungry, the poor, and the lost.

This is a vital foundation of the church. Every church should have a powerful program where they are giving full attention to Psalm 41:1-2. The world may reject and cast them out, but God loves them all and the church should love them too!

When we take care of the ones God says we MUST take care of, God takes care of us.

This is why I want to encourage you not to consider your own circumstances but begin to consider the difficult circumstances of others. You will always find someone who is worse off than what you are. By reaching out to them, you will find your own need met!

God wants us to bring the "Good News" to the broken hearted. To tell them that He is a wonderful Father and that He loves them and wants to provide for them, to lift their heavy burden off of their shoulders, and to reveal His glorious love and redemption!

Jesus loved the unlovely and touched the untouchable, He gave us power to reach out and minister to their needs.

April 18

For where your treasure is, there will your heart be also.
Matthew 6:21

Your Heart Is Your Measuring Stick

Whatever is absorbing your time is where your deepest affection lies! There is nothing wrong with having your own business or a great hobby but when these get all your love and attention something is definitely amiss.

What is a treasure? A treasure is your wealth, your fortune or your riches. Some folks have their children as their most special treasure and then when their children let them down they battle to recover. Others have their bank accounts as their treasure and when the local currency loses its value they are in a state.

There is only one treasure that will never devalue or let you down and that is your relationship with the Lord. No matter what happens in your life you should give Him first place.

Christians who have suddenly begun to prosper are in danger if their hearts are not fixed on the Lord. The blessings become their treasure and the Lord is somewhere in the background.

Realise who gave you the blessings in the first place; it is just as easy to lose them, as it was to gain them.

Keep your heart fixed on Jesus and never let it be distracted.

April 19

Don't become so well adjusted to your culture that you fit into it without even thinking. Instead, fix your attention on God. You'll be changed from the inside out.
Romans 12:1-2

Culture Comes Second

Many of the acceptable teachings of our different cultures do not agree with the Word of God. Wherever you go in the world you will find ways by which man lives that do not agree with the Word of God.

Our culture should not occupy the centre of our actions and our heart, but only the Word of God should have this most important position. When our culture demands something of us that is contrary to God's will, then we should decline and obey the Word of God. We are encouraged by this Scripture to think about what we do, and why we do it.

There are also a number of things that we do in our culture that is perfectly harmless and is a blessing to those around us. In these things we should excel to bring God's love to others.

When you gave your life to Jesus, you acknowledged that you had been bought by His precious blood and were joined to the family of God. From then on, your culture was no longer of this world; but of the Kingdom of God.

No matter the culture of others, we are to live in love, joy, peace, goodness and kindness toward all men. Jesus purchased your salvation and set you free from man's traditions, rules and regulations.

You are of Christ, it is in Him that you live and move and have your being.

April 20

I know that whatever God does, it endures forever; nothing can be added to it nor anything taken from it. And God does it so that men will (reverently) fear Him (revere and worship Him, knowing that He is).
Ecclesiastes 3:14

Know And Do His Will

When God says that He will do something He means it. That is why we need to pay the utmost attention to His Word. Because God is able to do what He says He will do, we ought to walk more circumspectly in this life. To know Him and to honour Him in everything we do is our "reasonable service" to show the Father of Creation how much we love Him.

Walking in God's will is an ongoing process of making the right choices with the help of the Holy Spirit. I heard Tim Storey say this, "Don't settle for good ideas when you can have God ideas." Why have it "good" or "better" when you can have the "best"!

Your heart must be hooked up to His will, then your life will be more stable and there will be more peace within you.

God never fails.

April 21

Therefore then, since we are surrounded by so great a cloud of witnesses (who have borne testimony to the Truth), let us strip off and throw aside every encumbrance (unnecessary weight) and that sin which so readily (deftly and cleverly) clings to and entangles us, and let us run with patient endurance and steady and active persistence the appointed course of the race that is set before us.
Romans 12:1-2

Get Rid Of Extra Weight

There is a great crowd of witnesses waiting to applaud your life as you serve the King.

When you first gave your life to Jesus, so many things in your life needed to change. Some changes were easier to make than others.

When I received Christ in my life most of the weights that were clinging to me just fell off. But, then there was my smoking that took a lot longer to be gone. I went to Rhema Bible Training Centre and was still smoking! But then one day I decided that it was ridiculous that I had become the slave of a piece of rolled up paper with some leaves in it! I immediately took the packet of cigarettes and broke everyone of them in two. It wasn't a week or so later that my weight began to blossom and I could not get my clothes on. I had rediscovered the beauty of tasty food! I had simply replaced my smoking with food! I was upset as I pondered which was the better sin to have. To smoke and be skinny and stink, or to be chubby and not stink!

It was faith that arose in me that helped me to get my flesh in submission to my desire, I was able to drop them both with ease.

Give your life fully to Jesus; He will finish what he started in you!

Jesus is the author, and finisher of our faith.

April 22

But you are a chosen generation, a royal priesthood, a holy nation, His own special people, that you may proclaim the praises of Him who called you out of darkness into His marvellous light.
1 Peter 2:9

I Am Royalty

You're not to be what the magazines say you should be, what your family or society says you should be, and certainly not what the devil says you should be. You must be what your Father God says you must be.

You are a royal priesthood, a special people.

There is within you the capability to accomplish anything and be everything that God wants you to be.

You can be the best parent, the best husband or wife, the best secretary; you don't have to put on a false front. Just seize the opportunity to excel in Him.

As you lean upon Him, your potential will increase; you HAVE the mind of Christ! As you ask Him for wisdom, your ability to know what is right will increase. Everything you do will multiply because of His Presence in your life.

You came to Christ because you needed His love. Along with His love came many things that you do not deserve but He gives them to you anyway!

We praise His name because He first loved us.

April 23

Therefore, you will fully know them by their fruits.
Matthew 7:20

Check The Fruit

The Father has given us a tremendous measuring stick by which we can discover whether someone is living a God-fearing life, before we let him or her into our lives. Not everyone who proclaims to be a Christian is a true Christian.

At times I become a little discouraged when I see what people do in the disguise of Christianity. They leave behind them a trail of hurt and confusion and are unperturbed by what they have done.

This is where you examine whether the fruit is healthy or rotten. Healthy fruit can only be grown on a healthy tree and if the fruit is bad then the condition of the tree is bad.

I am so grateful for this lesson that has helped me in my relationships. I can then make a wise decision about how close I can get to this person. We do not judge others, but we judge and examine the fruit in their lives.

The Word also tells us that there are wolves that feast at our tables. We are not to be ignorant but need to identify those who are real and others who have ulterior motives. We are to believe the best of every person but don't be afraid to look at the fruit. Are there any questionable signs, do you have a check in your spirit about them?

There are those who are out to destroy and there are those who are out to bless – be wise about who you let into your life.

April 24

*Test yourselves to make sure you are solid in the faith.
Don't drift along taking everything for granted.
Give yourselves regular check-ups.*
2 Corinthians 13:5

Have Regular Check-Ups

When is the last time that you evaluated yourself properly? A good check-up on "self" every now and then keeps you from getting way off the track. We need to examine ourselves and not each other.

If we are going to live for God then we must be above suspicion not only in the eyes of God but also in the sight of man. We must live pure, honest, upright lives that testify that Jesus is Lord!

When you hear a bad report about a Christian you always hear the words "but they are supposed to be Christians". Never mind what they have done, what are you doing with your life?

Are you living honestly, at peace with others, not abusing or misusing the favour that God gives you? When you do something wrong, do you swallow your pride and get it corrected as quickly as possible. Remember, truth prevails and will help you to live with yourself after you have dealt wisely with the problem.

It is a good exercise, if you have enough courage, to ask your family or a very close friend to talk to you if they notice anything in your attitude that has become offensive. A good friend should have your TRUST to be able to share some truths with you.

Check-ups clear your thinking.

April 25

Behold, You desire truth in the inner being; make me therefore to know wisdom in my inmost heart. Purify me with hyssop, and I shall be clean (ceremonially); wash me, and I shall (in reality) be whiter than snow.
Psalm 51:6-7

Turn On The Spotlight

It's very hard to have one foot in the Kingdom of God and the other in the world. Trying to keep both worlds happy will drive you crazy!

Make a decision to quit dabbling in sin and to purify your inner life. Allow God to work on the inside of your heart. You need to make a wise decision but you will have to first take off the mask and be honest with God and honest with yourself, not caring what anyone else may think.

The spotlight of God will leave no leaf unturned. Everything will be exposed. You may be aware of these things, and when you expose them openly to God, they will be exposed and God will help you deal with them!

When God touches the hidden things of your life, immediately you become stronger. In fact, your weakness becomes His strength in your life. Only by being open and honest will you be able to deal with the things that are holding you back.

The Father does not want you to be in bondage or a slave to anything. He wants you free to love and give of yourself to Him.

April 26

So that you may surely learn to sense what is vital and approve and prize what is excellent and of real value (recognising the highest and the best, and distinguishing the moral differences), and that you may be untainted and pure and unerring and blameless (so that with hearts sincere and certain and unsullied, you may approach) the day of Christ (not stumbling nor causing others to stumble).
Philippians 1:10

More Excellence

I am sure you have noticed that age has nothing to do with maturity. Many people have been saved for years yet they are still baby Christians!

In fact we know some "great men" who can preach up a storm, draw big crowds, heal the sick, pray in tongues and so forth, but have a weak Christian witness in their daily living.

We are to excel in ministry but not leave the fruit of the Spirit out of our excellence. Just because you talk in tongues does not make you a spiritual giant. You are a spiritual giant when you walk in love and others are drawn to Christ. This basic rule of loving one another is something so close to the heart of God. In fact, the Word says that people are able to tell that we are Christians, if we have love one for another.

Whatever you do, do it in the name of Jesus. Make sure that others are being drawn closer to God by your example.

Don't be the problem, be the solution!

April 27

Lord, who may abide in Your tabernacle, who may dwell on Your holy hill? He who walks uprightly, and works righteousness and speaks the truth in his heart. He is the one. The Lord is Holy. You are not going to dwell in the house of the Lord if you are not dealing truthfully with yourself and others. You will not dwell in His tabernacle if your path is one of destruction and unrighteousness.
Psalm 15:1-2

How Can I Abide In Your Tabernacle?

Think it through? You are going to have to come to God on His terms. To help you, He has written everything down and you have no excuse about what He desires!

Fall in love with Him with ALL of your heart. Don't let anything get in the way of your relationship with Him.

You can live as close to Him as you want to! He is longing for you to come into His Presence, not once a week but on a daily basis.

Get in touch with the Father through the Son. Call upon His name and He will save you! It's only by love and obedience that you will understand the stunning things He has planned for you.

Do not draw back and think that you cannot get to know the Lord, or that He is too distant for you to grasp, He is waiting for you to come!

If I can get close to God, believe me, you can too!

April 28

*Every way of a man is right in his own eyes,
but the Lord weighs and tries the hearts.*
Proverbs 21:2

Stand To Be Corrected

My mom and dad trained me and raised me in the English tradition. One of the areas was that meal times were family times and we would all sit down together, pray and then enjoy our meal. There was just enough for one or two extra folks if necessary. If folks were invited then there would be plenty for everyone.

It may be very different in other homes! Some may have six people sit down to eat, yet they have food for ten people. Or, there may be ten people in the family but just enough food for six to eat properly!

Whatever your upbringing, learn to celebrate the good things that you have experienced. Not everyone gets it right or should think that their way is the only way of doing things.

Some folk like to eat on TV trays and watch TV, while others like to sit down at the table and enjoy a family meal.

Whatever you do, enjoy being you and don't force your opinion on others. Perhaps they think that your way is weird!!

Celebrate your difference and learn to appreciate the difference in others. When there is something to be corrected, let it be something worthwhile and not something petty.

Be pliable in the hand of God and be reasonable with your family and friends. Your way is not always right.

April 29

Strengthen, (complete, perfect) and make you what you ought to be and equip you with everything good that you may carry out His will; [while He Himself] works in you and accomplishes that which is pleasing in His sight, through Jesus Christ (the Messiah); to Whom be the glory forever and ever (to the ages of the ages). Amen.
Hebrews 13:20

What You Ought To Be

Even though you may not be aware of it, God is always working on the inside of you. To strengthen, perfect and make you what you ought to be.

Not only is God working on the inside of you to make you what you ought to be, but he is also equipping you for everything that He is calling you to do. It would be unfair of Him to expect that if he did not give us the tools to do it with.

Everything that is necessary for you to do the job will be given to you, as you need it. You have quite a lot of it already if you are born-anew. These are what the Bible calls precious "fruit" of the recreated spirit: Love, joy, peace, patience, goodness, kindness, faithfulness, gentleness and self-control all work together for a greater victory in your life.

Having God work inside of you is a miracle.

It takes a lot of pressure off you to know that He will help you get things done the way they should be done!

April 30

For with God nothing is ever impossible and no word from God shall
be without power or impossible of fulfilment.
Luke 1:37

He Will Perform His Word

That says it in a nutshell. God's Word is reliable and you can bank your entire life on what it says. If God said it, He meant it and He will bring it to pass. When God makes promises, He does not back out. He is not a man that He should lie and He does not change His mind.

When I was believing for my first child, the Lord gave us a portion of Scripture in Kings that promised us a son in due season. I knew that it was going to take faith on our part for this child to manifest.

I needed to put action to my faith so I stuck the name Joshua on his bedroom door and when friends would visit they would smile at my explanation. The smile was on the other side of their faces when baby Joshua was born a few years later.

You are going to have to stand diligently on the Word of God for His promises to be made manifest in your life. If you keep wondering if God loves you enough or whether He wants to do it for you, you are never going to get anywhere. Realise, right now, that God loves you and sent His Son, Jesus, to die for you, how much more does God have to do to get you to receive His love.

God never fails. Don't give up when things do not come to pass immediately. You may need to wait a while, but it will come to pass if God has planned it.

May

Precious Gift

May 1

Learn to do right. Seek justice, relieve the oppressed, and correct the oppressor. Defend the fatherless, plead for the widow.
Isaiah 1:17

Do What Is Right

We need to be taught how to do what is right in the sight of the Lord. Every lesson that the Word of God teaches is a lesson well learned.

We are taught in this Scripture to plead for justice on the behalf of all those who are being misused and abused because of their plight. If they are being oppressed then we are to set them free, and teach the oppressor why he is wrong; this is quite a challenge as most of the times the oppressor thinks what he is doing is right. We are to defend the fatherless from those who would treat them with contempt, and stand in the gap for the widow who may have been left helpless.

It pleases the Father's heart when His people honour His desire and do what is right. Have you ever helped a widow or cared for a child who is fatherless? When was the last time that you helped someone that was being misused by another?

Jesus came to set the captives free, to provide for the poor, to comfort the widow and be a Father to the fatherless.

The Gospel is Good News to those who will receive it. You can be a part of that Good News if you use whatever opportunity opens up to you to contribute to someone's life.

May 2

For unto us a Child is born, unto us a Son is given; and the government shall be upon His shoulder, and His name shall be called Wonderful, Counsellor, Mighty God, Everlasting Father (of Eternity), Prince of Peace.
Isaiah 9:6

Precious Gift

These are just some of the wonderful names that have been given to Jesus. If you want to know more about His character and nature, then study His names.

Within each name is a revelation of who Jesus is. The Kingdom of Heaven describes Him perfectly; the Alpha and Omega – the beginning and the end. Jesus has been there all along. He chose to be called Saviour and to come and lay down His life for us. Not because we deserve anything, but because He loves us so much that He did what was necessary to redeem us back to the Father God.

We must rejoice in that we are now called children of God, and that we belong to the family of God. Through Jesus we have been made partakers of the Kingdom of Heaven and we are seated with Him in Heavenly places. Nothing has been left out of God's provision for us through the cross. He did it all for us.

Only Eternity will reveal the great love with which He loves us!

We will live for eternity with the King of kings and the Lord of lords.
What an awesome, humbling thought.

May 3

Those who see you will gaze at you and consider you, saying, Is this the man who made the earth tremble, who shook kingdoms.
Isaiah 14:16

Is This All He Is?

What will you think of Satan when you see him for who he really is?

You will wonder why you were so afraid of him. How you allowed him to torment you with all kinds of lies and abuse. When you see him you will say, "Is this he?"

His deception will be revealed, his subtleties will be exposed, and you and I will see the all powerful, mighty, blood of Jesus, and realise that the two could never begin to compare. How could we have been so blinded, how could we have been so deceived, how could we have been so stupid? What utter nonsense it is.

Nothing can stand against the blood of Jesus; nothing can overcome the love of God. You and I are filled with awesome power and authority that has already won the battle and destroyed the evil one's eternal plan. To think that he thought he could overthrow the Father is ludicrous!

You do not stand in your own authority against the devil and his hosts, but you stand in the name of Jesus and in the power of His blood. You are armed with more than atomic bombs. All you have to do is say the Word, and the angels will back you up.

Satan's place is under your feet, be sure to keep him there.

May 4

But none of these things move me; neither do I esteem my life dear to myself, if only I may finish my course with joy and the ministry which I have obtained from [which was entrusted to me by] the Lord Jesus, faithfully to attest to the Good News (Gospel) of God's grace (His unmerited favour, spiritual blessing, and mercy).
Acts 20:24

Endurance ~ Snail Style

How many Christians do we see that are so on fire for Jesus and three months later they are nowhere to be found. "What a Rock of Gibraltar"!

When you are squeezed what comes out of you? When the pressure and the storm are raging, can you stick around? Are you a "hundred yard sprinter" or a "marathon" believer?

The devil is going to try to move you. He will use things that you care about; friends, family, workplace, and finances etc. So stay fixed, unmoved, not tossed to and fro.

Get focused on the things that God has set out for you. Let Him plant you where you need to be. Once this is settled in your heart, you will not sway backward or forward; you will be steadfast and immovable, right in the centre of His will.

Endurance and long-suffering will produce character. God will often use situations to build "stickability' into your life, like a piece of Velcro that just won't let go no matter what!

"Without endurance the two snails would never have made it to Noah's Ark".
Charles Spurgeon

May 5

You will guard him and keep him in perfect peace whose mind (both its inclination and its character) is stayed on You, because he commits himself to You, leans on You, and hopes confidently in You.
Isaiah 26:3

Keep Your Mind On Jesus

Peace is one of the most precious greatest gifts that we can have on this earth. Daily, things around us billow and surge from all kinds of striving and confusion.

By giving the Lord our first attention, we will correctly analyse what is going on around us in the world. Often I will turn the television news off if I feel my heart beginning to get overburdened by what I see and hear. Now, that does not mean that we stick our heads in the sand like the ostrich! We must be aware of world news, but we cannot let it overcome us and we forget about our victory in Jesus.

Fear and depression go hand in hand. As an individual you can only do so much to help what is going on around you. Just a few of years ago, we did not have television in South Africa and we were a lot less aware of all the pain in the world. Today, as things happen it is sent to us in detailed pictures.

You are going to have to protect your heart and your thoughts if you are going to be of any use to anyone else. Being overcome by depression and fear will keep you down so low that you will be the one that needs help.

Keep your heart and eyes fixed on Jesus!

May 6

... And be not grieved and depressed, for the JOY of the Lord is your strength and stronghold.
Nehemiah 8:10

When The Going Gets Tough, The Tough Get Joyful!

The joy of the Lord is within us to sustain us. It is a fruit of the recreated spirit, the brand new heart, and the spirit that has been born-again!

Anyone can give in or give up when faced with opposition! But it is the joyful heart that seems never to be overwhelmed or disillusioned or discouraged. Joy is not a feeling or a shallow experience; it is what we receive when we receive Jesus as our Lord and Saviour. It comes from deep inside the Spirit man.

It's up to you to tap into it and use it as a powerful spiritual force in your life. Joy will usher in breakthroughs and answers to prayer in the natural realm.

When you hang onto joy, it doesn't matter what the devil brings your way or what tests and trials you go through, your joy in Jesus will be your stronghold and your strength.

> When tough times, are rough times,
> Don't let go of what you know.
> Doom and gloom are wicked;
> They wont let you in the flow.
> So wake up, and shake up that happy little heart,
> A Jesus "Toyi-Toyi" you need to start (African form of dance)
> I hear it; I hear it, a waking melody.
> The angels are singing, a three part harmony!

Look, look!
All the dark clouds are breaking, This victory song is in the making.

May 7

And the Lord said, For as much as this people draw near Me with their mouth and honour Me with their lips but remove their hearts and minds far from Me, and their fear and reverence for Me are a commandment of men that is learned by repetition (without any thought as to the meaning).
Isaiah 29:13

Relationship Not Religion

Is your relationship with the Lord purely good behaviour, or do you really know Him? Yes, God is out there somewhere, but is He unreachable to you? That's why Jesus came and died for you. By accepting Him as your Saviour, you will come into full relationship with God.

Attending church may help your basic God understanding, but to live in abundance you will have to connect your heart to God. Get hungry to know Him, reach out and call upon His name, and He will come into your life.

God wants a family, one to call His own. One who will serve, love and appreciate Him out of relationship, not out of compulsion or fear. Jesus is the link, the miracle. Through Him we walk and talk with God.

You can attend church every day of your life, but where is your heart? Is your worship only lip service to Him? Have you drifted from His companionship? Revelations talks about us being either cold or hot… but lukewarm, is just not on?

Only you can change the temperature of your intimacy with Him.

You cannot lose any more life without His Presence, hook your heart up to His heart, and live forever.

May 8

*Behold, I have indelibly imprinted (tattooed a picture of)
you on the palm of each of My hands; (O ZION)
your walls are continually before Me.*
Isaiah 49:16

Take A Look Through His Eyes

Would you even think that God could express His great love for us in this precious (vivid, dramatic, expressive) manner?

What were you thinking, imagining that He does not love you, or care for you. What a silly notion!

You need to see yourself as God sees you.

Don't just look at your weaknesses and bad qualities. See the potential that He sees. You have some strong qualities and special gifts, use them for His glory. They are lying dormant inside of you now, but tap into His power and there will be nothing that you can't do. The Helper will stand by you, and with Jesus on the inside, what more do you need?

If you are stale and bored, get with the Spirit. He never does things the same way... exciting is the word!!

Kick yourself out of bed and challenge the day. There are millions of possibilities in life. A surprise is just around the corner. In fact, one will be birthed in you today.

A child of destiny is what you are.
The loving Father is after you.

May 9

And when they had prayed, the place in which they were assembled was shaken and they were all filled with the Holy Spirit, and they continued to speak the Word of God with freedom and boldness and courage
Acts 4:31

Look Out! Here He Comes!

If you ever feel as though you are not coping with all the challenges that are before you, then you need to sit down, begin to praise the Lord, and see the delivering power of the Lord! Strength will come, courage will come, boldness will come, and peace will come.

Why is it that when we need encouragement, we wait until we are desperate before we go to the Lord. We should go to Him before we think of doing anything else. The same with our healing, when we are so sick and have contacted every doctor for an appointment, we finally use our faith to get well again.

The power of the Lord is always present for us. We must be aware of that fact. Nothing should be done without the Lord being involved. The Holy Spirit's work is to confirm that the Word of God works in our lives, when we believe it and speak it out.

You are going to experience God's Presence in your life in no uncertain terms when you determine that this is the way you are going to walk.

Expect Him to show up, look for His answers!

Are you ready? Blessings are on their way to you.

May 10

(The Lord God says) And the redeemed of the Lord shall return and come with singing to Zion; and everlasting joy shall be upon their heads. They shall obtain joy and gladness, and sorrow and sighing shall flee away.
Isaiah 51:11

Redeemed

We are the redeemed of the Lord. We are the ones to be singing and not sighing and sorrowing!

The Lord has delivered us from a certain eternity in a pit. He has given us a hope and a life beyond our simple understanding. How can we not respond to the joy of our salvation?

Joy and gladness must continually be in our hearts and praise on our lips. Rejoice in the One who has done it all for us.

> Jesus my life, my love and sweet peace,
> You lift my heart and heal my disease.
> When I reach out to you, O Lord, my salvation,
> You bring me abundance, my soul in elation.
> Each moment, a pleasure I cannot forget
> To touch your Presence, my path is well set.

Confession: "I am set free by the blood of Jesus. I will rejoice in the God of my salvation, and sorrow and sighing will flee away."

May 11

How beautiful upon the mountains are the feet of him who brings good tidings, who publishes peace, who brings good tidings of good, who publishes salvation, who says to Zion, your God reigns.
Isaiah 52:7

Beautiful Feet

What a thrill to discover that as far as the Lord is concerned, I have beautiful feet! I have always wanted to have beautiful feet! Actually, it's not by the bone structure that this beauty is defined, but by the dynamic message that my feet are carrying.

Feet do not often carry Good News. Mostly, they are about daily chores and business, some are even swift to mischief. But to have a divine calling is a miracle from the Father.

What you are carrying inside of you has no price, no measure. It is only to be released at an appointed time to set captives free.

Someone needs to hear. Someone has been longing to know the joy of eternity.

Be swift in your direction and do not be distracted along the path. When you need to get the message there swiftly, and get it delivered clearly and directly. The Helper will be with you, and He will prove your message true.

Your feet are beautiful because they carry the Good News.

May 12

Who led you through the great and terrible wilderness, with its fiery serpents and scorpions and thirsty ground where there was no water; but Who brought you forth water out of the flinty rock.
Deuteronomy 8:15-16

Toothpaste Christianity

"Who fed you in the wilderness with manna, which your fathers did not know, that He might humble you and test you, to do you good in the end."

When you squeeze a toothpaste tube – what comes out? What comes out of you when you are being squeezed by all kinds of pressure; work, relationships, finances, marriage, children? The complaining of the Jews in the wilderness, kept them in the wilderness.

Satan will offer you all kinds of excuses for your situation, but you will have to respond even as Jesus did in the wilderness, by rebuking the devil and using the Word of God.

What came out of Jesus in the wilderness was already in Him in abundance. He knew it; He believed it, and He spoke it against the enemy. He did not try and run away from the test but stood His ground and won the battle.

Today, in your own life you will have to find out what the Word of God says about your personal wilderness. You have to meditate on God's promises and get His Word on the inside of you, so that when you are squeezed, nothing but the Word of God will come out of you.

When the pressure is on, use spiritual warfare and let God's Word have the right of way.

May 13

Surely He has borne our grief's (sicknesses, weakness, and distresses) and carried our sorrows and pains (of punishment), yet we (ignorantly) considered Him stricken, smitten, and afflicted by God (as if with leprosy). But He was wounded for our transgressions, He was bruised for our guilt and iniquities; the chastisement (needful to obtain) peace and well being for us was upon Him, and with the stripes (that wounded) Him we are healed and made whole.
Isaiah 53:4-5

Be Healed!

Healing and well-being belong to you in Jesus' name. No sickness, disease, weakness or distress is sent by the Lord to try and test your faith. Abundant life is abundant health.

Jesus not only went to the cross for our salvation, He went to the cross to carry all our burdens and all our pains too. The cross was not payment for something that He did; He was not guilty; He did not sin. He went to the cross for something that we needed.

Take what belongs to you and don't settle for anything less. Divine health is yours as a child of God. You have the right to walk in it. If symptoms of sickness in your body come your way, don't sign for the package that does not belong to you, it's been sent to the wrong address!

Communion is a wonderful way to receive your healing if you are alone. Take the body, the bread and break it, giving thanks to the Lord for your healing, that the broken body of Jesus heals you. Take the cup symbolising the blood of Jesus and drink of it, thanking Jesus that He laid down His life for you, so that you are healed and have Eternal Life.

You are healed in the name of Jesus!

May 14

Looking away [from all that will distract] to Jesus, Who is the Leader and the Source of our faith (giving the first incentive for our belief) and is also its Finisher (bringing it to maturity and perfection). He, for the joy (of obtaining the prize) that was set before Him, endured the cross, despising and ignoring the shame, and is now seated at the right hand of the throne of God.
Hebrews 12:2

Looking Through Your Eyes Of Faith

When Jesus saw the cross, He saw the joy that it would bring. When you read the promises of God in His Word, you have to see it and receive it, before you actually have it! It may take a while and you will have to stand firm and strong.

You may need employment. By faith, you must see yourself working.

It might be for a child; by faith see yourself holding your child.

By seeing... you set your joy on what lies ahead, until the manifestation of your faith.

The devil will come and say to you, that it will never come to pass! Then YOU can say, "Oh no... just watch it happen!" Praise the Lord anyway, and don't get discouraged. Refuse to move, and you will be blessed.

Jesus endured the most grievous opposition and bitter hostility, and yet He still looked at the cross with joy. He knew what the end result was going to be. Adjust your focus, and keep looking through the eyes of faith.

Hold fast to the promises that God has for you.

May 15

...in Your presence is fullness of joy, and at Your right hand are pleasures for evermore.
Psalm 16:11

Don't Let Your Joy Go Out The Window

When you walk in joy – you walk in the anointing and you will not fear.

However, when you let your joy go out of the window, then depression and discouragement will come flooding in.

Jesus said to us, "All power in heaven and earth has been given to Me, therefore go and make disciples, and behold I am with you always." He also reminds us that He never leaves us or forsakes us!

God is always watching over His Word in your life to see that it manifests and produces what He said it would. No one on this earth is more committed to your happiness than the Lord. But, it's going to take you getting into His presence on a regular basis. His presence includes "fullness of joy". If you need the joy then you need His Presence.

When it comes to pleasures, God has them all. Get your priorities right and get your joy and pleasure from the right place – the world cannot offer this kind of pleasure to you.

Get all that you are looking for from the Supplier.

May 16

For though the mountains should depart and the hills be shaken or removed, yet My love and kindness shall not depart from you, nor shall My covenant of peace and completeness be removed, says the Lord, Who has compassion on you.
Isaiah 54:10

God's Love Will Never Leave You

The compassion of the Lord is greater than what we can understand. Even though we continue to do so many things that we know do not please Him, He continually forgives us and blesses our lives.

God is in covenant with us through Jesus. His response to us in the most horrendous of situations is that His covenant will never change. His Word to us will stand strong forever even though the mountains may crumble.

When the Heavenly Father commits certain promises to us, we are to take those as real as we would take the marriage vows by which we enter our covenant. Man's covenant is unreliable, that is why God had to cut covenant with Himself through Jesus.

You and I need to learn a good lesson from this Scripture. If God loves you, then nothing should change that assurance. Nothing. Not your thoughts, not your experience, not your feelings, not your challenges, not your friends, family or spouse and certainly ... not the devil.

God loves you and cares about you affectionately!

May 17

So then, brace up and reinvigorate and set right your slackened and weakened and drooping hands and strengthen your feeble and palsied and tottering knees.
Hebrews 12:12

Failure Is Not Fatal

Failure is not fatal with God. Even though you have failed, you are, able to get up and start again. Failure happens to everyone!

There are many reasons why we fail: we fail because we don't tap into God's will; we fail because we do stupid things and make stupid decisions, we fail because we are attached to someone who does something stupid and it is no fault of ours, but we bear the brunt! We jump into projects we know nothing about, and we fail because we lack wisdom and make impulsive decisions without seeking advice from God.

None of us is perfect, but the Word of God is. With the help of the Holy Spirit we obtain the wisdom to make the right choices.

Even though you may make a mistake, it is not the end of everything and God wants you healed. In the name of Jesus put your shoulders back, hold your head up high and walk by faith. If you have to fix something that has been wrong, then do it by faith. You can't pretend it doesn't exist and then hope it will go away. Be brave and face your failure head on. God will help you.

Failure is not fatal. It's how you handle the failure that is important. Many great men have failed hundreds of times, but they used the failure to make them stronger.

God's Word is your wisdom. Get up and live your life for God.

May 18

If you are willing and obedient, you shall eat the good of the land.
Isaiah 1:19

Dare To Prepare

How do you prepare for your destiny? You need preparation to help you follow through with God's plan for your life. You will need to become:

Disciplined: Hebrews 12:11
Diligent: Proverbs 22:29
Single-minded: Matthew 22:37
Patient: Hebrews 6:12
Hard working: Proverbs 6:6

These special attributes will make you great in the Kingdom of God. Tremendous opportunity is waiting for you to become what God has planned for you.

There is of course an important time of preparation where you will build character and values for the times ahead. Some of the preparation period can be unpleasant, agonising, and even distressing. You may feel like God has left you and rejected you, but He hasn't. He is preparing you for your destiny.

The "wilderness" experience was preparation for Moses and the Israelites – it also got rid of their rebellion. Does it feel like you are walking through the "wilderness"? Great! You are about to enter the Promised Land. When you are vulnerable, run straight into the arms of the Lord.

God wants the best for you.

May 19

Behold, they may gather together and stir up strife, but it is not from Me. Whoever stirs up strife against you shall fall and surrender to you.
Isaiah 54:15

Your Enemies Are In Trouble

God has never been the author of strife, confusion or any such thing. It is the devil that has a record of this kind of behaviour. If there is strife in your life, it is not from God.

When people come against you speaking lies, or stirring up strife, then confront them in love, and challenge the nonsense they are reporting. Christians get away with nonsense, and are hardly ever challenged for the words they so casually speak.

When someone shares some juicy information with you, be responsible with what you hear. You may have to challenge them to repeat it in front of the individual concerned. You will be amazed how quickly this attitude will stop gossip in its tracks.

God is not the author of strife and confusion. He does not have any of that stored up in Heaven to share.

Stories lengthen and get spicier as they go along. Eventually when they reach the one about whom they are told, they become life destroying. Caution yourself about the seeds that you sow.

Open your ears to the voice of God and close your ears to the voice of confusion and strife!

Let's work for God and spread the Good News.
Don't let others use your ears as trash cans.

May 20

Never lag in zeal and in earnest endeavour; be aglow and burning with the Spirit, serving the Lord.
Romans 12:11

Passionate, Stirred Up And Going Places For God

Life needs passion and you need to be passionate about your destiny in Christ.

What is passion? - Great enthusiasm, fire, strong emotion, fervour, intense excitement, deep desire.

People are not ashamed to show their passion at a sports match (especially if their kids are playing), or a movie, or a music concert. You hear them screaming and shouting and jumping around like wild animals over a ball. But, when it comes to passion about God they begin to "tip-toe".

Passion stirs us to action; it causes us to do something. I have never seen a couple who are passionately in love sitting miles away from each other or not show any affection. If you are going to show emotion, show it to the One who gave it to you in the first place.

What happens when passion is present? You cry, shake, shiver, shout, blush, sing, and dance. What does God think when we sit in His presence like dead ducks? We need to get free in God.

What is your passion level with God?
Cold… Lukewarm… Hot?

Fall in love with Jesus.

May 21

As a father loves and pities his children, so the Lord loves and pities those who fear Him [with reverence, worship and awe].
Psalm 103:13

Our Father's Heart

The Lord loves you. He wants to be a part of everything you do. He doesn't want to be a stranger.

Like any parent or child, in your relationship you do not want a void or distance between you. You want to talk with your children, to touch their lives, to bless them. So it is with God.

There is nothing complicated about getting to know God; it's like breathing – natural. You are His child and He is your Father; you want to know Him, and He wants to know you. Children are easy-going and straightforward; that is how our relationship with God must be.

God knows exactly what you need before you even ask Him. God made you!

The Father's heart is in love with you. If your earthly father never set a good example, or perhaps you never knew him, let God show you what a real father is like.

He loves you unconditionally, with an everlasting love. He wants you to be His child; He wants to be your Father.

May 22

...The earnest (heartfelt, continued) prayer of a righteous man makes tremendous power available [dynamic in its working].
James 5:16

Earnest Prayer

What is prayer? Prayer is talking to God, communicating with your Heavenly Father.

Prayer is part of the Christian lifestyle, getting into God's presence and talking to Him. But He wants us to be effective in our prayer life – to come out of prayer with victory, not wasting time with vain babbling.

Prayer is conversation… a two-way dialogue. It's talking, and listening!

You want to talk to God, and He wants to talk to you, but so often we rattle off a whole lot of requests, say "Amen" and walk away. You need to get into God's presence, speak to Him and allow Him to come and speak into your heart and touch your life.

Prayer is a very intimate time between you and God. The more time you spend with Him the better you will know Him.

James 4:8 says, "Come close to God." Prayer changes things; it doesn't change God, rather it moves us into God's will. Prayer provides the believer with authority and tremendous power through Jesus.

May I implore you to come into His Presence.
Seek out God's face and know His heartbeat.

May 23

For I know the thoughts and plans that I have for you, says the Lord, thoughts and plans for welfare and peace and not for evil, to give you hope in your final outcome.
Jeremiah 29:11

God Sees The Big Picture

God's thoughts about us are not usually our thoughts. If we are going to get anywhere in this life, then we need to pay attention to what God thinks and says about us.

He wants you to grow and increase in everything, not to be stagnant and ineffective. This is not the time to get comfortable, especially if you have been a Christian for 30 years. You especially should not be complacent. Stretch yourself in God, challenge yourself to grow and have vision. You need to see God move in your life every day because He wants you to increase.

Give God the opportunity to do what He needs to do in your life. Don't hang onto the things of old; God sees the big picture. You can no longer limit God with feeble thinking.

Our expectation is God's invitation.

May 24

Not that we (have the audacity to) venture to class or (even to) compare ourselves with some who exalt and furnish testimonials for themselves. However, when they measure themselves with themselves and compare themselves with one another, they are without understanding and behave unwisely.
2 Corinthians 10:12

Be Content

Don't compare yourself to others. If you do, you could land up discouraged and jealous. You are unique.

Don't see yourself as insignificant, even if your life may be filled with mundane duties. Measure your value by the fruit that your life is producing: personally, in your marriage and in your children. Trust in the Lord's wisdom.

If you think that you would like to do more for God, then take it to Him. He will open the necessary doors and bring His will to pass in your life. It's not important what others are doing; it's important what you are doing.

Be content with where God has placed you and don't wish to be some place else.

If you have been battling in this area it is going to take a concerted effort on your part to renew your mind and shake off that discontentment.

Be the best that you can be for God.

May 25

But no weapon that is formed against you shall prosper, and every tongue that shall rise against you in judgment you shall show to be in the wrong. This (peace, righteousness, security, triumph over opposition) is the heritage of the servants of the Lord (those in whom the ideal Servant of the Lord is reproduced); this is the righteousness or the vindication, which they obtained from Me (this is that which I impart to them as their justification), says the Lord.
Isaiah 54:17

Divine Protection

When the enemy comes in like a flood, God has promised you protection from weapons and lies that may be just as damaging.

Such crazy stories have been told about me over the years, that I could write a comedy. One such story was that I laid hands on a Porsche and charged a large fee. Thereafter, the car would never give any more problems. What a service!

This Scripture also talks about weapons. Living in South Africa during the most criminal of times, has caused me to know that this promise is alive. Many of my friends have faced knives and guns, but in the name of Jesus, they have all walked free from the perpetrators.

When God is your shield and your protector – look out devil!

May 26

Who is [He then] this King of glory? The Lord of Hosts.
Psalm 24:10

Royalty Check

He is the King of Glory.

When we come to God, we are to come on His terms.

You cannot boss God around. He is Who He says He is, but who are you? God is sovereign, majestic, and mighty. He sits on the throne in Heaven, while you sit down here on earth!

Show Him honour and respect due to His name. If you blame Him and reject Him, that attitude will get you nowhere? God loves you dearly and is able to move Heaven and Earth for you. He is NOT the One against you, but the One Who is FOR you.

We call Jesus our King. Is He truly King of your life? A king is in charge of his land; he is responsible for making wise and prosperous decisions for his people. The king's people wholeheartedly trust their king; they are committed to him and serve only him.

Let me ask you, how much more should we be in awe of our King Jesus? When we see Him we shall be like Him. We do not have to wait for eternity to do that, we can start right now.

When was the last time you took a royalty check?

May 27

I do not consider, brethren, that I have captured and made it my own (yet); but one thing I do (it is my one aspiration); forgetting what lies behind and straining forward to what lies ahead, I press on toward the goal to win the (supreme and Heavenly) prize to which God in Christ Jesus is calling us upward. Serve the Lord your God and do not be intimidated by man, the devil or circumstances. When you allow these things to interfere with where you are going, they will take a hold of your attention, and you will tend to please them and not the Master.
Philippians 3:13-14

Dead And Buried

Only God can shape a future for you that is prosperous and blessed. The more you draw near to Him, the more aware you will become of His plan and His will for your life. Outside of His plan, you are headed for disaster.

I want to serve Almighty God who causes me to reign, triumph and have victory in all of my circumstances. What has happened in my life outside of God is dead and buried. Only that which is alive in Him, will produce fruit in my life. Even my flesh is reminded daily that it is crucified with Christ and will not dominate my will or my choices.

What happened to you yesterday is past; it has gone; it is over with; it is done; you will never see yesterday again. Even if it was a good day, you cannot recapture it. Leave the past behind you. Accumulated old baggage will drag you back from where God wants you to go. It will deter you from your God-given destiny. Press on – look forward. Your life is precious don't waste it on nonsense.

Leave the rotten carcasses of the past buried where they belong.
Forgive yourself, forgive others and move on.

May 28

*I have told you these things, that My joy and delight may be in you,
and that your joy and gladness may be of full measure
and complete and overflowing.*
John 15:11

Hath God Said?

I have found that when God has given me a word, there will come a time where I will need to remind myself of what God has said.

I think about a prophecy that the Lord gave Rhema Church through Reinhard Bonnke many years ago. It spoke about Rhema Bible Church becoming the nest of the Divine Eagle where babies would be born, raised, and eventually would fly the nest to be useful in the Kingdom of God, in other places. God did exactly this, but to a far greater degree than I could ever have imagined.

It was not easy at the time, to see many of the Rhema children fly the nest to the many corners of the world. I would much rather have had them stay. To strengthen us, God gave this word of encouragement that it would happen and we should not worry about it.

Now when I travel abroad I am blessed to see my spiritual children working and producing fruit in many countries of the world. I have been fortunate to preach in many of their churches and celebrate what God is doing in their lives and ministries.

Don't base your joy on what happens around you as this is subject to change. Instead, put all your confidence and joy in the Lord and in His plan, and you will never be moved.

God wants your joy overflowing – keep it full in Him.

May 29

My son, do not despise or shrink from the chastening of the Lord (His correction by punishment or by subjection to suffering or trial); neither be weary of or impatient about or loathe or abhor His reproof.
Proverbs 3:11

Welcome God's Discipline

For whom the Lord loves, He corrects, even as a father corrects the son in whom he delights.

The other day I was thinking how wonderful it is for God to discipline us because when He does, we know He loves us. Parents, who do not care about their children, let them do whatever they like to the point of total danger.

When you are in rebellion or out of the Lord's will for your life, expect the Lord to show up. He will show you your error and discipline you because He is your Heavenly Father and He does not want your sin to kill you.

When God says NO or NO MORE, it's for your greater benefit!

Be courageous and welcome the Lord into your life to teach you how to live. His hands are very capable hands and His heart is filled with tenderness, kindness and mercy toward you. Don't rebel and run from His presence, you will make your situation worse and fill your life with torment.

Remember, that God cannot discipline you with evil. He has no evil in Him. He is a loving God and would chastise you as would a loving parent His own child.

Keep close to God and give Him the reins of your life. He is the one Who has your interests at heart.

May 30

Pray at all times (on every occasion, in every season) in the Spirit, with all [manner of] prayer and entreaty.
Ephesians 6:18

Practising Prayer

God's Word teaches us to practice prayer. To pray at all times – morning, noon and night; summer, autumn, winter and spring, at home, work and play ... all of the time.

You know that practice makes perfect. You don't become an incredible dancer if you never practice. You have to set time aside to train and exercise. The same is true with prayer. To get in the flow in prayer, you are going to have to practice, train and exercise your Spirit.

God exhorts us to pray for a reason as nothing He says is without purpose. When we pray we are performing spiritual warfare against the adversary and his host. When we pray: we keep our hearts pure and holy; we draw close to God; we do spiritual warfare; we keep out of temptation.

Prayer will reveal and confirm God's perfect will for your life. You can pray anywhere and at anytime. Be sensitive to your spirit and obey the Lord.

Pray with all kinds of prayer, and miracles will happen in the natural realm.

God says pray, so pray.

May 31

But the fruit of the (Holy) Spirit (the work which His presence within accomplishes) is love, joy, (gladness), peace, patience (an even temper), kindness, goodness (benevolence), faithfulness, gentleness (meekness, humility) self-control (self-restraint, continence).
Galatians 5:22–23

Basic Christian Character

We have the blessing of being anointed, filled with the Holy Spirit and thriving in God's Word, which builds our basic Christian character.

Character principles make us aware of our attitude, behaviour, discipline and manners. We learn character from living, reading, and meditating on God's Word and by being taught by other godly individuals.

Godly character is more important than what you achieve; takes a lifetime to develop; is what you are becoming; effects the decisions you make, words you speak, goals you set and actions you take.

After whom do you fashion your character? Not after man unless they live by the Word of God.

Godly character will help you make wise decisions, stay healthy and motivate you to greatness.

Godly character will set you apart from the rest.

June

Precious Seed

June 1

Whereas the object and purpose of our instruction and charge is love, which springs from a pure heart and a good (clear) conscience and sincere (unfeigned) faith.
1 Timothy 1:5

A Clear Conscience, Before God And Man

What a goal to set! To make 'love' our charge, and to couple it with a pure conscience, and a pure heart! Love never fails in our lives, and will keep our faith working!

Disguising impure motives means that you are not being honest with yourself. If the mask you are wearing hides insecurities such as fear, jealousy, bitterness, discrimination or revenge, the real you behind the mask will eventually be revealed!

God LOVES you too much to leave you as you are… He will set up situations whereby you will have the perfect opportunity to remove the mask. Be reconciled; restored and renewed by His Presence as He has already provided for your deliverance in Jesus. You can only hide for so long, God sees everything!

Keep your heart and motives pure. Make sure you keep good relations with everyone.

June 2

But be doers of the Word [obey the message], and not merely listen to it, betraying yourselves [into deception by reasoning contrary to the Truth].
James 1:22

Be A Hearer And A Doer Of God's Word

Studying the Word of God is good but not good enough. If you want to be established in The Word, you must start applying it in your life for it to work for you.

Getting your body in shape will take more than just reading books on workouts or studying every health diet you can find! You are going to have to put this information to work in your life, if you want to see results in your body!

The moment you start applying the Word of God and "doing" it, your whole life change. Fruit will begin to grow on your "branches" where there was no fruit before.

The Word will produce in every area of your life, if you will simply apply it.

If we would be as committed to understanding God's Word as we are to understanding our computers, we would have tremendous success.

Let your spiritual feet be firmly rooted in God's Word. When a dilemma arises, you will naturally respond with a corresponding 'Word' action that will bring you right through to your victory!

God's Word will NEVER fail you!

What good is it then only to listen? You need to action it!

June 3

Let this same attitude and purpose and [humble] mind be in you which was in Christ Jesus: [Let Him be your example in humility:]
Philippians 2:5

Humility

Humility: Unpretentiousness, humbleness, submissiveness. To follow Jesus is to walk humbly before God. He is our example. He doesn't want you competing with others or trying to imitate them. He wants you to follow Him, and be the best YOU – you can be.

Man is going to fail you, but God will NEVER let you down.

I have seen how people can shoot to fame as a rising star, but fall just as quickly.

Proverbs 11:2 says, "when swelling and pride come, then emptiness and shame come also, but with the humble are skilful and Godly wisdom and soundness." Pride will disgrace you and dishonour Christ. Humility is being submissive to God and the authorities He has placed in your life.

If you live a life of humility, the Word says you will be promoted, '… he who humbles himself will be exalted' Luke 18:14

What a pleasure to know that you don't have to go around striving or be in rivalry with others to excel, but rather live lovingly and peaceably, knowing that God will be the One Who elevates you to the next level.

Keep your door closed to pride. When you do well be assured that it is Christ in you who causes you to prosper.

June 4

Love one another with brotherly affection [as members of one family], giving precedence and showing honour to one another.
Romans 12:10

Love Your Brother

God desires that His children love one another. It seems strange that He would need to instruct us to do so, when we actually have His LOVE nature within us!

Daily we are faced with a decision to love one another and not enter into strife, no matter what the cost. Strife will destroy everything in its path and not care one bit about who may get hurt along the way.

There are dozens of opportunities to fight. Just don't do it!

Before the day starts, settle in your heart that you refuse to enter into conflict with anyone. The price is too high, and you need to keep your stress levels down.

Families are constantly under attack by inner competition, jealousy and bitterness. It's up to parents to refuse to allow these emotions to run rampant among children. A home filled with love will allow each member to feel as blessed and important as the other. Never favour one child above another.

When we honour one another, love will be our goal! We must look beyond the irritations and cords of difference, and love one another in the fear of the Lord.

We can only genuinely love one another, when we love God with all our hearts.

June 5

For just as the body is a unity and yet has many parts, and all the parts, though many, form [only] one body, so it is with Christ.
1 Corinthians 12:12

You Are The Body Of Christ

We all have a part to play in the Body of Christ. The Body of Christ is one Body, but with many parts. Each part has a function, just as a human's body-parts have specific functions; as the ear hears and the mouth speaks, so too is God's Church. You can't have the ear trying to speak. It just wouldn't make any sense. God places you in the body as He wills.

It is vital that each part finds its own place and is happy, not jealous or competing against the other. If you try and do something that is not in God's plan, you will make it hard on others and yourself.

Move only with God, and only when He tells you to move, don't move outside of God. As He initially placed you, then He will be the one to move you, and equip you.

At all costs – stay in harmony. If God moves you on to a new season in your life, then be sure to leave only with a blessing from your Pastor. Don't compare churches. Keep away from division. Work diligently at keeping the peace.

We are not to compete, but to complete one another
in the Body of Christ.

June 6

Seek, inquire for, and require the Lord while he may be found [claiming Him by necessity and by right]; call upon Him while He is near.
Isaiah 55:6

Seek The Lord

According to this Scripture there may come a time when the Lord may not be found.
After Adam sinned, a vacuum entered his life that we have all inherited. Only the presence of the Lord can fill that vacuum.

You are encouraged by God to seek Him with ALL of your heart while you can, and to require of Him whatever it is that you may need! He will take care of you, and when He does, be sure to give the Glory back to Him.

Your Heavenly Father is jealous for you and does not want to share your deep love with anything or anyone else. He wants prime position and prime time, with you!

Reaching out to God is part of what we were created to do, to be one with Him as Genesis 1:26 declares, that we are made in His image and after His likeness.

He wants to belong to us, just like we belong to Him. He wants to enter into Covenant with us through the shed blood of Jesus. That covenant means; whatever is His is mine and whatever is mine, is His! Not that I have anything much to offer Him other than my heart, which is exactly what He wants!

This is why Jesus died on the cross; to redeem us back to God through His blood covenant.

The Lord is near and we can call upon His name right now, at any opportunity, but don't take that for granted; treasure the fact that you are loved by God, and that He wants to walk with you and be in you.

Call upon Him while He can be found.

June 7

Behold, I am doing a new thing. Now it springs forth; do you not perceive and know it and will you not give heed to it? I will even make a way in the wilderness and rivers in the desert.
Isaiah 43:19

God Will Make A Way

When I look back on my life, I see the great things that God has done for me. He changed me from the inside out! From being a baby Christian in 1974, I have grown tremendously over the years and the things I thought I NEVER could do, I now find myself doing with ease!

God wants to do a "new thing" in your life. When it begins, don't wonder what is going on, but recognise that it is the Lord, and watch as the "new thing" unfolds and comes to pass.

God's mercy and kindness stretches out to you, and draws you into His Presence. He loves you more than you will EVER know. He wants to make a way for you, where there seems to be no way!

He desires to be an integral part of your life that will never fail you. He does not push you away, and He certainly has NO DESIRE to control your life. But He wants you to want Him, more than anything else! It's your hunger and desire for Him that releases His desire to nourish, provide and satisfy you.

God will move mountains to provide for you. He will bring water out of a rock, put a river in the desert and even make the crooked path straight; there is no limit to what God will do for you, when you call upon His name for help and you love Him.

Whatever your need, God's provision is greater. He promises that He will do what is necessary to satisfy your life. God is faithful in all things.

We are not to compete, but to complete one another in the Body of Christ.

June 8

And I am convinced and sure of this very thing, that He Who began a good work in you will continue until the day of Jesus Christ [right up to the time of His return], developing [that good work] and perfecting and bringing it to full completion in you.
Philippians 1:6

Jesus Began A Good Work In You

God is going to work His plan inside of you. Each day with God is a brand NEW day. Just when you think that you have got your whole life together, God begins a new work in you!

At times you will experience that "work" as clearly as you experience getting out of bed in the morning. Then at other times you may be a little slow at recognising it. Whatever change you are undergoing, He calls it a "GOOD WORK"!

He may desire for you to pick up the telephone and call a friend who is in need of help and encouragement. He may be "working" on you to forgive someone who has wronged you. Whatever it is, boldly obey the Lord when He directs. You can't afford to run away from the Master's moulding in your life.

There is always more for your life in God. Where you find yourself today is not necessarily where you will be tomorrow. When He starts that "work" in you, who knows what you will be doing in just a short while from now.

God's plans for you are perfect. He is educating you. Don't drop out, become the best you that you can be, for Him.

June 9

But without faith it is impossible to please and be satisfactory to Him.
Hebrews 11:6

You Can Walk By Faith

One of the wonderful things that I learned from Dad Hagin was how to believe God, and how to walk by Faith. I would hear him talk about the many things that he was standing in faith for, and pretty soon it would manifest.

I felt my own faith challenged as I began to grow in Faith and believe God for the many things that we needed for the ministry. I knew that was the only way that would please God, and the only way we would receive the manifestation of those things.

My greatest faith project was to believe God for my son Joshua. He was going to have to be a "faith baby" as the doctors had told me that it would take a miracle for me to be pregnant!

I stepped out in faith and put Joshua's name up on his bedroom door. Then each month, I would buy my son something from the baby store, even though at this time, I was not even pregnant! What a blessing to receive my precious son on September 25, 1983 a perfect gift from God.

Faith sees what the natural cannot see, and faith receives what the natural cannot receive!

Develop your faith and trust in God, know and accept His very best for you. You can walk by faith and when you do, you WILL please God!

As you continue to exercise faith, so your faith will increase.

June 10

So they are no longer two, but one flesh. What therefore God has joined together, let no man put asunder (separate).
Matthew 19:6

I Do!

God wants us to have happy homes. Every marriage can do with some adjustments in attitude, speech and behaviour. Marriage is a partnership of sharing responsibilities, of valuing, appreciating and celebrating one another, out of a flow of love.

If you allow abuse or misuse to dominate your marriage the enemy will move right in. God's order is that the man is the head of the home, but only because he loves as Christ loves the Church. When this order gets out of order, things do not go well.

This is what God asks of husbands and He repeats it THREE times in the book of Ephesians Chapter 5 "Husbands, love your wives as Christ loves the church, and gave Himself up for the church". Any man that would love and care for his wife in such a manner, would NEVER have an issue with her in marriage. Then he says to the wife for her to "submit to your own husband as unto the Lord".

It's a pleasure for a woman to submit to her own husband if he loves her as much as Jesus loves her. I cannot see how God would ask a woman to submit to a man who is abusive?

The only time a woman can change a man is when he is a baby! So don't even think about it? Only God can change your husband. If you fell in love with him the way that he is, then why on earth are you trying to change him? Just relax and enjoy him, and bring out the best in him.

Celebrate one another!

June 11

I am the Vine; you are the branches. Whoever lives in Me and I in him bears much (abundant) fruit. However, apart from Me [cut off from vital union with Me] you can do nothing.
John 15:5

Stay Vitally United To The Vine

Jesus is the Vine. We cannot survive, succeed, excel or produce fruit without Him. To make it in this life, we need to vitally abide, live and dwell in Him.

Jesus does not ask us to visit the vine, He asks us to dwell in the vine. In dwelling in the vine, we receive all the necessary sap that we need to produce MUCH fruit in our lives.

Fruit does NOT grow on the Vine it grows on the branches. Bearing fruit is a natural part of our lives when we are vitally united to the Vine, not only in one area of our lives, but in EVERY area of our lives; as woman, wives, mothers, business people, teachers, doctors, preacher etc.

Bearing fruit is a healthy sign that we are growing and doing well in God. The branch CANNOT produce fruit without the Vine.

Don't be like a branch that gets broken off or taken away. God's word says that if we are not bearing fruit and dwelling in Him, we will wither, be thrown into the fire and burned up.

As the branch gets its sustenance from the Vine, so we are to gain our strength and provisions from the Lord. Don't look in any other direction for your life; it will only come from Him, through the Vine.

Stay vitally united to the Vine and bear more rich and excellent fruit, for the Lord.

June 12

...And who knows but that you have come to the kingdom for such a time as this and for this very occasion?
Esther 4:14

Born For Such A Time As This

You were born for such a time as this. You are not here by accident, your parents' timing was perfect – God's timing for you is perfect.

God had you in mind long before you were born. There is a destiny that He has for your life, which is planned and perfected, designed and made just for you. Great possibilities and opportunities are there for you!

Look at Esther, she was a Jew living in Persia, her parents died when she was young and her uncle adopted and raised her. God had a destiny for Esther to bring the Jews back to Israel from Persia, as they were living there against the will of God.

The King of Persia was looking for a new queen. On advice of his aides he decided to have a beauty contest for virgins from which he could select his next wife. Esther's uncle entered her into the competition, Esther 2:17: ... the king loved Esther more than all the women, and she obtained grace and favour in his sight.

You had better believe that God has a plan for your life. God took a young Jewish girl, beautified her, and got the king of the land to fall in love with her so that His people could return to Israel. You may have to go through a time of preparation, but follow the plan of God for your life, and you will rise to greatness just like Esther.

Only you can fulfil the plan that God has for your life, and only you can stop it!

June 13

And he, gazing intently at him, became frightened and said, What is it, Lord? And the angel said to him, Your prayers and your [generous] gifts to the poor have come up [as a sacrifice] to God and have been remembered by Him.
Acts 10:4

Love The Poor

Jesus spent most of His time on earth in ministry helping the poor. He continually reached out to those in need and did what He could to help them in their plight.

When you pick up on the heartbeat of God you will be overcome by the goodness that He will pour into your life.

"Your prayers and your generous gifts to the poor have come up (as a sacrifice) to God ... " God is aware of everything that we do and the attitude in which we do it. Praying for the poor and doing what you can to provide for their need, in God's heart is a sacrifice of worship.

This action touches His heart so much that He remembers what you have done. The fact that the Word says, "and have been remembered by Him", expresses the love that the Father has for the poor.

Get out of your own little world and do something for someone else. It will touch your life more than you will ever know and you can bet your bottom dollar that God will provide for your own need while you are taking care of another's.

There are many helpless people in this world –
let's touch their lives with our love.

June 14

*This is the day, which the Lord has brought about;
we will rejoice and be glad in it.*
Psalm 118:24

This Is The Day That The Lord Has Made

This is a new day, with new opportunities, and new occasions to step out in God, and venture out a little. His Mercy is NEW every morning! No matter what has happened in the past, God has given you the "present" to enjoy, and a future to celebrate!

Stop looking at the past and the failures therein; we have all failed at some time, but we can't live in that failure forever. Determine in your heart that these failures are not going to keep you bound.

There is so much wonderful life to live. Do not let it pass you by, because of a few bad experiences. Complaining and murmuring will not get you anywhere.

If you are stuck in your ways, liven up, because you are the steward of your life; get excited about the years ahead. Your life will affect everyone around you positively or adversely. Don't build regrets.

The Word of God says in Psalm 89:47, that we must remember how short our time is. It ticks away with each tick of the clock. You cannot stop it; but only make the best of it.

Everything you do, do it with all your heart!

Be thankful for each moment that the Lord gives you,
and build a life that is a blessing to all.

June 15

Now in the present case let me say to you, stand off (withdraw) from these men and let them alone. For if this doctrine or purpose or undertaking or movement is of human origin, it will fail (be overthrown and come to nothing); But if it is of God, you will not be able to stop or overthrow or destroy them; you might even be found fighting against God.
Acts 5:38-39

God's Will Prevails

But if it is of God, you will not be able to stop or overthrow or destroy them; you might even be found fighting against God'. You cannot stop God!

When God does something in the earth, no man, no devil or demon can stop it. When God does something it will hold through Eternity until He chooses to change it. The sun still rises in the sky, and the waves will still crash on the shore. NOTHING can stop the plan of God!

As far as your personal life goes, God has given you the freedom of choice and only you can stop the plan of God for you life. He will NEVER force you to serve Him. Nobody would enjoy a relationship like that, not even God! He offers you the choice to serve Him.

God's ways are higher than our ways, and God's thoughts are higher than our thoughts. He wants us to come up to a higher advantage point where His will and our will meet.

Whatever needs to change, will change when God is involved. Everything will have to bow its knee to the name of Jesus. We never have to fear failure of any sort when we believe God at His Word. It will come to pass and it WILL prosper. If God calls it blessed, it IS blessed!

When God does something, it will last.

June 16

Let the wicked forsake his way and the unrighteous man his thoughts; and let him return to the Lord, and He will have love, pity, and mercy for him, and to our God, for He will multiply to him His abundant pardon.
Isaiah 55:7

Get Back To God

Many times you may feel that you just cannot live a Christian life anymore. That is the perfect time and season to get even closer to the Lord and live your life "flat out" for Him. Get serious about your heart decision and do not let anyone persuade you differently.

God's mercy makes the devil mad. He continually tries to keep you away from God's presence, but you have to know that you'll need some determination and guts in your decision.

One of my close friends went through a very bad experience that could have driven her away from God, but she chose to use it as an opportunity to run even harder into God's presence. Needless to say, I have great admiration for her and God has knitted her life into something beautiful.

You can use any excuse to drift from the One that loves you the most. Why aim your hurt and pain at the Lord? Thank goodness He does not treat us this way.

No, reach out to Him always and never misuse His love for you. The closer you live in Him the greater your fire and zeal for the Kingdom and God will be.

He welcomes you home!

June 17

For the time being no discipline brings joy, but seems grievous and painful; but afterwards it yields a peaceable fruit of righteousness to those who have been trained by it [a harvest of fruit which consists in righteousness – in conformity to God's will in purpose, thought, and action, resulting in right living and right standing with God].
Hebrews 12:11

Discipline In God

Spiritual discipline is necessary for Christ to grow and develop inside of you. Discipline is learning to say "no" when your flesh really wants to say "yes", and learning to say "yes" when your flesh wants to say "no".

A disciple is a disciplined one, one that is taught. Without discipline, our lives would be flaky, fruitless and out of control. God disciplines the ones that He loves. Discipline is a challenge for most of us, as we love to have a free will to do whatever we like. But an undisciplined life leads to trouble, and none of us want any of that!

Spending time in God's Word takes discipline. Our Bibles are on the night table next to our beds and hardly get read. We know the power of prayer, but how often do we pray? Worship lifts our faith and spirit; how often do we worship the Lord? Our hunger for God needs to supersede any distraction in our lives.

We need to be disciplined outwardly (our actions and words) as well as inwardly (mentally, our thoughts). A disciplined life is a rewarding life. Not a discipline of works or trying to earn something, but a discipline from the distractions and temptations that Satan would use for your demise.

Our lives speak, and resisting temptation spurs others on!

Giving discipline is one thing, accepting discipline is quite another. Both are needed.

June 18

His master said to him, Well done, you upright (honourable, admirable) and faithful servant! You have been faithful and trustworthy over a little; I will put you in charge of much. Enter into and share the joy (the delight, the blessedness), which your master enjoys.
Matthew 25:21

Faithful Over A Few Things

Perhaps your increase has not yet begun. You have stood in faith and are hanging on by your teeth. In fact, the past few months may have been the most difficult? Let me ruffle your feathers a little…

I want to remind you that your circumstances do not change the fact that God's Word is true. Your circumstances are subject to the Word of God and not the other way around. God is the God of increase; He will always be true to His nature. If something has to change, it will be your circumstances and not the Word of God.

So hold onto your faith and do not be discouraged. God's Word works in every situation, and it will work for you! God is always going forward, always multiplying. So do not let go!

Be diligent, be faithful with the things God has given you, continue to be a good servant, and you will increase. The Word works; it is alive, full of power and sharper than any two-edged sword, and it will lead you into victory.

Stand on His Word until you hear him say, "Well done, good and faithful servant, enter into the joy of the Lord!" God will always reward your diligence and your faithfulness. Get the idea that you think He cares about others more than you, out of your head!

God will multiply your life when you serve Him. It is His nature.

June 19

Cast your bread upon the waters, for you will find it after many days.
Ecclesiastes 11:1

Cast Your Bread

It is our nature to try and hoard and hold onto the things that we earn in this life. We suffer from the thought that it may be the last, so we hold onto it and NEVER let go!

The Bible says that what we try and hold onto we will lose, and what we let go of, we will gain back. This is rather the opposite of human thinking. The world says, "hoard it, and keep it in a safe place under the mattress in mothballs!" This fear has always been evident in human understanding. God says, "give it away and I will multiply it!"

The very thing that you scratch, fight and beg for, will slip out of your fingers; the devil will make sure of that.

When you cast your bread upon the waters, it will come back to you after a while, that is a spiritual law. You know when that beach ball is flung into the waves, before too long it comes back. Sometimes, you could get it back almost immediately, but mostly it takes time. A crop takes time to grow and ripen before it can be harvested. Just wait and see, it will surely come back. The more liberal you are, the more liberally you will receive.

When you become a giver, instead of a getter, you become a reaper and not just a keeper.

June 20

So shall My word be that goes forth out of My mouth; it shall not return to me void (without producing any effect, useless), but it shall accomplish that which I please and purpose, and it shall prosper in the thing for which I sent it.
Isaiah 55:11

The Word Will Never Return Void

The Word that God speaks shall never fail or not come to pass. God's Word is a container of life and manifests the life that God lives in. Whatever pleases the Father is done when He speaks. He does not change His mind as His mind was made up from the foundation of the world. What He says goes!

>The Word of God is full of power,
>It shall not fail at any hour.
>When sent in earnest, something to do,
>The Word will deliver, and even bless you!
>This awesome weapon we have in our mouth,
>Will destroy the enemy, his plan re-route.
>When spoken in faith, by one who believes?
>The Word of God will return, as He breathes!

Take the blessing that God has given you and let your heart hook into the power that lies in the spoken Word of God. Speak words of life and words of blessing!

Jesus used the Word against the enemy in the wilderness. Follow His example, have the victory.

June 21

And He said, the kingdom of God is like a man who scatters seed upon the ground, and then continues sleeping and rising night and day while the seed sprouts and increases – he knows not how. The earth produces ... first the blade, then the ear, then the full grain in the ear. But when the grain is ripe and permits, immediately he sends forth [the reapers] and puts in the sickle, because the harvest stands ready.
Mark 4:26-29

God's Season

Some of you have gone to bed at night and risen in the morning asking God, "What has happened to the seed I planted? I cannot see anything God, nothing is happening!"

It would be crazy for a farmer to plant his crop on the Monday and then on the Tuesday go out into the field and ask the Lord where is his crop? Every farmer knows that 'time' exists between seed... and harvest!

From the moment that the seed is planted things begin to happen, but you cannot see the changes because they are hidden under the ground. Spiritually it is the same. When you plant your seed something begins to happen even though you cannot see it with your natural eye.

Hold on because in just a short while, that little ear is coming out of the ground, especially if you have obeyed God by planting your seed in good soil. The fruit will manifest in due season – not our season, God's season.

God's timing is perfect. When He says put in the sickle the time is right.

June 22

Give, and [gifts] will be given to you; good measure, pressed down, shaken together, and running over, will they pour into [the pouch formed by] the bosom [of your robe and used as a bag]. For with the measure you deal out [with the measure you use when you confer benefits on others], it will be measured back to you.
Luke 6:38

Precious Seed

If you want a great harvest then you had better check your seed. Any farmer knows that you must choose the right seed – apple seeds will give you apples, wheat seeds will give you wheat. Seeds of kindness will bring in a harvest of kindness. If the quality is good, the harvest could be outstanding!

What kind of seed are you sowing? Are you sowing good seed or are you sowing weed-seeds? If you sow weed seed then you must expect a harvest of weeds. Strife will produce strife. If you need love then sow love, but do not sow the stuff you do not want.

When you sacrifice and sow your best that is precious seed. You've had to sweat and labor for it. Is there any better place to sow such precious seed than in the Kingdom of God?

Your seed is your wealth; in one seed is the possibility of many thousands of seeds. Be careful what you sow.

June 23

And He said, With what can we compare the kingdom of God, or what parable shall we use to illustrate and explain it? It is like a grain of a mustard seed, which, when sown upon the ground, is the smallest of all seeds upon the earth; Yet after it is sown, it grows up and becomes the greatest of all garden herbs and puts out large branches, so that the birds of the air are able to make nests and dwell in its shade.
Mark 4:30-32

Potential Power

Does your seed have potential? One of the seeds that have the most potential is the little mustard seed. It is one of the smallest of all seeds, yet after it has grown the birds are able to make nests in its branches. One tiny seed provides a home and shelter for many.

You might think that your seed is so tiny and insignificant that it cannot make a difference. Think of the widow who gave her two little mites in the offering. She too must have thought that her seed was small, but Jesus seeing what she put in the offering, spoke about the huge gift she had given – it was all that she had.

The little you give becomes much in the hands of the Lord. He is in the multiplying business.

Think of the little boy and the two fish and the five loaves of bread. It was little when looking at feeding over 5000 people. But, Jesus multiplied it and the little boy still had twelve baskets to take home to his mom.

Attach a mustard seed in the front of your Bible and every time that you look at it, you will be reminded of God's potential in your life.

June 24

But he who looks carefully into the faultless law, the [law] of liberty, and is faithful to it, and perseveres in looking into it, being not a heedless listener who forgets but an active doer [who obeys], he shall be blessed in his doing (his life of obedience).
James 1:25

Is Your Seed Dormant?

What have you done with the seed of the Word that has been sown in your heart over the years? What about all those conferences you have attended and the teaching tapes you have listened to? Do you remember what you heard? Has it changed your life? Have you grown?

When I preach I have spent much time in the Lord's Presence to get a word from Heaven for the listener's heart. He prepares the listener's heart for the message – it is an anointed word. If you are the listener, what have you done with that word? Did it fall into fertile soil? Did you do anything about it?

The soil of our hearts is our responsibility to prepare for the Good News to be planted!

We must not lose an opportunity to give the Word first place and to help us run our lives properly. To be what we desire to be in God is going to take the power of the Word to change our lives. But what good is it if we just hold the seed in our hand, and not plant it in our hearts.

Doing God's word is a great experience. From the moment you begin to apply it to your life and attitude you will feel the difference in your life.

It does not take long and you will really begin to grow.

June 25

There is a little boy here, who has [with him] five barley loaves, and two small fish; but what are they among so many people ... 5,000 in number. Jesus took the loaves, and when He had given thanks, He distributed to the disciples and the disciples to the reclining people ... When they had all had enough, He said to His disciples, Gather up now the fragments ... so that nothing may be lost and wasted ... they gathered them up, and they filled twelve [small hand] baskets ...
John 6:9-13

Nought Times Nought Equals Nought!

If you give God nothing then He has nothing to multiply. You have to give Him something to work with. Never mind your tiredness or your feelings of inadequacy. That is not something that should hinder you from receiving an abundance of what God has for you, to give to others.

He PROVIDES seed for the sower. If you are not prepared to sow, then you will not receive the seed that He is prepared to give to you to sow! That is His nature; He is always giving to us when we cannot even be faithful with what we have.

Trust God with what you have, give it to him with a glad heart and He will multiply it. He is God of the harvest and God of the increase.

God blesses us so that we can be a blessing to others. What good does it do if we hoard up our blessings? Sow your time, sow kindness, sow a listening ear, or love – find something that you can sow and be the blessing that God created you to be.

Giving back to God is the least that we can do for what He has done for us.

June 26

Strive to live in peace with everybody and pursue that consecration and holiness without which no one will [ever] see the Lord. Exercise foresight and be on the watch to look [after one another], to see that no one falls back from and fails to secure God's grace (His unmerited favour and spiritual blessing), in order that no root of resentment (rancour, bitterness, or hatred) shoots forth and causes trouble and bitter torment, and the many become contaminated and defiled by it.
Hebrews 12:14-15

Weeds In Your Seed

If you have weed in your seed get rid of it as fast as you can! Weed seed will do exactly what the bible says it will do. It will choke the good seed, and the good seed will eventually die.

Bitterness, anger, vengeance and jealousy are just the type of weed seed that will produce a bountiful crop of horrendous consequences and eventually choke the good crop that you busy trying to cultivate.

You can turn it all around by pulling out the weed seed, and beginning to nurture the good seed that you have sown in your garden. Don't be surprised if this becomes quite a task, as weeds do not give up too easily. Just when you think you have gotten rid of all of them, another one shows up! Never let this dishearten you, just stay with it until every weed is removed and before too long, you're good crop will be looking wonderfully healthy!

People's lives are destroyed because of the bad seed that they sow. When we begin to sow good seed and have a good harvest, then we can bless others around us.

Weeds will choke the good seed and life will be stunted.

Do what is necessary to win your brother, if you have to forgive then do so, if you have to root out bitterness then do it now – love never fails!

June 27

Therefore, my beloved brethren, be firm (steadfast), immovable, always abounding in the work of the Lord [always being superior, excelling, doing more than enough in the service of the Lord], knowing and being continually aware that your labor in the Lord is not futile [it is never wasted or to no purpose].
1 Corinthians 15:58

Don't Move!

When you come to terms with what the Lord wants in your life, you will stand strong and firm through every storm and circumstance. No matter what happens you will be anchored to the rock, and you will NOT be moved!

One of the MOST important characteristics of a mature believer is that his life is stable through every difficult circumstance, and that NOTHING moves him from his belief or his faith!

To be fully satisfied, you need to serve the Lord however you can, to give of your life unconditionally to Him. In so doing, you will begin to experience stability in our life that you have not had before. Abounding in the work of the Lord is commitment and accountability that keep you secure and in a safe place.

If you do not belong to a local church, then ask the Holy Spirit to lead you to one where you can get involved and serve the Lord. Let Him plant you.

You have gifts and talents to sow. If your gift is one which encourages others then do it with love, send a note, pray, show appreciation, be a blessing.

Go the extra mile; your work for God is never in vein; it has eternal value.

Give with everything you have in your heart, wholeheartedly, faithfully and willingly with a smile on your face, to God.

June 28

Be submissive to every human institution and authority for the sake of the Lord, whether it be to the emperor as supreme, or to governors as sent by him to bring vengeance ... to those who do wrong and to encourage those who do good service.
1 Peter 2:13-14

Stay Submitted

Submission is NOT a dirty word! When God speaks of submission He is speaking of protection, prosperity, growth and order.

Man needs rules and regulations by which to live or there would be total chaos in the world. Could you imagine what would happen if everyone just did their own thing!

At present, it is difficult to get man to obey the general laws of the land. Just drive down the highway and see how many cars pass you at ridiculous speeds endangering the lives of many.

The Pastor watches over the sheep and will give an account for their souls. He is not against you, but his calling includes protecting you from wolves that would do anything to destroy you.

In submitting to one another we honour the Lord. Submission is only successful when it is out of love, and not out of trying to control one another. Through submission, protection, help and the stirring of the gifts are provided.

Could you imagine an army without definite direction or leadership – they would never win in battle! Everyone would want to be in charge, likewise in the church!

You must stand in rank where God desires you to be. When He is ready, He will move you on.

June 29

But I say, walk and live [habitually] in the [Holy] Spirit [responsive to and controlled and guided by the Spirit]; then you will certainly not gratify the cravings and desires of the flesh (of human nature without God).
Galatians 5:16

The Work Of The Holy Spirit

The Holy Spirit is your greatest friend! He is called Helper, Counsellor, Comforter, Intercessor and Guide, his ministry is to help you to keep your life in Truth at all times.

He is also called "Teacher" and will teach you "how" to answer and what to say! Luke 12:12 says, "For the Holy Spirit will teach you in that very hour and moment what [you] ought to say."

There is absolutely nothing that you cannot accomplish in God's plan for your life, when you have the Holy Spirits help. The day that you accepted the Lord Jesus Christ was a life-changing event. So too is the day that you receive the Holy Spirit into your life as your Helper.

The Holy Spirit is gentle. He will never force His way with you or get you to do anything that would not be pleasing to the Father or that you do not desire to do. But if you allow Him, He will fill you to overflowing, and give you the necessary help to keep your life on track.

Listen, as He will show you things to come and prepare your heart for changes. Be aware of His presence and His support. The more you tune into His presence, the more you will experience His leading and know and recognise His voice.

The Holy Spirit is your personal friend and helper.

June 30

Consider it wholly joyful, my brethren, whenever you are enveloped in or encounter trials of any sort or fall into various temptations. Be assured and understand that the trial and proving of your faith bring out endurance and steadfastness and patience. But let endurance and steadfastness and patience have full play and do a thorough work, so that you may be [people] perfectly and fully developed [with no defects], lacking in nothing.
James 1:2-4

Hallelujah! Another Test

Consider it "wholly joyful" when you experience tests. Now I know that this goes against all of your natural, fleshly senses and logic, but who is smarter, you or God?

You have to mature as a believer and it's only through tests and trials that you truly develop Godly character. Simply put, it's like trying to develop muscles without a working out in the gym with weights!

When you walk out to your car in the morning and you have a flat tire, instead of complaining use the opportunity to praise the Lord. You can say, "I am joyful today and nothing is going to change that in Jesus name!"

You don't thank God FOR the difficulty, but you thank Him IN the difficulty. Your JOY should NEVER be subject to your circumstances. Your JOY is founded in Him.

God will NEVER test or tempt you with evil, as there is NO EVIL in Him. However He will test your love, your faith and your desire to serve Him.

Use trials and tests to raise your joy level!

July

Beauty For Ashes

July 1

He has made everything beautiful in it's time...
Ecclesiastes 3:11

Beauty For Ashes

You may be looking at a pile of ashes in your life and thinking that you could never truly live again! You have come through a tragedy, or a disastrous breakdown that has left you completely numb, and you don't know which way to turn, or how to begin again!

I have had a moment like this in my life when I felt as though NOTHING would ever fill the void in my life, or give me hope to go on again! A pile of dead ashes...

But once you have experienced the life of God inside of you, you simply cannot stay in a dead, dark, stuck place! The life of God inside of you begins to rise up and you realise that no matter HOW you feel, or WHAT is going on around you, "God is with you.

Today, I can boldly say, that God WILL breathe HIS life into your ashes and RAISE you up on your feet again. As long as you look to Him for your help, you will NEVER be left helpless! What Satan means for evil, God WILL turn it for your good, and for His Glory!

In a time of total confusion and tragedy, RUN to God! Draw your peace and your strength from Him! Allow His love to wash you through and through, until you are refreshed and renewed by His overwhelming and beautiful Presence.

You may think that you will never be able to live normally again, but time is a powerful healer, and God is a MIRACLE WORKING God. He WILL deliver you from your hurt, your pain, and your anguish.

Psalm 28:7 The Lord is my Strength and my [impenetrable] Shield;
my heart trusts in, relies on, and confidently leans on Him,
and I am helped...

July 2

But as it is, God has placed and arranged the limbs and organs in the body, each [particular one] of them, just as He wished and saw fit and with the best adaptation.
1 Corinthians 12:18

Soldiers In The Army Of God

If soldiers in an army are not prepared to submit to those in authority, they come under severe discipline! However the army does not function by LOVE, but by order of the law.

The Body Of Christ is called the Army Of God. It also functions with discipline and by Godly order, but in this case, it is governed by LOVE. Some folks think that because the church is a "love institution" they can do whatever they like, and the church must put up with it! If the Pastor tries to correct them they get mad and leave the church

The army of God needs to stay in the confines of the order of God for it to be blessed. Even the Gifts of the Holy Spirit have a working plan and order to their function!

However, if any abuse their authority then the necessary steps must be taken to correct that individual. Each one in authority must be under authority! But everything needs to be done in LOVE.

The Body needs every level of authority to help it function in the will of God. Thank goodness that the Lord is loving and merciful. But, He still requires order, respect, honour and discipline in His family. Why, even the angels are in ranks, look at Michael!

God sets you in the body as He wills. You may start out a private but end up a captain! Then again, maybe he has planned for you to be a General. Whatever He wills. Not only should you submit, but should lead in LOVE and with JOY.

Submit to one another in the fear of the Lord.

July 3

Therefore put on God's complete armor, that you may be able to resist and stand your ground on the evil day [of danger], and, having done all [the crisis demands], to stand [firmly in your place].
Ephesians 6:13

Don't Go Out Naked

If the Word of God tells you to put on the whole armour of God then there must be a reason for it. However, the weapons of our warfare are NOT natural or carnal weapons that one would use to wage war on this natural earth, like knives and guns, but they are supernatural weapons, that give us the victory before any natural war breaks out!

Now, we know that Jesus already paid the price for our victory, but we are going to have to claim it by faith. God's protection can be used as an example. Never allow the enemy to get you thinking that you are losing the battle – that's nonsense! You are MORE than a CONQUEROR in Christ Jesus!

Being a Christian is not walking around on flowery beds of ease but being strong enough to stand enduring hardship until the breakthrough in the natural!

At times, you may seem weak, but in your weakness God is your strength!

Stand and declare to the enemy, "You have no authority in my life because I belong to Jesus and He has already won the battle!"

You will not get away with wearing only part of your armour; you will have to wear it all, protection for your loins, your breast, your feet and your head.

Some folks have on their helmet but nothing else, they are naked, an easy target for the enemy!

Dress up in the spirit and be sure to wear every item of your armour;
Belt of Truth - Breastplate of Integrity and Righteousness - Feet dressed with Peace - Shield of Faith - Helmet of Salvation - Sword of the Spirit.

July 4

Behold, the former things have come to pass, and new things I now declare; before they spring forth I tell you of them.
Isaiah 42:9

Expect New Things In God

I have had some wonderful experiences with God where He has touched me, changed me, delivered and healed me in the most powerful way! However, as amazing as those experiences have been, I cannot live my life in the past, as there is a today and a tomorrow to enjoy!

Yes, we are to testify of God's goodness in the past, but we are to expect His goodness TODAY. To keep growing daily in the fresh new things that He has for us.

Some people not only live in past encounters with God, but in past disappointments, hurt and sorrows. You need to let go of everything that will hinder your progress in the Lord.

God declares that He will do a "new thing" in you and through you. He will take you by the hand and guide you, and empower you to fulfill all that he has prepared for you. Your destiny will unfold day by day.

Allow your relationship with God to be spontaneous, fresh and crisp.

Don't live in the 'same old, same old' as there is a wonderful today, and a tomorrow to celebrate!

Have you 'expector' switched on!

July 5

Now faith is the assurance (the confirmation, the title deed) of the things [we] hope for, being the proof of things [we] do not see and the conviction of their reality [faith perceiving as real fact what is not revealed to the senses].
Hebrews 11:1

Feelings Are Deceptive!

We don't always "feel" saved. Rather silly! Like waking up in the morning and not "feeling" married – one look at your husband and your "feelings" will have to change!

You may say, "I don't feel like praising the Lord." Well, that's when you need to praise Him more than ever, and keep praising Him until that "feeling" goes away. I don't feel like going to church and listening to another message. Yes, you do!

If faith were a feeling, then Jesus would not have hung on the cross for us. I'm sure He did not "feel" like it. He stayed there by faith, knowing that He was in the process of conquering death for us.

Faith is the substance that brings into reality the things we are hoping for. It delivers the result!

You cannot be moved by what you feel as your life will be like a yo-yo, up one day and down the next. Feelings are subject to change and need to be dominated by the Word of God.

Faith is active, progressive and fruitful every time it is set for an accomplishment. It is NOT founded on emotion, feelings or circumstances; it is founded on God's unchanging living Word that never fails.

Go beyond your feelings and walk according to the Word of God, by faith.

July 6

For we are not wrestling with flesh and blood [contending only with physical opponents], but against the despotisms, against the powers, against [the master spirits who are] the world rulers of this present darkness, against the spirit forces of wickedness in the Heavenly (supernatural) sphere.
Ephesians 6:12

Fight To Win

Our war is not a natural one. The Word tells us that we wrestle NOT against flesh and blood, but against the enemy of the air and his host.

The assignment of the enemy is to kill, steal and destroy according John 10:10. God has equipped us with supernatural armour for this battle that we don't fight from a position of defeat, but from a position of victory, as JESUS already defeated the devil 2000 years ago on the cross.

Even though we wrestle in the spirit, it is a rest! It is not a heavy burden or a hard yoke, but one that is light and easy because of the Jesus.

Stay filled with the Spirit of God and let the Holy Spirit work in your life to change you and to mould you, to cause you to become what you ought to be in God. Then when the enemy comes in like a flood to steal from you, tell him where he belongs.

He would like to distract you and keep your focus on what he is doing, but God's Word says give NO PLACE to the devil. If you give him a foothold he will take a stronghold.

Jesus disarmed principalities and powers (Col. 2:15) and He made a spectacle of them, triumphing over them in it!!!

You will find out who you are serving when facing temptation. Don't succumb!

You are an OVERCOMER in the name of Jesus!

July 7

For as the heavens are higher than the earth, so are My ways higher than your ways and My thoughts than your thoughts.
Isaiah 55:9

God's Ways Are Higher

God never takes the easy way out to solve the problem. He faces it head on, and always get the best results. We need to follow His example.

You cannot run away from issues in your life. If you try to handle them your way, you will dig deeper into the mire. Even if you think you are right, you need to go to the Word of God and handle them God's way to get the best outcome.

Proverbs 16:25 "There is a way that seems right to a man and appears straight before him, but at the end of it is the way of death." Nobody wants death as an outcome!

Just because your mom and dad handled issues in a certain way, does not mean that their way of doing it was right? Only God's way of doing things is right.

Knowing God's way takes training. Your mind needs to be renewed to His way of doing things, and that takes commitment and desire on your part.

Much of our thinking comes from natural wisdom, which is not on the level of walking in the wisdom of God. Wisdom that is from above is peaceable, fruitful, successful, productive and prosperous.

He has been around a long time and He knows ALL things, so why would you want to do it any other way! Wisdom that is from above is what you need if you want to have the edge on life.

The Word of God is your manual for life. Everything that you need to know is written on its pages. Take the time to discover God's plan for your life and do not compromise the wisdom that you have in your relationship with Him.

If you are going to make a decision, rather make the higher decision.

July 8

The upright (honourable, intrinsically good) man out of the good treasure [stored] in his heart produces what is upright (honourable and intrinsically good), and the evil man out of the evil storehouse brings forth that which is depraved (wicked and intrinsically evil); for out of the abundance (overflow) of the heart his mouth speaks.
Luke 6:45

The Heart Of The Matter

God knows the true intent of your heart. He alone knows where you are and how well you are doing. You cannot fool Him by acting out your worship, and praying vain words!

If your heart is full of anger, bitterness and strife, you can't go and share the treasures of peace and kindness. Whatever is inside of you, will emerge from within you. When you open your mouth to speak, those things will come out of you, especially if you are not on your guard!

A good man's heart brings forth good things, and an evil man's heart brings forth evil things. The heart reveals the truth about a man! Just like the physical heart pumps life into the body, so too the spiritual heart pumps life or death in the spiritual man.

Spiritually you can't survive if your heart is not full of God and saturated with His word pumping through you. The actions of man flow out of the heart:

Examine the condition of your own heart!

July 9

Be happy [in your faith] and rejoice and be glad-hearted ... (al¬-ways); Be unceasing in prayer [praying perseveringly]; Thank [God] in everything [no matter what the circumstances may be, be thankful and give thanks], for this is the will of God for you [who are] in Christ Jesus [the Revealer and Mediator of that will].
1 Thessalonians 5:16-18

Life's A Journey ~ Enjoy The Ride!

Make the most of every moment you have and learn to enjoy your life. Lighten up! You are going to make the journey anyway, so you may as well make up your mind to enjoy it.

I love the way my son says, "chill out mom"! Take a lesson from Josh… relax!

There are times when a little laughter will make the hard times easier! Learn to enjoy who you are in Him, and learn to laugh at yourself.

If a kettle can sing even though it's up to its neck in boiling water, then how much more can you sing with the Holy Spirit inside of you! When your circumstances are going crazy around you, get on your own with the Lord and have a little Glory moment! You will get supernatural strength and tremendous power to thrust you out of the doldrums.

Don't make a mountain out of a molehill! You can choose to see the negative side of everything and be eternally miserable, or you can choose to see the negative as a positive opportunity to break through into victory.

Joseph could have been depressed all of his life for what his nasty brothers did to him. But his brothers actually helped him to get to the Palace, so there was a big positive in the negative!

Living life is a bit like packing a suitcase.
Be careful what you put into it!.

July 10

For thus says the high and lofty One – He Who inhabits eternity, Whose name is Holy: I dwell in the high and holy place, but with him also who is of a thoroughly penitent and humble spirit, to revive the spirit of the humble and to revive the heart of the thoroughly penitent [bruised with sorrow for sin].
Isaiah 57:15

God Will Revive You

Our God is a Holy God. Sin cannot enter His presence. When we come to Him, we come to Him just as we are through amazing GRACE, and receive Jesus as our Lord and Saviour.

In Genesis 1:26 He tells us that we are made in the image of God and after His likeness. We were made to be in the intimate fellowship of God the Father, God the Son and God the Holy Spirit. When Adam and Eve fell we lost our position. Only God knew how He would win us back into His Family.

That is why we have John 3:16 … God sent His only begotten son so that in and through His blood we would come back into full relationship with the Father, Son and Holy Spirit.

GRACE is richer than you and I could ever imagine. It is not a 'something' but a person, it is JESUS. Thank God for GRACE and the amazing love of Jesus that paid the full price for our Redemption.

He is acquainted with all our ways. When you come boldly into His Presence with a humble heart, He says He WILL revive you.

He will cover you with His love.

He gives you a NEW HEART and your spirit is made alive for Eternity.

July 11

My flesh and my heart may fail, but God is the Rock and firm Strength of my heart and my Portion forever.
Psalm 73:26

Solid As A Rock

God is the Rock of my life; His Word is a Rock, a Rock that will not be moved or split in half. You can stand on His Word, and it will never let you down.

We need to be like the man spoken of in Matthew who built his house upon the rock, that when the rains fell, floods came, winds blew and beat against the house, it did not fall, because it was founded on the rock (7:24, 25).

When rain, storms and floods come and the enemy tries to bring havoc in your life, fix your heart on the Lord and you will not succumb to the pressure. When faced with temptation, turn your back and walk away. If you are grounded on the Rock, you will not stumble or fall.

The Psalmist writes that even when his body begins to fail, God will be his strength and his immovable tower. When you reach the end of your rope or are experiencing despair, know that God is greater than your circumstances.

God is your refuge, your ever-present help in times of trouble. Stand strong and do not move from your sure foundation.

You will not be crushed, when you are standing on the Rock.

July 12

In the morning You hear my voice, O Lord; in the morning I prepare [a prayer, a sacrifice] for You and watch and wait [for You to speak to my heart].
Psalm 5:3

New Every Morning

The Lord shows us mercy and loving-kindness when we come into His presence with joyful hearts of thanksgiving. He has done so much for us and only eternity will reveal the awesome ways in which He has kept us.

His Presence is a consuming fire. We cannot begin to think that we could walk into God's Presence without first being acceptable in His sight – we would be swallowed up just by the light that He emanates.

Everyday is a new opportunity for us to come closer to Him. Each morning is a fresh start! Do it right and give Him the honour due to His name.

God is always the same. He never changes His mind or gets confused; He knows what He is doing and where He is going. It's you and I that need the help and guidance to get through the day.

God's compassion is everlasting;
His blessings are new every morning.

July 13

And my God will liberally supply (fill to the full) your every need according to His riches in glory in Christ Jesus.
Philippians 4:19

A Great Supply

Since the day that I gave my life to Jesus, I cannot remember not having any seed to sow into the kingdom. Every time an offering plate passes my way I make sure that I have something to give. It does not matter how big it is, but it matters that I have something to give.

I rejoice at the pleasure of planting more seed. God is faithful and He has never left me without a harvest or seed to sow.

I discovered that it is according to His riches that I am blessed, not according to my little treasure. His riches are from everlasting to everlasting.

God wants to bless your life with His Presence. When you do your part in the relationship He fulfils His side. You can completely rely on Him, and you will receive your blessing.

When I was in Bible School, I was given a beautiful Kenneth Hagin Presentation Bible, something that I really treasured. While in a service that week the Lord spoke to my heart to give it to a lady sitting beside me. I was obedient! It wasn't but a few days later that I received another one, I cried!

Plant your seed into the Kingdom of God, and it will be multiplied.

July 14

You have made known to Me the ways of life; You will enrapture Me [diffusing My soul with joy] with and in Your presence.
Acts 2:28

Infectious Joy

When you are in the Presence of the Lord you can only smile and let your heart be full of joy. There is no stress, no fear or pressure, in His Presence.

It's like spending time with someone who has everything under control, all you have to do is relax and enjoy the company. You are a part of the magnificent eternal painting that is about to unfold.

When I think of this kind of joy, I think of a precious friend of mine who keeps me in raptures of joy when I am with him. It only takes one minute and I am doubled-over with laughter. What a special gift of joy to bring to the lives of others.

You don't have to be a comedian, or have the same gifting as my good friend, however you can still have the joy of the Lord that is contagious and spills off of you onto others.

If you struggle with your joy, then spend time rejoicing in the presence of the Lord. He will lift your spirit and give you something special to sing about.

Life is short, learn to treasure every minute of it! Don't forget your smile when you leave home in the morning.

July 15

You drew near on the day I called to You; You said, Fear not. O Lord, You have pleaded the causes of my soul [You have managed my affairs and You have protected my person and my rights]; You have rescued and redeemed my life!
Lamentations 3:57-58

In Days Of Trouble

If your life is hectic, then you need to call on the Lord. He is the one that will plead your case and stand by you as a strong tower.

The Lord ALWAYS knows what to do! He knows exactly what you are going through. He is there to protect you, plead your case and deliver you out of confusion and trouble. Trust His judgment and allow Him to speak a word into your heart; the end result will be the best for you.

When the Lord speaks He will always encourage you to "fear not". Fear will work against your faith and bring about bad results, as what you fear can come upon you. Fear not – is a command; you must obey!

When you yield your life to Him, He is in control. If God be for you, who can be against you? You have absolutely no reason to fear. Fear not!

Having the Kingdom of Heaven as your support is a powerful tool. Leaning on the wisdom of God to accomplish your vision will keep you safe and secure.

Call upon the Lord in times of trouble and do not yield to fear. He is able to deliver you and keep you from harm.

July 16

The voice of rejoicing and salvation is in the tents and private dwellings of the [uncompromisingly] righteous; the right hand of the Lord does valiantly and achieves strength!
Psalm 118:15

Joy Overcomes

Jesus had joy in His heart because He knew that victory was on its way. The devil could not stop Him. Persecution couldn't stop Him. They tried to kill Him when they wanted to throw Him off the cliff, but He just turned around in His authority and walked right through the middle of them.

With the anointing of the Holy Spirit and the joy of the Lord, you will walk through every type of opposition. God's joy will build endurance inside of your heart. When you walk joyfully in your Heavenly authority, you stand with the protection of Heaven at your side.

No demon, no person, no circumstance, no neighbour, no friend can stop you from getting where God wants you to be. The only one that can stop you from getting where you are supposed to be is yourself.

Don't become your own worst enemy but allow the Holy Spirit to bubble-up inside of your being, as you witness the will of God come to pass in your life.

Enjoy the victory that you have in Christ, now!

July 17

That they may walk in My statutes and keep My ordinances, and do them. And they shall be My people, and I will be their God.
Ezekiel 11:20

I Will Be Their God

Father God, your God, wants to be God in your life. He wants to walk with you, talk with you, and bless your life with His Presence. For you to have this astounding opportunity, you will need to worship and adore His Holy name.

Walking in fellowship with God is something that Adam and Eve were created to do. In the cool of the day the Father would come and talk with them, and walk with them. But they did not appreciate and value this amazing relationship, and rebellion was in their hearts. When they fell they suddenly became aware of the sin in their lives, and they ran from God in their guilt.

Through Jesus Christ we can have that awesome relationship back. We can enter into the Presence of the Lord through worship. His door is open; His love and mercy are everlasting and GRACE has saved us.

Your relationship with The Father is to be bold in the name of Jesus and open to the Holy Spirit. Don't cower away when things go wrong, and don't ever run from God – run to Him; He is the only One that understands and can help you to fix your problem!

Never be angry with God. Love Him and worship Him and you will have all your questions answered when the time is right.

July 18

Behold our shield [the king as Your agent], O God, and look upon the face of Your anointed!
Psalm 84:9

Always In The Anointing Of God

God's anointing in our lives will move in us and through us, as we live in His Presence. It is not some natural anointing. We need to live daily by the anointing so that we can fulfil the calling of God on our lives.

I do not want an anointing in my life that just breaks the yoke; I want the anointing on my life that destroys the yokes. To break is to fracture, crack, splinter or tear, but when you destroy something; it is gone forever, totally removed. The yoke of fear, discouragement, disappointment, insecurity and confusion, bitterness and disease must be destroyed.

When you pray for people with the anointing, you are going to see results. You will be confident in His ability flowing in you and through you, and the anointing of God will give you boldness and a freedom to speak His Word shamelessly.

The anointing of God will dispel all fear of failure, and when you are anointed God can use you to bring about miracles in the lives of others. The anointing gives us the ability to do something that we cannot do as humans in our natural ability – like Samson when he tipped the columns, and Daniel in the lion's den.

No success or victory is self-obtained. It is the anointing of God that flows through you, strengthening and sustaining you to do great things for His glory.

July 19

To everything there is a season, and a time for every matter or purpose under heaven...
Ecclesiastes 3:1

A Season Of Change

Life consists of many seasons that come and go. It's what we learn and how we go through and come out of each one, that makes us stronger. As a child one is constantly learning how to do things – tie your shoelaces, brush your hair, put on and take off your shoes. Eventually you graduate from that learning school to the next one.

Teenagers are subject to many hormonal changes that encourage emotional highs and lows. But when the season is over, they become men and women. There is not one thing in your life that will not change over a period of time. Constant change is here to stay!

The Word of God will build strong attitudes that will help you through all the seasons of your life.

Each experience you have will build strength for your future. Don't be robbed of the joy of the seasons of improvement in your life, however uncomfortable or painful. It's like the renovation of a building; at times it can be very inconvenient, and one can't see through the rubble. But when all is beautifully finished and everything looks good, you are thankful for the seasons.

Learn to work with the seasons of your life as you grow and change into becoming what God has in mind.

July 20

For we who have believed (adhered to and trusted in and relied on God) do enter that rest.
Hebrews 4:3

Rest

Rest - an intermission from labour, a break, to patiently wait, a place of peace. Trusting God will bring you to a place of rest, a rest that He has promised. I have seen many Christians unable to rest in God, unable to trust God.

When you are standing in faith, you need to simply rest in Him and confidently trust Him to do whatever it is that He has promised. If you are prepared to trust your doctor or your lawyer, how MUCH MORE should be able to trust the Lord.

Faith is not about frustration, impatience or a works programme. Faith is simply trusting and resting in God's promises, where your heart is governed by His peace. Faith in God is actively exercising His Word, not lazily sitting by singing "whatever will be, will be"! You know in your heart, when you are living in faith and resting in God. The Bible doesn't speak of "striving in God", it talks about "resting in Him".

During the years I have needed to trust God for many things. I can honestly say that He has never failed me or let me down. Everything that He has promised has come to pass and I have no regrets.

When you give something to God, don't take it back, by worrying and trying to sort it out yourself. Leave it in the Lord's capable hands, and rest in His arms.

Rest is an expression of your faith.

July 21

So for the present you are also in sorrow (in distress and depressed); but I will see you again and [then] your hearts will rejoice, and no one can take from your joy (gladness, delight).
John 16:22

Joyful Tenacity

You don't know the future – only God does! You don't know what is going to come your way in your lifetime, or how your life may change, because of circumstances or sudden change.

I can assure you of this one thing, if you have the joy of the Lord in your heart it will give you a bulldog tenacity in the middle of the most trying times.

Joy is like a river that is filled with living water. It will flow from your inner most being – up and upon you, and lift you out of all your difficult circumstances. Nothing can touch you or defeat you.

When your focus is on the Word of God, your eyes look straight ahead of you toward the goal of the upward call in Christ Jesus. This focus is solid under any stressful situation and is rich in the knowledge of the cross and will not be distracted.

Use whatever ability you have in God to come out on the other side of the mountain. Joy will keep your strength high, and depression out.

Joy will be your cheerleader and it will help you never to give up on God.

If you give up, you could lose the moment of your biggest breakthrough.

July 22

Trust (lean on, rely on, and be confident) in the Lord and do good; so shall you dwell in the land and feed surely on His faithfulness, and truly you shall be fed.
Psalm 37:3

Totally Trusting

How much do you trust the Lord?

If you want to live a fruitful and fulfilling life with God, then to trust Him is the only way to go. To "say" you trust God is not going to be enough.

Trusting God requires action, utter reliance upon Him, putting your total dependence on Him. When you trust God you will do good; you will prosper; and you will be abundantly blessed, because His peace will sustain you. To trust God is to place your life in His hands entirely.

Don't think that you are trusting God, and the moment an issue arises – you stress about your finances, health, home and relationships and then you begin to scheme and plan out ways to get through it all. In your walk with God, you are to surrender to Him completely.

Just like a little child who jumps off a wall into his father's arms and is not afraid, but will not jump into a stranger's arms, so it must be with you as child of God. You must leap into the arms of God, who knows and understands every fibre of your being; to lean on Him in every situation, to rely on His love and mercy and to be confident that He wants only the best for you.

Exercise your faith in God, He will astound you with His trustworthiness.

July 23

There he found a man named Aeneas, who had been bedfast for eight years and was paralysed. And Peter said to him, Aeneas, Jesus Christ (the Messiah) [now] makes you whole. Get up and make your bed! And immediately [Aeneas] stood up.
Acts 9:33-34

You Are Whole In Jesus Christ

Jesus Christ makes you whole! Perhaps you have been aware of His goodness and blessings, but you have not moved into them and applied them in your life. You have watched life pass you by from a distance. Well, it is time to get up and make your bed; it is time for you to stand up as God has made you whole.

God wants you to have SHALOM, peace - nothing missing, and nothing broken in your life. He wants you to grow and move forward, to rise above and walk in wholeness, to GET UP and make your bed!

It's time to get out of your 'stuck'. Listen to what He says to you:

> 2 Corinthians 12:9: ... My grace (My favour and loving-kindness and mercy) is enough for you [sufficient against any danger and enables you to bear the trouble manfully]; for My strength and power are made perfect (fulfilled and completed) and show themselves most effective in [your] weakness.

God wants you whole in your spirit - Through the New Birth
God wants you whole in your soul - Through the renewing of your mind
God wants you whole in your will - As His will becomes your will
God wants you whole in your emotions - Align your emotions to the Word Of God
God wants you whole in your body - By His stripes you were healed

July 24

Let be and be still, and know (recognise and understand) that I am God. I will be exalted among the nations! I will be exalted in the earth!
Psalm 46:10

Too Busy!

If you are racing through the drudgery of the day, and you don't have any time for the Lord, then you need a serious life evaluation. If you are busy being busy, then you are simply too busy!

You cannot sacrifice your life in God for something that will not last forever. Get to grips with your time and decide that you will give place to the Father, and nothing will interfere with it.

A loving relationship takes time and commitment. Your roots must be planted in eternal value. Anything that has your utmost attention and distracts you from a loving relationship with the Lord is not from God. Concentrating on your own needs, day and night, will make you "self-centered" and not "God-centered"

God's Word instructs you to be still, and know that He is God!

To live your life in order, you must have your life ordered of the Lord.

July 25

And this is the confidence, (the assurance, the privilege of boldness) which we have in Him: [we are sure] that if we ask anything (make any request) according to His will (in agreement with His own plan), He listens to and hears us.
1 John 5:14

Confidence In Prayer

God hears you always when you pray.

When you pray to the Father according to His Word and His will, He will not refuse your request. God is incapable of breaking His Word; His promises are forever settled in Heaven. Calling on His name in times of need is right where He wants you to be.

When you ask the Father for something, go to His Word and find out if what you are asking for is scriptural. If it is then He immediately hears you. Confidently speak to Him as a Father and then thank Him for all that He has done for you.

When my daughter was five years old, she asked me for a new dress and I agreed to bring one home for her, she simply believed me. She was confident in my words; she didn't question me or doubt me. Her mommy said so, and that was enough for her.

You may need to exercise such childlike faith with God, and confidently be assured that "your Daddy said so" in His Word, and He is bound to that.

Appropriate the many promises of God,
by confidently praying His will.

July 26

And Jesus stopped and said, Call him. And they called the blind man, telling him. Take courage! Get up! He is calling you.
Mark 10:49

He Is Calling You To Change

Just when you think you have everything together, get ready, because the Lord is about to bring about some change in your life. Jesus doesn't want you relaxing in your comfort zone, because when you are there you are no longer walking on the water but sitting in the boat.

God will give you a little "come" just like He gave Peter, and Peter stepped out of the boat and walked on the water. When Jesus says, "come" to you, you will find out what is in your heart.

God is not satisfied with you being mediocre. He wants you to be stretched to capacity in your walk with Him, to be effective, and productive in the Kingdom of God.

He knows that you have the capacity to succeed in Him and whilst you are here on the earth, you will continually be changing, growing and developing in your relationship in Christ. He wants your life to be clean and beautiful so that you may testify of His goodness and all He has done in and through you.

The Lord continually calls and encourages you to change, not to be afraid but to step out with Him. We need to be like the blind man; he heard the call of God, leapt to his feet and was healed. You may need to get yourself out of a rut and follow God, and do what ever is required of you. He is calling you.

Don't settle for the good; go for God's best.

July 27

All has been heard; the end of the matter is: Fear God [revere and worship Him, knowing that He is] and keep His commandments, for this is the whole of man [the full, original purpose of his creation, the object of God's providence, the root of character, the foundation of all happiness, the adjustment to all inharmonious circumstances and conditions under the sun] and the whole [duty] for every man.
Ecclesiastes 12:13

Fear God And Worship Him

The wisest conclusion that man can come to is to "Fear God". Everything in life revolves around this principle, our joy, our peace, our wisdom, our destiny, our satisfaction, and our eternal life.

Every circumstance that you and I face is solved in the knowledge of fearing and knowing God. He is all wisdom and all-powerful, He is the beginning and the end of everything; He is the one who was and is and is forevermore. He IS our happiness and our Joy.

Giving your thoughts and desires second place is the most natural thing to do when you are dealing with Almighty God, Creator of Heaven and Earth. Come to Him and let Him show you the avenues of life.

Put God first, honour and worship Him forever.

July 28

But let all those who take refuge and put their trust in You rejoice; let them ever sing and shout for joy, because You make a covering over them and defend them; let those also who love Your name be joyful in You and be in high spirits.
Psalm 5:11

Tell Your Face What Is In Your Heart

Putting your trust and refuge in the Lord is going to release your joy. It starts on the inside and rises up from your spirit until your whole being is rejoicing.

Learn how to thrive in your relationship with the Lord; just being with Him is thrilling. When you get around folk, look for the little things that bring you pleasure – there is so much to enjoy! People are precious and each one is so very different.

Church is another place that I make up my mind to enjoy. I get filled with strength and encouragement for the week to come, and it shows on my face.

When you walk into a room, make an effort not to look as though you have just attended God's funeral? He is alive and so are you. The more time you spend giving praise to the Lord, the more that smile will stay on your face. If you do not worship the Lord, then the Word of God says that the trees of the field will wave and clap their hands in worship of Him.

Put a spring in your step, a song in your heart, and a smile on your face. Let the joy of the Lord grow inside of you. We all have good and bad days, but it's what you do with them that count.

God wants you to be in high spirits as you live for Him. How else would you be with God on your side?

July 29

So let us seize and hold fast and retain without wavering the hope we cherish and confess and our acknowledgement of it, for He Who promised is reliable (sure) and faithful to His word.
Hebrews 10:23

The Promises Of God

God's Word is full of promises to the believer. The day you accepted Jesus Christ into your life, you stepped into His grace and mercy. Automatically you qualified to inherit His promises.

A person does not receive his inheritance when he dies, but when the owner of the estate dies. Jesus left you an inheritance when He died – you are the rightful one to claim what He has promised. Jesus not only gave you eternal life, but healing, peace, joy, abundant life, and a family, and so much more. It's there for you today.

People so easily make promises, "I'll do it today. Leave it to me!" However, the quality of a promise is not in the way it sounds, but rather in the one who makes the promise. Every promise Jesus ever made is a quality promise; it is founded in the written Word of God and there is no shadow of turning in His ways.

So if you believe God's promises you have a sure blessing. Always keep your word if you promise to do something for someone. You are only as good as your word!

The promises of God are sure, they will never fail, just as sure as today becomes tomorrow, and day becomes night.

July 30

*Yet, O Lord, You are our Father; we are the clay, and You our Potter,
and we all are the work of Your hand.*
Isaiah 64:8

The Potter And The Clay

Some of the changes in your life happen gradually, and then again others happen suddenly and turn out huge. Just like the pot in the potter's hand – if there are any rough edges or uneven sides, he will mould that pot until it is perfect.

Gradual changes are easier to handle, because we slowly get used to them. Sudden changes stress us, as they are challenging and unexpected. Don't get nervous when things around you get out of control – God has your life in His hands; He is able to keep you. What you need to do is to hold on tight to Him and get through it.

Marriage changes all of us; we have to work on certain things: the toilet seat being put down, fighting over blankets, (you know what I mean!) Sudden change can come through losing a precious loved one and everything around you seems to collapse. Keep your eyes on Jesus and make sure you have strong friends who will encourage you, and lift your heart. It will be painful, but you will get through it with the help of the Holy Spirit.

Allow the Potter to work the necessary changes in your life. In the end you will be a beautiful, pure vessel, fit for the Masters use.

July 31

We are assured and know that [God being a partner in their labor] all things work together and are [fitting into a plan] for good to and for those who love God and are called according to [His] design and purpose.
Romans 8:28

Are You Ready For Change?

t's always time for change, even though you may not readily think so.

A friend of mine relocated with her husband to the UK a few years ago. I remember when she told me that they were emigrating I was not happy about losing my friend. Yet, I knew that God had some things planned for their lives and even though it was hard for me, I eventually had to release them to what God was going to do in their lives.

As a child of God you have the assurance that the work God is doing in you is a good work, and one in which He is looking out for your best interests. God will never do anything to hurt or harm you. The changes, although you may not see it now are for the better, to make you stronger and more dependent on Him.

Change in your life will cause you to grow up in the things of God. It would be weird to see a man of 30 still holding onto his blanket and drinking from a baby's bottle.

If God arranges change, you can't fight it or resist it.

Change is positive when God is in it!

August

Flourish In God

August 1

And there shall be stability in your times, an abundance of salvation, wisdom, and knowledge; the reverent fear and worship of the Lord is your treasure and His.
Isaiah 33:6

The Treasures Of God

When God gives you treasures, you get to keep them. When your husband comes home with a box of chocolates for you, how often does he "help" you eat the chocolates?

God's treasures are forever! When we are in fellowship with the Lord, and are consistently seeking after Him, we will see the treasures of God overflowing in our lives.

The treasure that Isaiah is talking about in this scripture are not natural treasure that rust and moth will decay, like cars and houses, jewellery and clothing. It is talking about rich treasure that lasts for Eternity. A treasure that NO MAN can break in and steal, and NO fire or flood can destroy. It is a treasure that only worshipping Him and knowing Him will provide.

Wisdom and Knowledge, the reverent fear and worship of the Lord is the GREATEST TREASURE and it is yours and it is His. You belong to Him and because you do, your life will exude the greatest of His richest treasures.

Having God in your life brings stability to everything. Jesus settles all the dust and keeps your feet firmly planted on the rock. Your union with God is your most valued treasure; no material possessions or temptation can match the worth of the riches you have in Christ Jesus.

No wealth can compare to Christ's treasure.

August 2

*There is a way, which seems right to a man and appears straight
before him, but at the end of it is the way of death.*
Proverbs 14:12

God's Pathway Of Life

There are no shortcuts with God. There is a right way and a wrong way; even though the right way seems longer, it is still the right way.

The route God has planned is the correct one. If you make your own plans, and you think your plans are better and quicker you will be sorry.

Preparation is a vital part of life, and walking God's pathway helps you to build the characteristics that go hand in hand with God's blessings. When things come too easily and you are not prepared for them, you will lose them just as quickly as you attained them.

Taking the wise route is bound to bring blessing your way. It is much nicer to enjoy the riches when you are more ready to do so. What a waste to rush through something, to have done it incorrectly and to have to start all over again.

Any path without God is the wrong path. The Lord has to be at the centre of every decision you make. He is the One who must lead and guide you.

Never detour from God – keep your feet on the right path.

August 3

Arise and go down to the potter's house, and there I will cause you to hear My words.
Jeremiah 18:2

The Potter's House

When you go to church you must go with the attitude that God is going to speak into your life, and give you direction and wisdom for the week.

We get a tremendous amount of blessing from spending time alone with the Lord in His Word, but there is nothing like getting into a corporate meeting where the man of God has prepared a powerful message to speak into your heart.

The message is not always one that you want to hear, but one that you NEED to hear. If it is the Word of God, it will carry the necessary characteristics of The Word. It will quicken you, correct you, refresh and revive you, and most amazingly, it will discipline you. God's Word is sharper than the surgeon's knife, and it is able to separate the soul from the spirit. NOTHING else has the power to do that!

I get direction from attending church; in fact there is nowhere else that I would rather be on a Sunday, and I always learn something, even if it is what not to do!

It is good to belong to a local church and give of yourself in service to the Lord and to the Body of Christ. Attending seminars and conferences and other inspirational and challenging events will encourage change in your life.

Allow the Potter to mould the pot and change your life. Be pliable in His hands and let Him do His work in you.

For this to happen, you will have to be obedient and pliable.

August 4

*Now when I arrived at Troas [to preach] the Good News (the Gospel)
of Christ, a door of opportunity was opened for me in the Lord.*
2 Corinthians 2:12

You Have The Keys

Just as the keys to your home open different doors, so do the keys that God has given you to His Kingdom. Some keys open the locks pretty easily; then again others truly test your patience.

God has already given you all the keys that you will need for your new life in Him. Each key will unlock various doors that you must go through. These doors are not going to unlock automatically; you are going to have to take a step of faith, find the key and open that door.

If you need to get the lawnmower from the garage, you are not going to unlock the garage door with the laundry room key. If you need forgiveness, you are not going to get it by paying your tithes. You will have to study forgiveness and then follow the necessary steps to deal with it.

By avoiding opening the door, you will keep the things locked-up that you desperately need. Believers were given a set of keys when they went through the door of salvation, but sadly many of their keys are hanging up, rusting and collecting dust.

You have the keys to unlock the door of opportunity in your life. Be bold, and put that key in the lock; you will marvel at what God has in store for you.

August 5

And in all matters of wisdom and understanding concerning which the king asked them, he found them ten times better than all the [learned] magicians and enchanters who were in his whole realm.
Daniel 1:20

Ten Times Better

Everything that is in you should be growing and improving. Nothing should be holding onto your life, that you should have gotten rid of a long time ago. If this is true, then you need to get your actions and thoughts together and do something serious about these little foxes.

When God changes your life, almost immediately you are at least ten times better. His Word tells us that old things pass away, things like a broken heart, tormented mind, addictions, hatred, fear and insecurity, depression, discouragement… that makes you at least ten times better than before! He gives you a brand new heart and a desire to love.

Even though so much falls off of your life, there will be things that will take a little longer, but you will keep on getting better and better.

A good example of being ten times better is the story of Daniel's men who were found ten times better than the men who were partying at the king's palace. They were eating tasty food and drinking fine wine while Daniel's guys were on a healthy diet, training their bodies and worshipping their God.

Live right, do right, and never lose sight of the Excellent One who did it all for you in the first place.

You don't know how good you are looking, until you get a glimpse of your past.

August 6

Now the Lord is the Spirit, and where the Spirit of the Lord is, there is liberty (emancipation from the bondage, freedom).
2 Corinthians 3:17

Freedom In Change

ou will experience FREEDOM where the Spirit of the Lord is.

When everyone else around you is falling apart due to unforeseen circumstances in the workplace, they will see you standing with a smile on your face and strong in God. What a testimony of God's goodness, freedom and peace.

No situation that you encounter takes God by surprise! So rest, and surrender yourself to Him. Don't let pressure weigh you down. If you are a believer, there has to be something different happening on the inside of you.

You can use change as a growing opportunity. Ride the tidal wave and don't become depressed and burnt out like those around you, when God is doing a work in you. Use the time to develop, and perhaps to discipline your mind and speech. Grow through the experience.

Welcome change and embrace it. If you don't, you are going to fight it and become weary and tired. How you come out of the change on the other side, depends you and on your attitude toward it.

Embrace change, it will bring greatness to your life.

August 7

And I sought a man among them who should build up the wall and stand in the gap before Me for the land, that I should not destroy it, but I found none.
Ezekiel 22:30

Will You Stand In The Gap?

Are you prepared to pray? Are you prepared to pray for your nation and to stand in the gap?

God is seeking those who will present the circumstances of the nation to Him in prayer – not so that He will find out what is going on, but so that He is given, the right to act on our behalf according to the Word.

You see, Satan has a lease on this world and even though it belongs to God, he is still the god of this world. Adam was given that right until he sinned.

Our responsibility, as children of God, in the authority that lies in the name of Jesus, is to raise-up a standard against the works of darkness. Are you prepared to be a part of that standard?

2 Chronicles 7:14 "If My people, who are called by My name, shall humble themselves, pray, seek, crave, and require of necessity My face and turn from their wicked ways, then will I hear from heaven, forgive their sin, and heal their land."

We are to pray according to His Word and Will. This unleashes power to get things to change in the earth. When God seeks someone to stand in the gap, will you be available?

Let's stand together against the darkness for the Kingdom of God to increase.

August 8

In conclusion, be strong in the Lord [be empowered through your union with Him]; draw your strength from Him [that strength which His boundless might provides].
Ephesians 6:10

Victory In God

There are instances in your life when the devil will tempt, and try to overcome you with evil. When this happens, take command of the situation and conquer him by doing good works. Take the Word of God and apply it to your situation.

We see in 2 Chronicles 20, the Moabites, Ammonites and Meunites came against the tribe of Judah to battle. The Lord spoke to the people of Judah, saying, "Be not afraid or dismayed at this great multitude, for the battle is not yours, but God's".

Perhaps you are in the midst of an immense battle right now and you can barely see above the clouds; listen to me, no matter how big the battle is, it is NOT yours – it is the Lord's!!!

You do not need to fight, stand still and see the deliverance of the Lord. Just as the tribe of Judah began to sing and praise the Lord, so should you.

Rejoicing lifts burdens off your shoulders, it infuses confidence in you, and opens doors to your victory.

The darkest hour is just before dawn. Hold tightly to God and His Word, morning is about to break!

August 9

But the Lord is with me as a mighty and terrible One; therefore my persecutors will stumble, and they will not overcome [me]. They will be utterly put to shame, for they will not deal wisely or prosper [in their schemes]; their eternal dishonour will never be forgotten.
Jeremiah 20:11

The Lord Is With Me

Belonging to God gives you a tremendous advantage over your enemy. I know that we do not like to think of the possibility of having enemies, but when the Lord begins to bless your life, the devil and people get mad.

Yes, you are a child of God, and if anyone is going to protect you it is going to be the Lord. Don't meditate on evil thoughts against your enemy, as you will develop a heart filled with anger and bitterness.

Matthew 5:11-12 Blessed (happy, to be envied, and spiritually prosperous— with life-joy and satisfaction in Gods favour and salvation, regardless of your outward conditions) are you when people revile you and persecute you and say all kinds of evil things against you falsely on My account Be glad and supremely joyful, for your reward in heaven is great (strong and intense), for in this same way people persecuted the prophets who were before you

41-44 And if anyone forces you to go one mile, go with him two [miles]. Give to him who keeps on begging from you, and do not turn away from him who would borrow [at interest] from you. You have heard that it was said, You shall love your neighbour and hate your enemy; But I tell you, Love your enemies and pray for those who persecute you,

Treating enemies the way God commanded is the most productive way with an enemy. Your enemy is a test of the depth of your understanding of your love. Loving your enemy disempowers their hold over you. Your freedom is in forgiving and letting go.

Let's stand together against the darkness and for the Kingdom of God to increase.

August 10

And let us not lose heart and grow weary and faint in acting nobly and doing right, for in due time and at the appointed season we shall reap, if we do not loosen and relax our courage and faint.
Galatians 6:9

He Will Sort Them Out

When you are continually doing what is right, and you feel as though nothing is working out for you, do not lose courage and give up on your faith. When you lose heart, there is basically no hope left.

Your heart is where inspiration, vision and dreams are birthed. The Word promises that if you do not let go or get tired, you will see your dream come to pass. Take this difficult period as a wonderful opportunity to grow and to gain fresh vision from the Lord.

When continual pressure is applied to your life how do you respond? Are you challenged by it, or do you give up after the second or third time. Does your faith get stronger, or do you begin to waver? Then hold tight and do not let go of your faith.

You may need to learn to stretch and discover that there is more inside of you than you realised. Until you get the opportunity to test that inner-strength you are unaware that you have it. I guarantee that if you have been planting the Word in your heart for a period of time, it will rise up when you need it.

You WILL reap, when the season is right and you will receive the reward of your faith.

The first time you went to the gym it was difficult to pick up even the lightest weights. After the tenth time, it becomes a lot easier.

Never quit!

August 11

If I say, I will not make mention of [the Lord] or speak any more in His name, in my mind and heart it is as if there were a burning fire shut up in my bones. And I am weary of enduring and holding it in; I cannot [contain it any longer].
Jeremiah 20:9

I Cannot Keep Quiet!

When God has given you such a beautiful life you cannot be quiet. You will want to shout it from the rooftops! No matter where I am or what I am doing, if there are people around, I find myself sharing about just how AMAZING and good my Father God has been to me.

The Love of Jesus CANNOT be shut up in your bones! I remember many years ago when I was attending a wedding with a friend, a lady came up to us and asked us what was so different about us. We took her in a private room and began to share the love of Jesus with her. She accepted Jesus as Lord right there, and then she ran out of the room inviting everyone to come and hear about this amazing Jesus! Needless to say, before too long, the whole wedding was listening to our testimony!

Our world is lost and lacking in love. It does not take much to get their attention. Don't be shy to share about what Jesus means to you, and what He has done for you. You don't need to be forceful or overbearing, but just a sweet gentle word will open the door for many questions.

There are also times when the Lord will tell you not to say a word, but to let your face and smile do all the talking! However God leads you, SHINE with His Glory! It comes from deep within and will impact others as they encounter His Presence in you.

Go tell it on the mountain, over the hills and far away that Jesus Christ is Lord – that is the Good News.

God's Presence is everywhere.

August 12

Behold, I stand at the door and knock; if anyone hears and listens to and heeds My voice and opens the door, I will come in to him and will eat with him, and he [will eat] with Me.
Revelations 3:20

Knocking On The Door Of Your Heart

Getting to know Jesus is life changing, He will be the best friend that you have ever had. He will encourage you, support you, cheer you on along the way, stick with you through thick and thin, and one thing I can promise you, He will NEVER EVER leave you!

I received Jesus as my Lord and Saviour just before my 19th Birthday in March 1973. Immediately my life took on new meaning and began to change.

I recognise today that there were many times that I had heard Him knocking, but did not know that I needed to open the door and invite Him in. The day that I did, I ran to the Altar to receive Him as my Lord and Saviour. It was the BEST day of my life!

Life is busy and our attention is all over the place. I have invited the Lord to never stop knocking on the door of my heart for my attention. Even though He is in my heart, I still get distracted and forget about the MOST important relationship that I have, the one I have with Jesus.

I hear Him knocking… "I need time with you!", "Let's do this together!"

We need to be busy for the Lord, encouraging and telling others of His love for them and bringing them to the cross.

When you hear Him knocking, open the door!

August 13

Do not be deceived: God is not mocked, for whatever one sows, that will he also reap.
Galatians 6:7

Be Careful What You Sow

*E*very day of your life you will be sowing seed. As that seed is watered it will begin to grow and eventually you will have a harvest. This works in areas both good and bad.

As a mature Christian I have become very aware of this spiritual law. I decided a number of years ago that I was going to be very wise about what kind of seed I was sowing in my life. It takes a number of things for seed to grow, good soil, water and some very special TLC (tender loving care).

You certainly do not want to sow bad seed, never mind watering it and feeding it compost! I believe we sow bad seed by our actions and words, then we water and compost the seeds by coddling them, being sure that we feel justified by our actions, that we are always right no matter the consequences and try our best to tell everyone why we are the way that we are!

The less weeds you have in your garden, the better the good fruit will grow. Weeds choke good seed and stop its growth. So too with bitterness, anger, fear, discouragement and pride that we may have. Human nature is always to take care of "self".

God's Word instructs us how to behave and what kind of seed will bring us the best fruit. There just is no place for things in our lives that break us down and destroy us.

The quicker you pull those weeds out before they become trees, the better off you will be!

My heart is ready to receive all the good seed that I need to sow!

August 14

Am I a God at hand, says the Lord, and not a God afar off?
Jeremiah 23:23-24

You Cannot Keep A Secret From God

"Can anyone hide himself in a secret places so that I cannot see him? Do not I fill heaven and earth?" says the Lord. God is Ever Present. There has never been a beginning to His presence. He is the alpha and omega, the Great I Am, the all in one. How could you ever hide anything form Him?

You cannot get away from Him, no matter what you do. Running away from Him only causes you to run into Him. That's exactly how He wants it, for you not to run from Him but to run TO Him

So you had better get used to the idea that He is always going to be wherever you go. You cannot think that if you hide under the bed and sin, God will not be able to see you? The more open that you are with God; the more He is able to help you.

During my teenage years at school I played truant one day. While listening to the radio, I heard the back door slam as my dad arrived home. I dived under the bed and hid away. Fortunately, because my dad was not God, he did not see me or I would have been in very hot water!

Not so with God… He knows and sees EVERYTHING!

God LOVES you enough to not leave you as you are!

August 15

Blessed and fortunate and happy and spiritually prosperous (in that state in which the born-again child of God enjoys His favour and salvation) are those who hunger and thirst for righteousness (uprightness and right standing with God), for they shall be completely satisfied!
Matthew 5:6

Hungry And Thirsty For God

You will only be satisfied and lacking nothing in your life, when God fills the vacuum in your being.

To discover all of who God is, you are going to have to hunger after Him and His Presence. You are not going to get by with riding on your mother's or your friend's relationship with God. You will need to discover God for yourself. God has no grandchildren.

Develop your own relationship with Him and get to know Him intimately.

If you really want what God has for you, you will have to take it from Him yourself. Do you want righteousness, right standing and uprightness with God? He is giving you the opportunity to have all of these in your life. How? By longing to have His Presence even stronger in your life.

If your body is hungry, you will do just about anything to get some food into your stomach. Only the Lord can fill the spiritual hunger in your heart.

Always be hungry and thirsty for His Word and His Presence.

Hunger after God, without Him there will be no satisfaction or fulfilment in your life.

August 16

Then you will call upon Me, and you will come and pray to Me, and I will hear and heed you.
Jeremiah 29:12

Call Upon God

There are so many promises in the Word that tell us that God hears us when we pray. Do not spend your time in repetitious prayers as God does not have a bad memory and He is not deaf either.

Once you have prayed, give thanks to the Lord for whatever it is that you have prayed about. Prayer is the most powerful tool that you have, and it will accomplish the miracles that you need in your life and others around you.

There is nothing as beautiful as talking to the Father in the name of Jesus. The Word of God declares that this action makes tremendous power available to us. Developing a healthy prayer life is the most practical thing that any Christian can do to stay in touch with the Father's heart.

If you are in strife or any confusing circumstances you will find it hard to pray. First clear the air so that there are no blockages in your communication with the Lord.

Living a prayer-filled life will cause you to grow strong in just a short space of time and keep you sensitive to issues that are important to the Father's heart.

"Our Father, who art in Heaven hallowed be Thy name..."

August 17

And his master saw that the Lord was with him and that the Lord made all that he did to flourish and succeed in his hand. So Joseph pleased [Potiphar] and found favour in his sight...
Genesis 39:3-4

Flourishing In God

Joseph was serving in the house of Potiphar, even though he was a slave, he was a successful man. Joseph was hungry for the things of God. He loved his God and was walking in a close relationship with Him. The blessing of the Lord was upon Joseph's life. Whatever he did, prospered and flourished.

Flourishing means: growing, increasing, succeeding and abounding.

It's time for you to flourish in God. When you are flourishing in God, there is favour upon your life. When you are seeking Him first, all that you do and touch will prosper because of His blessing. This blessing that will flow onto you will pass onto others, your husband, children and your friends. Of course, the tests and trials will come, but you will grow through the difficulties, and come out flourishing and the glory of the Lord will be evident in your life.

My prayer for you is that you will hunger and thirst and flourish in your life in God, that the favour of the Lord, will embrace you, as you abound in His presence.

August 18

Who [with reason] despises the day of small things?
Zechariah 4:10

Dynamite Comes In Small Packages

I never thought that God would be able to use my life the way that He has. Even though I am only 1.6 metres (5' 3") tall, God has me travelling around the world preaching the Good News. It does not matter how tall you are, or how young or old you are, God will use your life for His Glory.

I am so grateful that I was given the opportunity to study at Rhema in Tulsa, Oklahoma. If I did not go, who knows where I would have been today?

When I returned to South Africa from Bible School, we started a Church. It took small, baby-steps of faith and obedience to God and the calling, and now today I am still reaping off of those baby steps of obedience! You have to be faithful in small things for God to trust you with the bigger things.

Everything you go through today is preparation for tomorrow. Nothing you do or experience today is in vain. Each day's activities are planting seeds for the crop tomorrow. Keep happy in your planting now and do not think that it's the crop that will make you happy. It's planting that satisfies your heart.

Let me assure you even the small things are vital. What would an extravagant building be worth, without the foundations? We don't see them, but without them – a beautiful looking building would just crumble to the ground.

Every small step you take is a future you are about to make.

August 19

[For my determined purpose is] that I may know Him [that I may progressively become more deeply and intimately acquainted with Him, perceiving and recognising and understanding the wonders of His Person more strongly and more clearly]...
Philippians 3:10

Determine To Know God Better

It does not matter how long you have been walking with the Lord, you will always need to progressively get closer to Him. It's an on-going desire for you and for Him. He wants you to learn how to trust Him, listen to Him and draw your life from Him.

Our God is amazing. His personality, character and ways are too stunning for words; it will take a lifetime to fully comprehend His Greatness, but He gives us the opportunity to understand and know His love and miraculous power by coming into close contact with Him.

Just as it takes time for you to develop a close natural friendship, it will take the same commitment to get to know the Father. The more time you spend with Him, in His Presence, the more you will develop your understanding of Him. When you are intimate with God, it is just you and Him.

God does not hold back on you. His story is written for all to read. He has nothing to hide from you.

August 20

*Then you will seek Me, inquire for, and require Me (as a vital necessity)
and find Me when you search for Me with all your heart.*
Jeremiah 29:13

Seek God With All Of Your Heart

Drawing close to God takes commitment and desire on your part. When you have a definite need to know Him more intimately, you will experience His Presence.

Not only does God want you to seek Him, but to ask Him about anything that you need to know. Once you have done that, He desires for you to take Him at His Word and to need Him in your life as much as you need air to breathe.

When you have been away from His Presence for a period of time, you will feel a tremendous lack in your life. He is the only one that can fill your life with everything that you need.

His peace should overcome you; His joy must be your continual strength; your desire for His love should never grow dim; His presence should be with you always.

God wants to be in our lives by choice, not by habit or ritual. He wants to know that we really desire to be close to Him, to be in love with Him always.

He wants you to trust Him and to keep your desire
and heart fixed on Him.

August 21

He answered, Behold, I see four men loose, walking in the midst of the fire, and they are not hurt! And the form of the fourth is like a son of the gods!
Daniel 3:25

Who Is In The Fire With You?

Are you standing in the midst of a fire right now? May I ask you if you are alone in the fire, or is someone in the fire with you?

Can you believe that you can have a friend who would be prepared to go through your hottest hour with you? Jesus was the fourth man in the fire with Shadrach, Meshach and Abednego. King Nebuchadnezzar was horrified when he noticed that they were walking around in that furnace.

Satan will be horrified when he sees you walking around with your best friend Jesus, in the hour that he just thought would finally destroy you.

Don't try and get through the fire on your own. You do not have the supernatural ability to do it. When you call on the name of The Lord and He is by your side, you can go through anything and not be affected.

Another miracle is that God revealed His Presence to everyone who looked in the furnace at these three young men. He will do that for you too.

When you look like you are about to be consumed, Jesus will reveal to others that He is with you in your fire.

August 22

Do you not know that your body is the temple (the very sanctuary) of the Holy Spirit Who lives within you, Whom you have received [as a Gift] from God? You are not your own. You were bought with a price [purchased with a preciousness and paid for, made His own]. So then, honour God and bring glory to Him in your body.
1 Corinthians 6:19-20

Does God Own You?

You are precious to God and He wants to own you. He wants to be the Keeper of your heart and for you to be His child. He paid a high price for you, revealing His serious need of getting you back into His household.

When you buy a car, you are the proud owner thereof. You have chosen it, the colour, the upholstery, sound-system, everything. You own the car. You paid a lot of money for the car, so you are careful where you park it; you maintain it well and keep it clean and polished. You will not stand by and watch your car being vandalised or stolen – you will fight for it.

Christ paid for you; He owns you; He chose you – just as you are. He wants to keep and protect you, nourish you in His Word. He is not going to stand by and allow the enemy to destroy you. He wants the best for you. The only difference between you and the car is that you are "alive" and have the right to choose your owner.

Let Christ take care of you – you are His treasure.

August 23

For I desire and delight in dutiful steadfast love and goodness, not sacrifice, and the knowledge of and acquaintance with God more than burnt offerings.
Hosea 6:6

Love Is Better Than Sacrifice

Unless you are doing your work for God out of love and a desire for goodness, your motives are wrong.

When you think that you are doing God a favour by serving Him, you have just missed the boat. Running off to church on a Sunday to cover-up for your bad living is not going to work for very long. Eventually, your bad living catches up with you and brings troubles your way. Going to church should be a part of your heart's desire and something you do out of love and not sacrifice.

When you ask a friend or your child to do a favour for you and they reveal their lack of desire, you will not want them to do the favour. However, when you ask someone to do something for you and he or she kindly answers, "It's a pleasure!" your relationship is blessed.

You cannot serve God thinking that you are doing your share and He should be satisfied by your sacrifice. Remember it is by GRACE that you are saved!

He is God and you are human – get the picture.

August 24

Man's steps are ordered by the Lord. How then can a man understand his way?
Proverbs 20:24

God Orders Your Steps

God receives you just as you are. When I went to Bible School, I was a new Christian and still smoking. I am so grateful for God's mercy that rescued me and ordered my steps without me even understanding what His plans for my life were at the time.

Jesus will take your hang-ups, bad habits and if you will surrender to Him, He will establish something precious in your life.

Only God will take someone with old baggage and a bad history and give them sunshine and a future in Him. He doesn't want anything in return – He does it unconditionally. His love for you stretches beyond all of man's knowledge and understanding. It's called GRACE… God's Riches At Christ's Expense.

In Isaiah (55:8-9) the Scripture teaches us that God's thoughts are not our thoughts and that they are much higher. His plans are more than what you and I expect in life. He has purposed a destiny for you, far above all your creative thinking and scheming – you can rest in Him. You will have to do your share to get there, but you will get there with His help and support. This cuts down on the stress levels.

God's purposes for your life are not in vain. They will accomplish all that He has planned.

August 25

Even upon the menservants and upon the maidservants in those days will I pour out My Spirit.
Joel 2:29

God Pours His Spirit Out On Everyone

I really enjoy reading this Scripture as it tells me that NOBODY is exempt from receiving His Spirit, if they desire to be touched by Him.

Not only does God pour out of His Spirit on the men, but on the WOMEN too! I am glad that I qualify to receive an abundance of His Spirit. The servants, who could be classed as the least in man's eyes, are just as privileged as anybody else.

There is no discrimination in the Kingdom of God; if you want to receive anything from the Lord you can have it. It does not matter if you are young or old, single or married, chubby or skinny, male or female, black or white, tall or short, English, Italian, Jewish or Russian – you can get everything that God has for your life.

One day when my daughter Krissy was a little girl, she invited me to pray with her in God's language. She boldly began to pray… shadda, shammer, shishkad in her little way and then she stopped and said, "Mommy, I must not say "shuddup!" I had a good laugh about it when I went to bed, as it was the cutest little moment for me! At the tender age of four years she was filled with the Spirit.

There are no limitations in God – you can have it all if you love and serve Him.

August 26

There is [now no distinction] neither Jew nor Greek, there is neither slave nor free, there is not male nor female; for you are all one in Christ Jesus.
Galatians 3:28

Rise Up, Woman Of God!

Woman of God, it is time for God to use you in a powerful way. Although men and women are both spirit-beings, there are noticeable differences in the natural, as I am sure that you have noticed! God is not concerned about your gender but that you will serve and obey Him.

The Word is filled with many great women of God in the Old Testament, also the women that Jesus blessed to spread the Gospel in the New Testament. Some were single, some married with children but all were mighty ministers of God: Hannah was a strong woman of faith.

Rahab is listed in the genealogy of Jesus, she was the only person saved, when her city was destroyed. Deborah was a judge over Israel, she led the army into battle and they would not go without her. She gave the glory of the victory back to God and was a mediator between God and His people. Abigail was a wise and wealthy businesswoman, who would not comprise God's will for her life. Esther was crowned Queen of Persia and used by God to deliver her people.

Do not let your gender hinder you from serving God.

Obey Him and get rid of the fear of man.

August 27

But the saints of the Most High [God] shall receive the kingdom and possess the kingdom forever, even forever and ever.
Daniel 7:18

Saints Of Blessing

Who is going to inherit what you have been able to accumulate in this life when you go to Heaven? Are you going to leave it to a stranger and leave nothing for your children? Surely not! You are going to leave an inheritance to the ones that matter to you the most and who have meant everything to you, your children, and if you do not have any, a very special friend or a family member.

That is what Jesus did. He left His inheritance to the ones that mean the most to Him, the ones whom He laid down His life for His family, the children of God. Anyone that does not qualify does not share in the inheritance or the blessings.

By belonging to the Kingdom of God through receiving Jesus as Lord and Saviour of our lives, we not only receive the blessing, but we possess the Kingdom of God not just for a time after we die but forever.

The Word of God talks much about leaving an inheritance for your children's, children's children. Three generation to come will receive the blessing.

If you are a child of God, do not leave your inheritance in the bank, but use it wisely and give thanks to the Lord for what He has done for you everyday.

August 28

Hannah prayed, and said, My heart exults and triumphs in the Lord...
1 Samuel 2:1

Honourable Hannah

In the Word of God, Hannah is known as a strong woman of faith; she knew how to believe God; she was faithful to her Master and loved worshipping Him and being in His Presence. Hannah's husband, had another wife, but he preferred Hannah, because in her he saw a godly person, he honoured her righteousness, her love and her compassion.

One thing Hannah never had, was a child – this became her faith project. She prayed and promised God that if He would bless her with a child, she would give her child back to Him, to serve Him. Hannah fell pregnant with Samuel. When he was born she presented him to the Lord, and she began teaching Him to worship God. Samuel served the Lord all the days of his life. Hannah is our example of motherhood.

It was by faith that she conceived Samuel. It was her righteousness that gave her favour with her husband, and made her the awesome woman that she became.

You will get blessed too when you love the Lord. Nothing will shut out His divine favour. When you receive the blessings, follow through on your commitment to the Lord and never take the credit for yourself.

A woman of God who fears the Lord will be praised.

August 29

... What eye has not seen and ear has not heard and has not entered into the heart of man, [all that] God has prepared (made and keeps ready) for those who love Him [who hold Him in affectionate reverence, promptly obeying Him and gratefully recognising the benefits He has bestowed].
1 Corinthians 2:9

The Unveiling Of God's Ways

When is the last time that you looked at someone and wondered why does God choose to use them? They seem so unimportant.

I am sure the people of Jericho did this to Rahab. She was a gentile, an outcast by the Jewish people, a prostitute, a woman! She heard about this God of Israel, and she believed in Him. God chose Rahab to hide the spies; His favour and His hand were upon her life. When the city was destroyed she was spared. She is listed in the genealogy of Jesus Christ.

God does miracles with our lives when we love and serve Him. He will take a life that is headed for disaster and turn it into something so beautiful. All that He wants is your heart, your love and adoration.

There are heights that you will climb, and visions that you will accomplish by making Him your Lord.

God loves you so much. Give Him His rightful place in your life and watch what will happen to you.

August 30

... Let not the wise and skilful person glory and boast in his wisdom and skill; let not the mighty and powerful person glory and boast in his strength and power; let not the person who is rich [in physical gratification and earthly wealth] glory and boast in his [temporal satisfactions and earthly] riches; but let him who glories, glory in this: that he understands and knows Me [personally and practically, directly discerning and recognising My character], that I am the Lord, Who practices loving-kindness, judgement and righteousness in the earth, for in these things I delight, says the Lord.
Jeremiah 9:23-24

Revel In Jehovah

It does not matter how great you think you are. You can have untold riches and accomplishments, even be voted the "greatest human ever to have lived". What measure can it hold when it comes to the greatness of Almighty God? If you are going to boast, then boast in Him. He measured the waters of the earth in the palm of His hand. When did you last do that?

Embrace the complete sovereignty of God in every facet, and huddle into the fullness of life contained in Jesus. When you are in a close and intimate relationship with Him, your boast will be well directed. Brag on all that God has done and provided in life for you, not on your "self" achievements or worldly gain.

You only have, what you have, because God let you have it.

Glory in God, His love, kindness and mercy. Thank Him for giving life to you to appreciate and enjoy.

August 31

My God has sent His angel and has shut the lions' mouths so that they have not hurt me, because I was found innocent and blameless before Him; and also before you, O king, [as you very well know] I have done no harm or wrong.
Daniel 6:22

God Has Shut The Lions' Mouths

What a surprise for Daniel to find himself innocently in the lions' den. Have you ever landed in a place that you least expected and had to stand by faith to save your life?

God's Presence in Daniel's life was so awesome that the lions were struck dumb. They completely lost their appetite. When you are so full of God, and the enemy wants to destroy your life all you have to do is let God shine through you. His Presence in your life will confuse your attackers and make them bow before you or run away in stark terror.

It is not before men that you are to be found blameless but before Almighty God. He will be your shield and your great protector. With a two-edged sword in your mouth which is the Word of God spoken – you are already in the winners seat.

Do not allow sudden fear to grip your heart; stand your ground; submit to God and resist the enemy; he will flee.

No matter what circumstance you find yourself in, God will deliver you from your enemies.

September

Dare To Dream

September 1

*And whoever shall call upon the name of the Lord
shall be delivered and saved...*
Joel 2:32

Salvation For All

What's our wonderful God, always reaching out to us with His unconditional love.

The Kingdom of God belongs to anyone who will call upon the name of the Lord. It does not matter what your background is, or from what culture you come, the Lord is there for you.

Once you have discovered His precious love, you will desire to walk with Him. His Presence in your life is vital for every day. Under the Old Covenant, only the sacrificing of a spotless Lamb once a year could save the Jews. Thank God that under the New Covenant and through the shed blood of Jesus, ALL are welcome to come to Jesus and be saved.

The priority of the Holy Spirit is wooing people to Christ.

Over the years I have become more and more aware of the Great Commission. Every believer should be equipped to share the Gospel and lead others to Christ. Jesus came chiefly to save sinners

There is absolutely nothing that can keep you from the love of Christ and the desire of God to have you "abide" in Him. It comes by a simple decision, one that will set the platform for the rest of your life.

Anyone who will call on the name of the Lord will be saved.

September 2

Multitudes, multitudes in the valley of decision. For the day of the Lord is near in the valley of decision.
Joel 3:14

Do Not Delay, Decide Today

You cannot live in the valley of decision. If you live there you will be discouraged and confused. Procrastination keeps you in the midst of failure.

The sooner you decide that you are not going to compromise what God is doing in your life for a lesser pleasure, the sooner you will rise above the mire of the pit. Making a decision for God will always set you free and build your spirit. Giving Him the "go-ahead" to rule and reign in your life is the most important step you will take.

When I was faced with the choice of leaving South Africa and attending Bible School in the USA, I seriously stood in the valley of decision. I was confronted with a choice – yes or no! I was not given a couple of weeks to think about it or pray about it. I had to give an answer there and then.

James says that a double minded man receives NOTHING of the Lord.

I am so glad that I made the right choice – saying yes to God always is the right thing to do. Getting into partnership with God will give you the best outcome.

Do not be afraid; go with God all the way. Saying yes to Him will bring you out of the valley of indecision.

September 3

Then Jesus answered her, O woman, great is your faith! Be it done for you as you wish. And her daughter was cured from that moment.
Matthew 15:28

According To Your Faith

Our faith has much to do with what we receive from the Lord. When we know what God's Word says He will do and we believe it, we will receive what He has promised. But if we do not believe it we will not receive it. So many people know that God can do it, but will He do it for them?

This precious woman mentioned in the book of Matthew knew how to get her answer to prayer. She had obviously heard about the Healer and the Miracle Worker Jesus, and that God would do it for her. She made a fuss to get Jesus' attention; she was loud, troublesome and begged Him to heal her daughter. When He did not answer her, she said aloud, "Lord help me."

She was determined to get her child healed by the Master. How determined are you to get what God has already provided for you? Jesus said to her, "O woman, great is your faith."

She demanded His attention and was prepared to go to whatever lengths necessary for her faith to work.

Faith is a measure in many ways; strong faith, weak faith, little faith, no faith, great faith

God cannot ignore "great faith" – not letting go of His Word, is one way to stand. This woman's daughter was healed from that very moment.

Be strong and confident in your faith, trust the Lord.

September 4

As for you, you thought evil against me, but God meant it for good, to bring about that many people should be kept alive, as they are this day. Now therefore, do not be afraid. I will provide for and support you and your little ones. And he comforted them [imparting cheer, hope, strength] and spoke to their hearts [kindly].
Genesis 50:20-21

What A Heart!

Joseph's brothers were terrified after their father died thinking that Joseph would repay them for all the evil that they had done to him. But Joseph knew and understood the plan of Almighty God so well, that he forgave them and invited them in to bless them.

After all Joseph had been through he still longed to have a relationship with his brothers. As they stood before him he wept when he saw their distressed and dismayed faces, that was when they realized it was Joseph that was in charge in Egypt.

How would you react if your family disowned you and had you sold as a slave, which led to you being thrown into prison for many years? After God delivers you and puts you in a place of authority, would you be able to welcome and share your prosperity with your enemies? God's heart is for us to see the bigger picture, to know the greatness of His plan and His will.

When we get to the place of being able to look past the natural hurting circumstances, we are beginning to mature in our walk with God.

September 5

*And the Lord regretted that He had made man on the earth,
and He was grieved at heart.*
Genesis 6:6

God's Grace Abounds

Whenever I read this Scripture, it hurts to think that God was disappointed and regretted having made mankind. The best of His creation, given the power of choice to love and obey Him, would turn their backs on Him and walk away.

"But Noah found favor in the eyes of the Lord." Thank goodness for Noah, and Praise the Lord for Jesus. What a terrible state we would be in if the Father had never given us a second opportunity, to get it right.

Finding GRACE in the sight of the Lord opens all kinds of doors to His heart, and makes all things possible and available to you to succeed in this life. Nobody knows better how to get through this life successfully other than the Lord.

Each time you choose to serve Him above your own desires you are choosing life, grace and mercy. When His heart shines upon you, you are guaranteed the best outcome. Do it right. Never return to the life that left you miserable and failing, it will eventually kill you.

Prayer: "Father, I desire to walk pleasing in Your sight, help me to walk in Your divine plan for my life".

September 6

God is not a man, that He should tell or act a lie, neither the son of man, that He should feel repentance or compunction [for what He has promised]. Has He said and shall He not do it? Or has He spoken and shall He not make it good?
Numbers 23:19

God Cannot Lie!

You need to settle in your heart the fact that God cannot lie. If you have any doubts about His credibility, you had better get your thoughts sorted out very quickly.

When God spoke this world into existence, every fiber, every molecule, every cell had to obey His Word and become what He said it must become. If nature is submitted to God, then what is wrong with us? God is infallible, but man continues to make mistakes in all areas of life because he is man.

For God to say that He is not a man that He should lie, He is telling the truth. The first man that He made lied to Him. Adam hid from God because he had done wrong, and when God asked who had disobeyed, he blamed Eve, and Eve blamed the serpent. None of them were prepared to tell the truth.

There is no sin in God. When He says He will do something, you can be guaranteed He will do what He has promised!

You are the one who has to make up your mind about the Lord;
The Lord knows exactly Who He is, and He cannot lie.

September 7

Now to Him Who, by (in consequence of) the [action of His] power that is at work within us, is able to [carry out His purpose and] do super-abundantly, far over and above all that we [dare] ask or think [infinitely beyond our highest prayers, desires, thoughts, hopes or dreams].
Ephesians 3:20

Dare To Dream

My mom will tell you that I am not the same daughter that I was the first 19 years of my life. I was shy, and very self-conscious, until I gave my life to the Lord. I have never been the same since.

God wants to do something special with your life too, far beyond your desires, hopes and dreams. God will take your life and multiply and increase it, and make it dynamic.

Without God, you are not complete; without Him, you cannot become what you ought to be. Do you know that you have the ability to excel and produce at the highest level in the Lord; total satisfaction.

Ask God and He will do super-abundantly in your life. You are unique; there is only one of you. Only you can do what God has purposed for you to do. You are the only one who can accomplish great things for God in your life.

God will not disappoint you; His Word is His bond. See yourself as He sees you, and never hold back from His blessings.

September 8

And moreover, some women of our company astounded us and drove us out of our senses. They were at the tomb early [in the morning] but did not find His body; and they returned saying that they had [even] seen a vision of angels, who said that He was alive!
Luke 24:22-23

Astounding Women

The amazing story in this Scripture is that even though the men are a little floored by the women, they do mention that the women were a part of their team. Today, I believe that men need a better understanding of women, who are more than welcome in the Presence and Ministry of God.

No wonder Jesus appeared to the women first, if it had anything to do with the men they would have been convinced that Jesus was a hallucination, or a dream! Poor guys needed the ladies to show them the way, jokes aside!

A great part of the Body Of Christ is not at work in the Kingdom of God because of man's denial that God would use them. Yet God gave women the first opportunity to preach the RISEN CHRIST!

I know of a church in Virgina USA that still believes that God does NOT use women in leadership. They are not even welcome to work in the children's ministry?

The devil is able to nullify the potential of over half of the Body Of Christ through misconception and ignorance. Thank God things are changing and the whole army of God is rising up.

Because of your female sensitivity you may often be mocked by the opposite sex. Don't let it get to you, keep your emotions in agreement with the Word of God!

The heart of a woman is wise, tender and precious in the hands of God.

September 9

But test and prove all things [until you can recognize] what is good;
[to that] hold fast.
1 Thessalonians 5:21

Test It!

I would like to seriously urge you not to accept everything you hear and see in Christian circles as from the Lord. There is a tremendous amount of deception going on in the disguise of Christianity and the people perpetrating the confusion do not have your best interests at heart, but their own. You are going to have to be responsible for the path that you follow.

The testing and proving of all things will do you good until you are mature enough in the Word of God to know what is right. You are encouraged throughout the Bible to:

- Find out what God has planned and purposed for your life;
- How you are to live; and
- What is and is not acceptable behavior.

If anyone tells you any differently from what you have learned and know, then you are to graciously ignore them.

Always pursue that which is good, this is the will of God. Anything that you may feel a little discomfort about will not be right in the sight of God. You are born of the Spirit of God and are perhaps a lot farther down the road to good understanding than what you realise.

The Holy Spirit will teach you the difference between right and wrong in the Kingdom of God.

September 10

The blessing of the Lord – it makes [truly] rich, and He adds no sorrow with it [neither does toiling increase it].
Proverbs 10:22

Blessings Of The Lord

Every blessing that you have ever had comes from God. The fact that you have life is the first blessing – that you can breathe is a gift and an opportunity that God has given you.

When you know that your blessings come from the Father, you will handle them differently and a new outlook on life will be birthed in your heart. A heart of thanksgiving, appreciation and gratefulness explains why there is no sorrow with the blessings God.

When you think that the blessing is of your own doing, you get sorrow with the blessing. Some of the richest men on earth are blessed with great wealth, but do they enjoy it? No, they live in total fear that they may lose everything they have, or that they may die and leave what they have behind.

One of the richest men of our age made his son use a public telephone that was installed in his house, how very sad! Blessings are there to be shared and not to be hoarded up.

God will do things the way He chooses to,
no matter what you may think.

September 11

The Lord is good, a Strength and Stronghold in the day of trouble; He knows (recognizes, has knowledge of, and understands) those who take refuge and trust in Him.
Nahum 1:7

Mighty In His Strength

Jesus is the strength of your life; when you are weak physically, emotionally, mentally, spiritually – Jesus will sustain you, lift you above, enable you to rise higher in Him. He will be your confidence, your security, your love and joy; everything that you may need will be found in Him.

The areas in my life that I have handed over to God do great, but the one's that I try and hold on to, are my weakness. Give everything to Him; learn a lesson and don't be stubborn.

God's strength will sustain you in difficulties; take hold of your heart; radiate from within you; energise you to overcome; nourish your inner man and guarantee a peaceful mind. You do not know your strength in God until you need it!

His energy is boundless, mighty and everlasting.

Be strong in the Lord.

September 12

Pay attention and always be on your guard [looking out for one another]. If your brother sins (misses the mark), solemnly tell him so and reprove him, and if he repents (feels sorry for having sinned), forgive him.
Luke 17:3

Help Your Brother

Keeping your life on track is a challenge. There are so many temptations that if you are not careful you can drift away from the Lord, and not be aware of what is happening to you.

You do not have to be doing anything wrong, but just not being in the Lord's Presence will affect your daily attitude, your behavior, your thinking and your life.

Whenever I would go on holiday and not be in corporate worship and hearing the word for a week or two, I would find myself irritated and short tempered at the slightest of things. The moment I would get home and back to my routine, everything would settle again.

The best way, to stay strong, is to have a special friend who will act as a "policeman" in your life. One that you will not get mad with when she tells you a few little truths!

Sometimes good old-fashioned advice is necessary. Helping each other walk with the Lord is a wonderful defense against temptations and distractions.

If you have a friend that has offended you and they repent, show them a little love and mercy and forgive them. Don't let something ride for weeks and weeks keeping them in a broken place. Help them back on their feet. God will take care of you!

Let's look after, and keep one another out of the clutches of the wicked one.

September 13

That you may walk (live and conduct yourselves) in a manner worthy of the Lord, fully pleasing to Him and desiring to please Him in all things, bearing fruit in every good work and steadily growing and increasing in and by the knowledge of God [with fuller, deeper, and clearer insight, acquaintance, and recognition].
Colossians 1:10

On The Increase

When God gets hold of your life, you will increase in many areas. Your life will have far more meaning, and your desire to walk uprightly in all that you do will be constantly pulling on your heartstrings.

Growing in God is something that God loves you to do, gaining wisdom and knowledge, and excelling in good-works, being productive and successful in life.

To "increase" is to expand, enlarge, multiply, grow, improve, extend. As a believer, you are to increase spiritually, that you may be full and running over with the Spirit of God in your life. But many Christians are on a diet spiritually they are unhealthy; skinny and starving, spiritual beings. They can hardly make it through the day.

You are to "steadily increase" in the Spirit and NEVER stop growing. Keeping your focus on Him, gaining in strength and power to overcome. Even the worst storm in your life will not be able to stop you, as you will be as solid as a rock in God.

If you are growing in God it will be noticeable to others.

When the world sees a crisis, you will see an opportunity.

September 14

He who is faithful in a very little [thing] is faithful also in much, and he who is dishonest and unjust in a very little [thing] is dishonest and unjust also in much.
Luke 16:10

Little Is Much In The Master's Hand

What you do with a little you will do with much.

The little bits always start with a thought – "I think if I keep it quiet no-body will know." When you start out on the wrong foot, before too long you will be walking and running on the wrong foot.

Always choose to do what is right, and before long you will be walking a life filled with honesty, justice and uprightness. What started out as a challenge becomes easy the more you practice it? They tell me, it takes approximately 30 days to develop a habit, good or bad. The bad ones you do not want.

I developed a tremendous habit with yoghurt recently. I would come home from work and go straight to the fridge and grab the yoghurt. I was not satisfied until the whole tub was finished. After a while I realised that I needed to take a detour in the kitchen when I came home from the office. It worked! Yoghurt is good for you in moderation.

When you become aware of something that is controlling your life, then take hold of it, and get it to line with the Word.

Keep your life in submission to God's will and blessing!

September 15

And He died for all, so that all those who live might live no longer to and for themselves, but to and for Him Who died and was raised again for their sake.
2 Corinthians 5:15

Receiving A Great Life

Within the death, burial and resurrection of Christ, you have received deliverance from certain death and an abundance of certain life. Jesus not only died for you, but for all. That is the Gospel, the Good News.

Why would one want to settle for a second rate life, when you can go first class all of the way. It's not even a choice?

Jesus paid a high price to deliver you from your past, present and future sin. The innocent blood that He shed for you at Calvary is life changing and powerful, and still speaks today of the miracle of the Cross. To have everlasting life in the Kingdom of God did not come cheaply. He gave up everything.

Jesus took on every sickness and disease when He was nailed to the cross, so that you can be healed. The stripes that were lashed upon His body set you free. You and I were the ones who should have paid for our own sin, but He chose to do it for us. That is what the love of God is all about. Jesus was raised from the dead, so that you can live for eternity in the presence of Almighty God.

May the miraculous, resurrection power of Jesus become revelation to you. His blood will never fail to speak of His dying love for you.

September 16

And those sown on the good (well-adapted) soil are the ones who hear the Word and receive and accept and welcome it and bear fruit – some thirty times as much as was sown, some sixty times as much, and some [even] a hundred times as much.
Mark 4:20

Good Soil

When I first heard about my heart being fertile or unfertile soil, I realised how simple the Word of God is to understand. I am quite a keen gardener and love to see my garden grow! Good healthy soil is vital; soil without clay, weeds, stones and too much mush. After a long period of rain one year, my garden turned into a swamp and everything died.

When you hear the Word of God accept it, welcome it into your life and let it begin to bear its fruit. You are what Jesus called good soil! Some of those who are good soil will produce at lease 30 times the amount which was sown, others 60 times and some even 100 times!

Good soil has to be prepared. You do not often come across soil and say "wow, that soil is perfect, it needs no attention"!

Good soil has to be worked over, fertilized, and rid of any strange roots or weeds. Before you can be that good soil, you are going too have to do some work on it. Then when you plant good seed, you will have a bumper crop!

Prepare your heart for the wonderful seed that God wants to sow into you life. Stretch for the 100 times fruit production!

September 17

For the kingdom of God consists of and is based on not talk but power (moral power and excellence of soul).
1 Corinthians 4:20

A Distinctive Mark

"A distinctive mark", that is how the Webster's dictionary defines character. Character is an essential feature. Character is nature, the total sum of qualities that make up individuality – your individuality. It is what you are that makes you into the character or mark that you are.

Over the years you have built up a character, a reputation. People know that you do or do not keep your word; you pay or do not pay your bills; you do or do not always tell the truth. You are spoken of as having honor, integrity, strength and uprightness or the opposite values.

All these characteristics are part of your character; they make you, you! If the you that you are right now, does not match up to the you, that you would like to be, then you can start right now to adjust the areas that you do not like about you. It's no good talking the talk when your life does not match up to what you are saying.

The Kingdom of God is not based on how you talk, but rather how you walk – your character. You carry a distinctive mark! The day you told your family you were born again – you marked yourself.

Let your light shine before men that they may see your good works and glorify the Father in Heaven.

September 18

If any of you is deficient in wisdom, let him ask of the giving God [Who gives] to everyone liberally and ungrudgingly, without reproaching or faultfinding, and it will be given him.
James 1:5

Know Jesus, Know Wisdom

God wants you to be wise. He wants you to operate in this life not as walking around in darkness or confused by the circumstances, but wise in Him for every situation.

We see that God gives plenty of wisdom to those who simply ask. He doesn't go around selecting a few, He says, "Whoever asks, will receive My wisdom, liberally and ungrudgingly". The wisdom of God is a free gift and belongs to the children of God.

The Bible speaks of King Solomon, as being one of the wisest of his time. We see his wise judgment (1 Kings 3:16-28), when the two harlots came to him fighting over a child. He asked that a sword be brought to him, that he may divide the child in two, that each may have a half. The birth mother, pleaded before him to not kill her child, but rather to give it to the other woman. King Solomon wisely assessed the situation and knew that no mother would stand by and watch someone kill her child. He was very wise.

If you are facing a particular issue and you are not sure which way to turn, ask God to help you with as much wisdom as you need.

Jesus promises you wisdom. He will give it to you.

September 19

For He satisfies the longing soul and fills the hungry soul with good.
Psalm 107:9

Fully Satisfied!

Each one of us has the need to be increasing and going places with God in this life. We need to be fulfilled, productive and to be an asset to the Body of Christ.

Daily we need to be stretching, not just sitting around bored and going nowhere. If you desire to improve your situation, then do so; stop procrastinating; take the initiative and do something about it.

Life without Jesus is meaningless and has no real purpose. Without Him guiding all that you do, you will be empty and everything you do will be in vain. The moment you allow Him to direct your path, your vision will increase, you will have the assurance that what you accomplish has greater meaning and purpose.

Jesus comes to satisfy you; He will fill your hungry soul with goodness. He will give you hope for the future. You will be fully satisfied, plugged into your Source.

Nothing will satisfy you, like Jesus. He completes the meaning to life and gives you divine understanding to the reasons why you are here.

Complete satisfaction comes only from being in relationship with your Creator, and fulfilling the purpose He has created you for.

September 20

And God blessed them and said to them, Be fruitful, multiply, and fill the earth, and subdue it (using all its vast resources in the service of God and man); and have dominion over the fish of the sea, the birds of the air, and over every living creature that moves upon the earth.
Genesis 1:28

Be Fruitful And Multiply

When God made Adam and Eve He put them in the garden to tend, guard and keep it. He gave them complete authority and held nothing back from them. Not only were they to guard it, but to multiply and increase and bear much fruit.

In the center of the garden was the tree of the knowledge of good and evil, and the tree of life. Amazing how both of them were in the middle of the garden where they would see them each day.

God gave man authority in the earth not to make bad choices but to make right choices according to His Will. God planted both trees. All He required of them to do was to follow His clear instructions. But as we know man always wants to do his own thing, in spite of tremendous warnings, and then the consequences of actions.

Even the earth's vast resources were to be used in the service of God and man. What an opportunity to be a friend of God, to fellowship with Him and walk and talk with Him.

I am so grateful that God did not leave us in a fallen state, but He made a way for us.

Jesus brought back a hopeful relationship for us in God. He re-opened the doors that were closed through disobedience. Today, we can come into the throne-room of Grace boldly, just as if we had never done anything wrong – enjoying all the benefits that God gave us in the first place.

God wants your life to be fruitful and to multiply in the blessings, be sure to make good wise choices in all that you do.

September 21

Moses told the people, Fear not; stand still (firm, confident, undismayed) and see the salvation of the Lord which He will work for you today. For the Egyptians you have seen today you shall never see again.
Exodus 14:13

Delivered Forever

Can you imagine the strength of this Scripture today? God tells Moses to tell His people, "Do not be afraid, stand still, see the salvation of the Lord." That is all we need to do – stand by and watch as the Father works it out for us.

God is in the miracle working business – He built the Word of God on miracles – miracles that delivered His people time and time again. Every time the enemy tried to destroy the people of God and their love for Him – God comes onto the scene and gives His people a miracle that in the natural is totally impossible.

The greatest part of this tremendous Scripture is that God rejoices in the fact that His children will never have to worry about this problem again.

The devil that has been trying to destroy you is going one way and one way fast – you are on the upper hand and that hand has already delivered you. Stand still and see the mighty, miraculous, delivering hand of the Lord.

God is an "ever present" help in times of trouble.

September 22

Blessed (happy, to be envied, and spiritually prosperous – with life-joy and satisfaction in God's favor and salvation, regardless of your outward conditions) are you when people revile you and persecute you and say all kinds of evil things against you falsely on My account. Be glad and supremely joyful, for your reward in heaven is great (strong and intense), for in this same way people persecuted the prophets who were before you.
Matthew 5:11-12

Persecution Makes Your Day?

The Lord calls the fact that you are being persecuted a blessing! Some of His ideas might seem a bit peculiar to us, but they work. When folk come against you and say all kinds of bad things about you, put a smile on your face (as hard as that may be), and let the Lord sort them out.

Innocence cries a loud cry in the spirit world – all of heaven pays attention to a child of God who has been wronged. You do not have to get into a state and wonder how to defend yourself; let your Father handle it for you.

When I was a young girl in junior school, if I had any problems I could not handle, I would let my dad sort it out. I was very secure and confident in his ability. It is the same with the Heavenly Father; He is more than able to deal with wrongdoing. In fact, He is the expert.

When Satan took one third of the Heavenly host with him when he fell, it did not shake the Father – He still rules and reigns.

Love never fails, and God's got your back!

September 23

That is why I would remind you to stir up (rekindle the embers of, fan the flame of, and keep burning) the [gracious] gift of God, [the inner fire] that is in you by means of the laying on of my hands [with those of the elders at your ordination].
2 Timothy 1:6

Reach Out!

Timothy was told to stir up the gifts that were within him. We can say the same: stir up the gifts that are in you! If your child comes to you feeling sick, lay hands on him and pray the Word of God over your child that he may be well. If your friend is feeling low, get a hold of her and speak an encouraging Word that will lift her spirit.

We need to get serious about doing our part to minister to hurting people. We cannot see pain and just sit back. You could bring healing or a breakthrough into someone's life.

You are the hands, feet, eyes and voice of God. He will use you to touch and restore hearts, to minister His Word to the dying and lost souls, and you will bring the sweet fragrance of Christ to those you encounter.

There is so much work for all of us to do in the Kingdom of God. If each one of us will do our share, we can change the lives of all the folks around us.

Stir up the gifts that Jesus has deposited in you, and reach out to those who need the Master's touch.

September 24

And God saw everything that He had made, and behold, it was very good (suitable, pleasant) and He approved it completely. And there was evening and there was morning, a sixth day.
Genesis 1:31

God Saw It Was Good

Everything that God made was perfect and complete; He approved of it.

We live our lives in the will of God because that is our choice. We came to Jesus because of a better way. The closer we walk in His Presence the more we will experience His approval on our lives and the things that we do.

God cannot approve and be satisfied about something that is not justified, correct or righteous. When we get out of His will and begin to get confused, God will not bless us in our confusion. We first have to sort out the things that are not pleasing in His sight and then we can go on.

God is a good God. He will not side with evil or strife. He lives in the realm of love and mercy and expects us to have the same compassion and understanding that He has.

He knows that we are going to make mistakes, so He has made a way for us to stay in His Presence... by GRACE are you saved, through faith, it is the gift of God.

Walking close to God will cause everything that you do, to be successful and good.

September 25

And I will bless those who bless you (who confer prosperity or happiness upon you) and curse him who curses or uses insolent language toward you; in you will all the families and kindred of the earth be blessed [and by you they will bless themselves].
Genesis 12:3

Your Enemies Are Defeated

God promised Abraham these blessings if he would follow and serve the Lord.

Those who loved Abraham and were behind him, God would bless and those who were jealous and cursed him, God would take care of them.

The blessing that came upon Abraham was because he chose to obey God. Obeying God will bring tremendous favor your way, not only from your Heavenly Father, but from man too.

The wonderful thing about God's blessings is that when your life is touched so are all the lives around you, and the continuation goes on right down to you children's children. You are a catalyst for blessing.

There were many reasons why God told Abraham to get away from his kindred. You may have to get away from some of those who have a bad influence on your life too. If you are strong enough to handle them, then you may be able to stay strong in God. But if they encourage you to compromise and lose a grip on your life in God, then its best that you let them go.

Make your choice and walk in His ways, you will be blessed.

September 26

Bring forth fruit that is consistent with repentance, [let your lives prove your change of heart].
Matthew 3:8

A Change Will Do You Good!

If you belong to Christ, what sort of fruit are you producing in your life; peace, love, patience, kindness, goodness and joy? We are to bring forth good, healthy fruit, fruit that is consistent with repentance from the old life. Let your life prove your change of heart.

People can see by your lifestyle whether you really did change. If you are praying and prophesying, then you must stop lying and cheating.

Step outside yourself and say, "you lost your temper today; you were rude and unmannerly but this is not acceptable, examine your "self", repent and make a decision that you are not going to compromise your God-given ability for any more nonsense.

Most problems in relationships come from a lack of discipline of "self", refusing to change or adjust to the other person. Marriages fail when one party wants their own way and the other will not oblige. Friendships break down when one will not forgive the other.

Being truthful to your "self" is wise.
It will help you to make right decisions.

September 27

I will cry to God Most High, Who performs on my behalf and rewards me [Who brings to pass His purposes for me and surely completes them]!
Psalm 57:2

Climb The Ladder Of Destiny

God wants you to succeed in all that you do. He may call you into a male dominated work place, where the pressures surrounding you are enormous. If you find yourself in such a situation know that if God has placed you there, you will be able to accomplish all that is required.

Deborah was such a woman. God put her in a position of authority as judge over Israel; men would come to her for advice. Deborah raised such a standard of excellence that judges came from afar off to get advice from her. Deborah was called by God to deliver His people – the chief of the army would not go to war without her in the front line with him, knowing that God was with her. This she did and they won the battle. She gave the glory back to God.

Deborah was also a wife and a mother. This did not hinder her life and calling; in fact, her husband recognised that she was called as judge over Israel; he was in agreement with her, and he blessed her.

Don't let your gender hold you back.
If God is for you, then who can be against you.

September 28

And he shall be like a tree firmly planted [and tended] by the streams of water, ready to bring forth its fruit in its season; its leaf also shall not fade or wither; and everything he does shall prospers.
Psalm 1:3

Prosperity In Adverse Conditions

"Blessed is the man, who walks not in the counsel of the wicked." Psalm 1:1-3 is one of my most favorite Scripture passages in the Bible. It speaks of the blessings of the Lord that you receive when you give your life to Him fully and completely.

When you think of the beauty of a tree that is planted near a river – it is healthy, strong and bears fruit. Not only is it planted, but Psalms speaks about it being firmly planted – not one root in and the other out of the soil.

For us to be like this awesome tree, we are going to have to firmly plant our lives in the Word of God, to walk closely to His heartbeat, drinking from the rivers of life.

Bearing fruit should be easy for us, just like it is for the tree. You may not be bearing fruit all the time but you will bear fruit in your season, and the fruit will be good fruit. As for your leaves, they shall be healthy, green and lush. Everything that you touch will prosper in Him and in His love.

Plant yourself in God's will, and you will bear much fruit.

September 29

For You are not a God Who takes pleasure in wickedness; neither will the evil [man] so much as dwell [temporarily] with You.
Psalm 5:4

Refuse To Compromise!

God does not take pleasure in wickedness; He will have nothing to do with it. When you choose to go your own way and walk away from the Lord, you cut yourself off from God. He does not cut Himself off from you as He is always there for you, but He cannot compromise His stand against evil and wickedness for your benefit.

God wants all of you – your heart, your soul and body, and your worship.

Now if you have erred along the way, remember that God loves you more than you will ever know and His desire is for you to soar in this life and not to fail. When you recognize you are in the wrong place you can turn around and run back to Him. He will welcome you home like the prodigal sons father, put a robe on your back, a ring on your finger and sandals on your feet.

When you turn back to God, 1 John 1:9 will be you're greatest blessing. "He is faithful and just and will forgive our sins and cleanse us from all un¬righteousness". He is a loving, forgiving Father who wants to walk in fellowship with you.

Take courage, and become all that God has destined for you to be. If you compromise and find yourself in a not so good place, run back to God. Compromise is the thief that will rob you of your great inheritance in Christ. Be bold, break free from the bondage that holds you, and urgently seek His attention, which is the only attention that you really need.

Reject the bait the enemy throws out to you; it will only destroy your life.

Grab hold of God; never let go of anything He represents.

September 30

Give, and [gifts] will be given to you; good measure, pressed down, shaken together, and running over, will they pour into [the pouch formed by] the bosom [of your robe and used as a bag]. For with the measure you deal out [with the measure you use when you confer benefits on others], it will be measured back to you.
Luke 6:38

Give And It Shall Be Given

Giving is second nature to a Christian. At every opportunity and in every circumstance that the Lord opens to you, BE a giver! When you stop giving you become a swamp from where no life flows.

Jesus walked that way. He was constantly giving into the lives of all those who reached out to Him, not only by touching their spiritual needs, but by taking care of their physical needs too. Feeding five thousand with the little boy's lunch and then still having leftovers. Isn't that just like our God? He multiplies everything that we give, far above all that we can ask or think.

Being selfish or stingy is the heart of the evil one – he did his utmost to get all the riches for himself – illegally. When we give to God, He blesses our giving and multiplies it abundantly – good measure, pressed down, shaken together and running over!

You will find that God will often use people to give back into your life. Look out, for your blessings, they are on the way!

With the heart attitude that you measure,
it shall be given back to you again.

October

Be Of Good Cheer

October 1

And they went out and preached everywhere, while the Lord kept working with them and confirming the message by the attesting signs and miracles that closely accompanied [it]. Amen (so be it).
Mark 16:20

The Lord Works With Us

When you serve God you never do it on your own. No man is an island unto himself, but each must have the Presence of the Holy Spirit to confirm the message that is preached.

It is the responsibility of the Lord to see that when we preach His living Word, that the Holy Spirit with miracles and signs and wonders confirms it. The Word of God is powerful, full of life, and as sharp as a sword with a double edge. But it is the Holy Spirits assignment to confirm and work the Word that is preached.

When we speak the Word of God, God backs it in our lives, it will come to pass and fully accomplish what God sets it out to do.

If you think that you can deliver some garbled message, one that does not agree with the Word of God and think that God will bless it, you are confused. It is only the Word that God speaks that carries any weight.

Preaching the Word of God is a great honour especially when you know that it is the Lord who must bring it to pass, and for the Holy Spirit to confirm it.

October 2

Then the just and upright will answer Him, Lord, when did we see You hungry and gave You food, or thirsty and gave You something to drink? And when did we see You a stranger and welcomed and entertained You, or naked and clothed You? And when did we see You sick or in prison and came to visit You? And the King will reply to them, Truly I tell you, in so far as you did it for one of the least [in the estimation of men] of these My brethren, you did it for Me.
Matthew 25:37-40

You Did It For Me

Reaching out to hurting people is where you will find Jesus. The poor, the sick, and the lame were always mentioned wherever He went. He did have friends who were affluent and had great influence in the area, but His concern was for the hurting.

You and I have been given the same commission. If we belong to God then we have His desire in our hearts to do our share in touching the world with the love of Jesus.

Giving yourself as often as possible to any worthy cause is a powerful force in your life. Putting "self" aside and thinking of others will enrich your life with joy and peace.

When you give to the poor you lend to the Lord. What an effective way to obey the Lord on a daily basis. Just do what you can; it is vital to the Lord.

October 3

But Jesus, knowing within Himself that His disciples were complaining and protesting and grumbling about it, said to them: Is this a stumbling block and an offence to you? [Does this upset and displease and shock and scandalise you?]
John 6:61

Protesting Disciples

Something happened here that you and I can hardly believe. The disciples, after hearing Jesus preach one of His most powerful, anointed sermons, were heard grumbling and complaining!

Often when we hear the Word of God preached it challenges us about certain things that we are doing in our lives. It will raise a positive response from us, or we will grumble and complain just like the disciples did!

As Jesus was aware of what was in their hearts, He is aware of what is in our hearts today. There are things that will take us a while to understand, but as long as our heart attitude stays right we will remain teachable, and eventually we will get the revelation of the message down the road.

God knows best how we should do life because He knows the beginning from the end, and He understands all things.

Keep your heart open to instruction from the Lord, and stop moaning when you do not understand the reason why you have to do something a certain way.

Obey God and you will get the most wonderful results.

October 4

How God anointed and consecrated Jesus of Nazareth with the [Holy] Spirit and with strength and ability and power; how He went about doing good and, in particular, curing all who were harassed and oppressed by [the power of] the devil, for God was with Him.
Acts 10:38

Jesus Did Good

Jesus walked around anointed of God for a purpose. He was able to do the will of God in every situation that demanded liberty, healing, deliverance and the meeting of needs.

We have the same calling as Jesus – to do good, and to bring blessing and life to people in every avenue of life. The anointing upon our lives is given to us through the power that was invested in the name of Jesus. It is not in our own ability that we can touch lives but in the name of Jesus.

God equipped Jesus with strength, ability and power in the Spirit that enabled Him to heal and deliver those who reached out to that anointing. Like the woman with the issue of blood!

The devil oppresses people, but God wants to set them free. You and I are instruments in the name of Jesus for such a wonderful ministry, "these signs shall follow them that believe, in My name" (Mark 16:17, 18)

Each one of us has a responsibility to obey the Word of God, do not be afraid.

Do you believe? Then you can help others.

October 5

Therefore I always exercise and discipline myself [mortifying my body, deadening my carnal affections, bodily appetites, and worldly desire, endeavouring in all respects] to have a clear (unshaken, blameless) conscience, void of offence toward God and toward men.
Acts 24:16

Clear Conscience

Your conscience is the voice of your recreated spirit. If you listen to your heart you will know the right thing to do. When we willingly and continuously choose to do the wrong thing, eventually our conscience may be seared.

If you are walking close to God and the opportunity arises and you tell a lie, you will feel terrible for a long time. If it happens again, in a short space of time, you will probably feel less guilty until eventually you can lie without it bothering you very much. When we ignore our conscience in the first lie, the first steps to compromise are taken.

How wonderful to walk around with a perfectly clear conscience. To not have anything on your heart to correct or apologise for.

In this Scripture the flesh is aptly described with its appetites, desires and affections. You need to put down the rules of behaviour that are acceptable to God. Your flesh does nor like discipline, but you must let it know beyond a shadow of doubt, who is in charge of the situation.

To have a clear, blameless conscience is a blessing, and can only come from inviting the Holy Spirit to walk with you.

October 6

And I will ask the Father, and He will give you another Comforter (Counsellor, Helper, Intercessor, Advocate, Strengthener, and Standby), that He may remain with you forever.
John 14:16

The Great Comforter

We have the ability to walk in this world with supernatural support and help. When Jesus was raised from the dead and went to be with the Father, He did not leave us comfortless but sent the Holy Spirit to do a work for the Father in our lives.

Whatever you need, the Holy Spirit is there to give you that support. There is tremendous ministry available to us. When you do not know how or what to do, the Holy Spirit is there to help you. When you are discouraged, He is there as your Strengthener. When you are lonely and confused, He is your Comforter and Counsellor, and He will stand in the gap for you, and finally, when you need justice, He is your faithful Advocate.

To have a member of the Trinity at all times as your support system means you have supernatural help, and no excuse not to do the will of God. The rest of the promise is that not only will the Holy Spirit be with you, but He will be with you forever.

Your life is fully supported by the power of the Holy Spirit to help you to accomplish the perfect plan and will of God for your life.

October 7

But love your enemies and be kind and do good (doing favours so that someone derives benefit from them) and lend, expecting and hoping for nothing in return but considering nothing as lost and despairing of no one; and then your recompense (your reward) will be great (rich, strong, intense and abundant), and you will be sons of the Most High, for He is kind and charitable and good to the ungrateful and the selfish and wicked.
Luke 6:35

Love Everyone

To be kind and to do good, is quite a message to preach to believers! You would think that this would be something believers do naturally? The Word of God is explicit in how we should treat other human beings on the earth.

Loving those who love you is an easy task, but loving someone who is an enemy is another thing altogether. You will have to put your emotions and feelings aside and draw on the wisdom and strength of the Lord, to love an enemy with God's love. Agape is supernatural and upheld by the Spirit. It is unconditional love that loves expecting nothing in return.

Your life is to bring benefit to others; by doing good to those who hate you, sharing kindness with the ungrateful, the selfish, and the wicked.

Although these actions take supernatural ability, they are some of the most powerful responses against the work of the devil and his host.

If you want to confuse the devil, this is the perfect way to do it.

October 8

For I am not ashamed of the Gospel (Good News) of Christ, for it is God's power working unto salvation [for deliverance from eternal death] to everyone who believes with a personal trust and a confident surrender and firm reliance, to the Jew first and also to the Greek.
Romans 1:16

I Am Not Ashamed!

How can you be ashamed of the Gospel? How can you be ashamed of God who gave His best, and loves you unconditionally? That should cause you to brag and not to be ashamed.

I would often embarrass some of the members at Rhema when they brought a first time visitor, and I had everyone singing Father Abraham and doing all the hand and feet actions. This is not talking about that kind of embarrassment.

Peter was embarrassed and ashamed, and felt threatened when he was asked if he knew Jesus; he denied knowing Jesus three times. I pray that in a similar situation we would not do that!!

The Gospel is the most powerful message on the earth, why would one be ashamed of it or of the name of Jesus, when both are able to deliver and save souls from damnation. Often when saying a prayer in a restaurant folk pray as if they have a headache, hiding their closed eyes.

Without Christ, we would be lost and without hope for eternity.

Whenever you sense the urging of the Lord to share the Gospel with someone, do not be embarrassed or ashamed, just pose a simple question and you will see that they will respond to the love in your heart. Go ahead and ask them 'Has anyone ever told you that God has an amazing plan for your life...'

Never force your message on someone, but if they want to hear, then gladly share the Good News with them.

October 9

So if when you are offering your gift at the altar you there remember that your brother has any [grievance] against you, leave your gift at the altar and go. First make peace with your brother, and then come back and present your gift.
Matthew 5:23-24

Say, 'I Am Sorry'!

God is not so desperate for your gift that He will allow you to pay your way out of your trouble. When you come to God and present your offering, God would rather you go and make right with the ones you have wronged, and then bring your gift.

Many folk think that by going to church on a Sunday, it relieves them from any responsibility for their actions during the week. Yes they may repent before the Lord, but they have left a pile of hurt people in the workplace or possibly at home. Strife is something that we need to nip in the bud before it grows out of control in to full bloom.

That is why this scripture is such a blessing. A simple "I am sorry, will you please forgive me?" works wonders with people! Then you are FREE to bring your gift to the Lord.

God cares about the condition of your heart much more than the gift that you bring to Him.

Many times I have given an offering and have thought of a problem in a relationship and realised that I needed to get it in order. By faith, I pray and ask the Lord to first forgive me, and then I do my best to sort it out with the person.

If they do not forgive, then they will have to answer to God.

A humble heart is a healthy heart.

October 10

Then the cares and anxieties of the world and distractions of the age, and the pleasure and delight and false glamour and deceitfulness of riches, and the craving and passionate desire for other things creep in and choke and suffocate the Word, and it becomes fruitless.
Mark 4:19

What Chokes The Word?

You can read about your life in Scripture. These are the main reasons why you get confused, discouraged, angry and bitter. These bad influences must be identified and resisted with all your heart, as they are out to steal your joy, liberty and blessings in the Lord.

- Cares and anxieties of the world and distractions of the age
- Pleasure and delight and false glamour
- Deceitfulness of riches

Choking the Word here is like an ivy plant growing up a tree. The tree can be a giant but eventually when that ivy plant gets a good hold, it will choke the life out of that huge healthy tree.

Cares of the world (worries, anxieties of life), deceitfulness of riches (if only I had more money I would be happy) and the lust of other things (I would steal for that car), are powerful enough to choke and stifle the Word of God in your life.

We are reminded that we are drawn away by our own lust. Living our lives as close to God as we can will keep us from these fleshly distractions.

Be on your guard – the devil is out to choke the Word of God in your life. Don't be mislead or blinded, do what is right.

October 11

And Simon (Peter) answered, Master, we toiled all night [exhaustingly] and caught nothing [in our nets]. But on the ground of Your word, I will lower the nets [again] ... For he was gripped with bewildering amazement [allied to terror], and all who were with him, at the haul of fish which they had made.
Luke 5:5-9

At Thy Word

Simon Peter soon learned to obey the Lord when He spoke. After the first opportunity when Jesus told him to launch again in the deep for a catch, and then he panicked when the blessing of obedience was so much that it nearly sank his boat.

Are you ready to follow the instruction of the Lord? What price will you have to pay? Does it go against your logic? If the Lord is speaking to you, you will have the right results and not a disaster on your hands.

I have watched people follow instructions that could not have been from the Lord; marrying the wrong person, buying the wrong business, moving to the wrong town.

If God speaks then the necessary fruit is evident in the end result, and there is not a hint of a question in the deal. If you miss God then repent and go on, it is not the end of the world. Others have made mistakes before you and are back on their feet.

Peter never doubted the Lord, he went ahead and did what He said, and the results were astounding, not confusing.

October 12

And whenever you stand praying, if you have anything against anyone, forgive him and let it drop (leave it, let it go), in order that your Father Who is in heaven may also forgive you your [own] failings and shortcomings and let them drop.
Mark 11:25-26

Forgive... Let It Drop!

You cannot pray and ask the Lord for any help until you have your heart right with others. Just like when you bring your gift. God wants you walking around as a well person, not sick with grudges, bitterness, hatred and jealousy.

This is the best description of getting rid of your little "things" or emotional baggage that you are holding on to. Let it drop. Simply, let go and get on with your life. Holding on to ancient "stuff" will wear you down and make you sick.

Once you have done that, you may have to do some "damage control" by going to the individuals if they are aware of the problem, and making it right. Then you can go to the Father in prayer with a clear conscience.

If you choose to keep your "stuff" then perhaps the Lord will keep a note of all the "stuff" He has on you. When you forgive then it opens the door for the Father to forgive you of all of your wrongdoing.

Learn to forgive and do it quickly. Drop the "junk" as it will weigh you down and keep you in bondage...

October 13

So everyone who hears these words of Mine and acts upon them [obeying them] will be like a sensible [prudent, practical, wise] man who built his house upon the rock. And the rain fell and the floods came and the winds blew and beat against that house; yet it did not fall, because it had been founded on the rock.
Matthew 7:24-25

Where Are You Building Your House?

What are you building your life on? Where did you learn to lay your foundations, from your family or friends at school, or from rumours or a newspaper?

Your house will fall if a novice builds it. You will have to build the way the Master-builder teaches you to build if you want it to survive the biggest storms, and get through the toughest times. Your opinion really does not matter when it comes to eternity.

When we build our lives on the Word of God, we will survive any storm that comes our way. Our roots will go down deep and our walls will be solid. Nothing will shake us and nothing will be able to break us down.

Watch the fruit of those who build their houses on their own advice and the advice of others who are not experienced; they use pride as a foundation and self as the walls; when any of these fail, they are left homeless.

But the house that the Lord builds will stand forever.

October 14

And the Lord God caused a deep sleep to fall upon Adam; and while he slept, He took one of his ribs or a part of his side and closed up the [place with] flesh. And the rib or part of his side which the Lord God had taken from the man He built up and made into a woman, and he brought her to the man. Then Adam said, This [creature] is now bone of my bones and flesh of my flesh; she shall be called Woman, because she was taken out of a man.
Genesis 2:21-23

Wow! What A Chick!

he reason why men do not understand women is because they were asleep when God made us!

God said "It is not good for man to be alone" so God put him to sleep and took Eve from a rib from his side. Not from under His feet where he would stand on her, but from His side so she could partner and stand alongside of him.

When God woke him up and brought her to him as a handmade gift, Adam did three things; he saw that she was different from the animals, he recognised that she too was made in the image and likeness of God just like he was, and then he celebrated her, 'now this is bone of my bone and flesh of my flesh'!

Eve was NEVER single and Adam woke up married! What a big surprise! But they became one flesh just like God designed. There was complete harmony and unity between them. There was no jealousy or competition.

That is how marriage is supposed to be, a great blessing of a union between a man and a woman.

Never marry for the wrong reasons and marry someone who loves God as much as you do.

October 15

He who believes in Me [who cleaves to and trusts in and relies on Me] as the Scripture has said, From his innermost being shall flow [continuously] springs and rivers of living water.
John 7:38

Living Water

When you get in touch with God you will come alive with the living water from which you are drinking. Deep down in your heart you know that no matter what goes on around you, everything is going to be just fine.

When I was baptised with the Holy Spirit it took a little while for me to receive my heavenly language. Part of my problem was that I was shy and self-conscious and I had also seen some crazy things done, I was also afraid that something strange would happen to me!

John 7:38 'from his innermost being shall flow [continuously] springs and rivers of living water'.

The devil will try and do all that he can to keep you from receiving the 'living water' that comes from being filled with the Holy Spirit. It seems strange when you try and understand it with your natural thinking, because your natural thinking cannot understand things of the spirit.

The night I received my prayer language I was completely on my own just talking to God, when I got determined to receive my prayer language. I asked the Lord to baptize me and I began to make sounds as the spirit gave me utterance. I received my gift as He promised I would!

Don't be afraid, the Holy Spirit's presence in your life will encourage that river to flow. It's your gift from God, and it gives you so much more power to pray the will of God.

Get on your own with God and ask Jesus to fill you. Obey the Holy Spirit's prompting and you will speak in your Heavenly language. It's a free gift from God!

October 16

Jesus Christ (the Messiah) is [always] the same, yesterday, today, [yes] and forever (to the ages).
Hebrews 13:8

The Good Old Days!

There is only one who never changes and that is the Lord.

There is no such thing as the "good old days". If you really think back you will remember that there were many problems in the good old days! It's amazing how your soul only remembers the good things but does not remember all the difficulties that you had.

God has equipped you to live in the now. He has given you the strength and power to cope with the tests of this present world. The greater the challenge you face, the greater the victory – Hallelujah!

When you get so caught up with how good things were, you lose out on the glorious moments of the present and the abundant life that God has planned for you now.

It is not an accident that you were born during this time – God planned that in eternity. You were born "for such a time as this". God is not confused; He will not lead you where his grace cannot keep you.

The past is the past and that is where it must stay, let bygones be bygones. Live your life in the Lord with great expectancy for today, and the great days that lie ahead.

With God on your side you have nothing to fear.
He is the same God as He was yesteryear.

October 17

I have told you these things, so that in Me you may have [perfect] peace and confidence. In the world you have tribulation and trials and distress and frustration; but be of good cheer [take courage; be confident, certain, undaunted]. For I have overcome the world. [I have deprived it of power to harm you and have conquered it for you.]
John 16:33

Be Of Good Cheer!

I love the way the Lord says "good cheer" and not just "cheer". It is an indication that the level of joy that He has called us to walk in is higher than the norm. He has made provision for us to be carefree and joyful, yet we continue to carry all kinds of burdens and troubles of the day. Jesus overcame these things 2000 years ago.

If you are in Christ then what He has provided belongs to you. Make your stand. Take your place. Walk in the joy of the Lord and don't let the worst of circumstances steal your joy. If you lose your joy, you will lose your strength and determination to fight – the joy of the Lord is your strength.

Jesus overcame the world (the whole world) for you, and He deprived it of power to harm you. Undoubtedly, the troubles and pains, stress and heartaches will come. Get a hold of your thoughts, emotions and self-control and let the power that lies in Jesus' name rise up inside of you, and help you to overcome the troubles of the day, as you walk by faith.

Empowered by the Spirit you will walk in joy
and walk free from troubles.

October 18

But God – so rich is He in His mercy! Because of and in order to satisfy the great and wonderful and intense love with which He loves us.
Ephesians 2:4

Jesus Makes You Beautiful

Before you knew Him you were pretty ugly! In fact, the Word of God says you were once dead, but now you are made ALIVE in Jesus. His awesome presence in your life will change you as you draw close to Him. His marvelous light will deliver you from all the works of darkness that are trying to keep their grip on your life.

Can you believe that God would still love you even with all your ugliness, and still desire to have you in His family? Well He does, and He continued to reach out to you and to 'woo' you into His Presence.

His Mercy and Grace abounds toward us and will never fail us. It's His mercy that gives Him the power to forgive and forget. If He did not love us, He would not be able to show us any mercy, and we would spend eternal life without God and be damned forever.

The mercy of God is rich, and powerful, nothing can equal it.

Even when you were at your worst He touched you. When you least deserved His love, He loved you. You were ugly but now you are BEAUTIFUL because you are His child.

Praise Him for His love and thank Him for His Mercy that brings you into His Presence for eternity.

October 19

You must submit to and endure [correction] for discipline; God is dealing with you as with sons. For what son is there whom his father does not [thus] train and correct and discipline?
Hebrews 12:7

Fully Comprehensive

Are you at the place in your life where you mean business with your life? When God comes into your life He means business. He wants to see you grow and become all that He has provided for you in His Word.

He does not want any of your old ways to have a hold on your life. In fact, He will keep working on you until the day you leave this earth, stripping away and stripping off all the things that need adjustment and change.

Give Him every opportunity to do what needs to be done. Don't harden your heart otherwise you will just make your life more complicated.

As time goes by you will notice how your desires and attitudes are changing and you will have so much more peace than ever before.

Being disciplined by God is proof that He loves you and wants to walk with you.

October 20

Consider well the path of your feet, and let all your ways be established and ordered aright. Turn not aside to the right hand or to the left; remove your foot from evil.
Proverbs 4:26-27

Keep Your Feet On The Right Path

Compromise will lead you away from the Presence of the Lord and give your conscience many troubles. If you ignore your better judgement and submit to walking in the wrong direction, you will pay the painful price.

The Lord wants you to walk on the straight and narrow path (with Him), trusting Him all the way. This certainly is the harder path, and will take far more discipline and determination than walking the easy, wide road that leads to destruction.

Think about your path, consider it well and then establish the way you are going to walk. Do not be distracted by what is going on when you think about the right and left hand of the path. Fix your gaze and your feet to walk straight ahead without any wandering. God wants you walking on His path, He is a jealous God and will not share you with another.

God's path will lead to blessing.

October 21

And since we have [such] a great and wonderful and noble Priest [Who rules] over the house of God, let us all come forward and draw near with true (honest and sincere) hearts in unqualified assurance and absolute conviction engendered by faith (by that leaning of the entire human personality on God in absolute trust and confidence in His power, wisdom, and goodness), having our hearts sprinkled and purified from a guilty (evil) conscience and our bodies cleansed with pure water.
Hebrews 10:21-22

Sprinkle Your Heart And Purify Your Body.

Jesus has wiped the slate clean, given you a fresh start. Not only has his mercy dealt with your past, it has also dealt with your future before you have lived one day of it!

This assurance gives you the wonderful opportunity to come to God with a pure and clean conscience. Be open and honest in His Presence and serving Him wholeheartedly with your body.

Don't hide away from God like Adam and Eve did when they sinned. Come to God and get your life back into a good place. He wants to finish the good work that He started in you. A guilty conscience will lead you to run away from His Presence and anyone who may be a light in your darkness.

You are not going to go forward if you keep thinking about and regret your past.

October 22

Blessed (happy, fortunate, prosperous, and enviable) is the man who walks and lives not in the counsel of the ungodly [following their advice, their plans and purposes], nor stands [submissive and inactive] in the path where sinners walk, nor sits down [to relax and rest] where the scornful [and the mockers] gather.
Psalm 1:1

Counsel From Above

Sinners are always ready to give advice to everyone, and if you do not want to get the wrong advice, then whatever you do, do not ask them for help. It would be like going to a bad insurance sales man and asking him to train you to sell insurance? Their spirit has not been made brand new by the power of God and their thinking will not come from a righteous point of view.

The Lord says that you are blessed, happy and enviable if you do not get your counsel from anyone but Him. He is the greatest counsellor and He has been around for a very long time. Nobody understands your situation like He does, and with His advice you will get the most dynamic results in your circumstance.

You are also blessed, happy and enviable when you do not submit yourself and play an inactive part when you are around sinners, or sit down and relax in the presence of people who will mock and jeer at your God.

Ask God for Wisdom.

October 23

And the Lord God took the man and put him in the Garden of Eden to tend and guard and keep it.
Genesis 2:15

Tend, Guard And Keep Your Garden

You are aware that you are going to work while you are on the earth. Sitting around and looking at your circumstances is not the way to prosper.

God instructed Adam to take care of the things around him. He was to tend and to guard and to keep the garden.

Tend – to take care of, watch, and keep.

Guard – preserve, safeguard, shield.

Keep – maintain, mind, and observe.

God blesses us with wonderful things in this life to enjoy and share with others. Because of this, we are not to take this for granted but to have a heart of thankfulness and appreciation.

If you give someone a gift and they hide it away or let it lie out in the garden, what would you think of them?

God is going to put you in a place of blessing. Be wise in how you handle it when it comes – don't abuse it or misuse it.

October 24

Therefore I tell you, stop being perpetually uneasy (anxious and worried) about your life, what you shall eat or what you shall drink; or about your body, what you shall put on. Is not life greater [in quality] than food, and the body [far above and more excellent] than clothing?
Matthew 6:25

Keep Your Priorities In Order!

We keep using up so much energy worrying about endless lists of things that we need to do. If we had to reverse our attention and put it on God we would find out that our anxiety levels would drop dramatically.

Giving your life to God makes the statement that you trust Him and are willing to let Him work out everything for you. By taking all these concerns back you are actually saying that you are not sure whether God is able to do what He says.

You need to get your emotions and your desires under control and put your love and affection where it belongs, on the living God. He will not allow you to go around naked and without a morsel of food to eat. You may have experienced difficulties, but knowing God, you will never go without.

When I was at Bible School all that was left in the house to eat was a tin of baked beans and corn, a few slices of bread and half a bottle of cool drink. At the same time a group of people were praying and God had them receive and offering for us. It was so much that we were able to live off it for two months.

God is faithful!

October 25

Then Mary said, Behold, I am the handmaiden of the Lord; let it be done to me according to what you have said. And the angel left her.
Luke 1:38

Mary Receives The Word

Could you imagine what it was like for this young lady, to have an angel appear to her and tell her not to be afraid? This was the first challenge. To hear and receive his message, was another.

I would have been quite shocked, and you? Not only shocked by his presence but also by his message. Me pregnant, an illegitimate child and you call this favor?

The angel waited for her answer, "... be it unto me according to the Word". She accepted the favor of God and welcomed the Word into her heart.

It was through her obedience that she was able to give birth to the most precious gift that the world has ever received. I believe that the Lord must have prepared her for this amazing task by having her raised in a God-fearing family.

You have similar opportunities in your life everyday, obviously not nearly as grand, but whereby your efforts and welcoming of the Word will have eternal results.

Are you listening? Are you prepared to receive that Word and see the wonderful results?

October 26

The Lord sets free the prisoners...
Psalm 146:7

No Longer A Jailbird

You are no longer a prisoner to natural circumstances and difficulties. You are only a prisoner of Christ, to do His will. God's purposes and plans must be the plans that come to pass in your life, He wants you free, fulfilling what He has called you to.

Don't allow bad and hurtful experiences to imprison you and don't stay in bondage to the pain of the past. Use the incident as a challenge to change; grow through it and become a more excellent person. Disappointments and frustrations will come, but learn to kick open the prison doors that hold you back, and walk straight out to the freedom that is yours.

If you stay imprisoned, you are going to lose too much; the price is high, and why should you pay so dearly for something that you can be released from? Don't bow down and surrender to the chains of bondage. Get free.

Don't let some relationship incarcerate you. Take the Word of God and His destiny for your life, apply God's Word and forgive and break loose. The enemy is the binder, but the Lord is the liberator. Walk free from aching bitterness, jealousy and rejection, and put on the cloak of righteousness that is yours in Jesus.

The prison doors are wide open, what are you doing inside?

October 27

But the Lord was with Joseph, and he [though a slave] was a successful and prosperous man; and he was in the house of his master the Egyptian. And his master saw that the Lord was with him and that the Lord made all that he did to flourish and succeed in his hand.
Genesis 39:2

God Is With You!

Joseph was a dynamic young man. Through all his challenges and heartache, he stood strong and faced each mountain as an opportunity to be somebody and to do something. The devil tried to destroy him, but it was not to be. In the end, it was his life that saved the ones who had betrayed him, his family.

His power of forgiveness was awesome. Even though he had been abused, abandoned and betrayed, he walked in the strength of his God.

Life, today, presents so many mountains that need to be climbed and many that need to be removed. With the power of God in our lives, and the love of God in our hearts, there is nothing that we cannot accomplish.

Even though Joseph was a slave, he was prosperous and successful. Your circumstances cannot hold you back; you will be blessed right in the midst of your darkest hour if you serve the Lord.

God's favor will be evident in your life for all to see. Keep your heart pure, turn bitterness away, and love your enemies.

October 28

You have not chosen Me, but I have chosen you and I have appointed you [I have planted you], that you might go and bear fruit and keep on bearing, and that your fruit may be lasting [that it may remain, abide], so that whatever you ask the Father in My Name [as presenting all that I AM], He may give it to you.
John 15:16

He Chose You!

God is waiting for you to come to Him. You did not choose Him, but He chose you long before you were even born. All you have done is to welcome Him into your life, and that opened the doors of blessings and deliverance. By your coming to Him, He appoints you to bear good, healthy and lasting fruit in your life.

He wants to be your great support so that you can live abundantly and be as productive and successful as possible. Every step that you take, coming closer to His Presence, opens doors of blessings to you. To protect and take care of you is His desire, just as you would do for your own child.

Jesus invites us to come to the Father, and to not be afraid when you present your requests. Come, not in your own ability but as being in Christ, He is your confidence. That is how you come – in Jesus name. With this in mind, the Father will hear your prayer and bless your life.

Bearing healthy good fruit is part of your inheritance in Jesus and brings glory to The Father.

October 29

The work of each [one] will become [plainly, openly] known (shown for what it is); for the day [of Christ] will disclose and declare it, because it will be revealed with fire, and the fire will test and critically appraise the character and worth of the work each person has done.
1 Corinthians 3:13

It's Time To Work For God

It's a pleasure to give my life in service to the Lord. Nothing is more important. Wasting precious time with trivial things and waking up when it is too late is disastrous. I count my time for God as the most valuable thing I can do, is my reasonable service. What are you doing?

To add to the encouragement, you are to do your best; not second, or third, but your absolute best for Him. Our God is an excellent God and He deserves our best.

If you are not sure where to start, begin by helping others. You could ask your Pastor where you could serve with your gifting. As you begin to sow as an act of your worship, you will reap so much fulfillment, joy and happiness.

But do something. Knowing that you are serving God. You do not have to be full-time for God, but you must give some time to God.

Your secular job is a blessing but has no eternal value.
Working for God is immeasurable.

October 30

So too the [Holy] Spirit comes to our aid and bears us up in our weakness; for we do not know what prayer to offer nor how to offer it worthily as we ought, but the Spirit Himself goes to meet our supplication and pleads in our behalf with unspeakable yearnings and groaning's too deep for utterance.
Romans 8:26

Help Us To Pray

The Holy Spirit is our Helper, Comforter and Teacher; what a gift to have when you do not know how to talk to the Father about a specific need.

When you pray you want to be as effective as possible, pleasing the Father. The Holy Spirit knows exactly how to do this as He has been with the Father since before time began. He will teach you how to pray.

On occasions the Spirit of God will lead you into spiritual warfare as you pray against certain areas of darkness. You may cry, mutter, moan or groan aloud in the spirit – just as if you were in travail, with child. It's all in order and has its purpose.

You may know what you are praying about and then there are times when you do not know what you are praying about, but you will feel the unction of the Holy Spirit. Do not draw away or back-off, let the Holy Spirit pray through you. You may be a little surprised at what comes out of your mouth, but you will know that it all has very specific spiritual significance.

Yield to the help of the Holy Spirit when you pray.
You will be moving mountains.

October 31

So repent (change your mind and purpose); turn around and return [to God], that your sins may be erased (blotted out, wiped clean), that times of refreshing (of recovering from the effects of heat, of reviving with fresh air) may come from the presence of the Lord.
Acts 3:19

Times Of Refreshing!

Anything that draws you away from God is NOT from God. The devil will do whatever he can to keep you away from Gods Presence.

Psalm 16:11 *Thou wilt shew me the path of life: in thy presence is fulness of joy; at thy right hand there are pleasures for evermore.*

When you are heavy laden and do not know which way to turn, run to the Lord. He knows exactly how you should handle your difficulties and will help you to overcome them, without being so distracted that you are totally out of His will.

The moment you turn to Him you will feel the effects of the heat begin to subside – refreshing will flood your soul and great peace will be yours. The presence of the Lord does wonders for your life, it calms, delivers and strengthens your soul. It will also heal your body from anxiety and fear.

He promised you that He would never leave nor forsake you, so do not let your heart become captive by the enemy.

There is nothing like a time of refreshing in the Presence of the Lord; turn around and run to Him when the heat is on.

November

For His Good Pleasure

November 1

For God so greatly loved and dearly prized the world that He [even] gave up His only begotten (unique) Son, so that whoever believes in (trusts in, clings to, relies on) Him shall not perish (come to destruction, be lost) but have eternal (everlasting) life.
John 3:16

God Loves The World!

Salvation is for all. When scripture says, 'For God so loved the world', He means that He loves everyone, He may not love what he or she does, but He LOVES them.

When God sent His son Jesus to die for us, He sent His most treasured possession – His Son. Jesus had to be involved in the plan to obey God. He knew that by His victory over the devil on earth, He would pave the way for us to come back into relationship with the Father.

Nothing that we can do will ever earn us the privilege of belonging to God. Only by GRACE and through God's Mercy in Jesus, are we saved. By believing in Him we walk in the blessings that are ours through the cross. We are delivered from spiritual death to life, from sickness to health, torment to peace, fear to faith and depression to joy.

The Bible says that anyone who calls on the name of the Lord will be saved. It does not matter what your age, colour, or gender is. It does not matter what you may have done, God's anointing in your life is able to break the yoke of any bondage you are entangled in.

As you walk in newness of life reach out to others who are still in darkness – give some of your life to others and life will be multiplied back to you.

November 2

My brethren, pay not servile regard to people [show no prejudice, no partiality]. Do not [attempt to] hold [and] practice the faith of our Lord Jesus Christ [the Lord] of glory [together with snobbery]!
James 2:1

Prohibit Prejudice

Prejudice if practiced, is straight from the pit of hell. It is ungodly, and brings bondage into your life and the lives of others; it causes despondency, discouragement and failure. We see prejudice among religion, race, gender, almost anything and everything. Whatever it is, it is not from God.

We are to see people through the eyes of Jesus, and hold them in the same esteem as He does. He commands us in His Word to love one another, not to dominate one another. But man likes to set up his own rules and conditions by which he will love. Jesus holds no prejudice in His heart, and He does not intimidate or manipulate anybody.

The Body of Christ is not a clique. We are one Body, and each one is just as important as the other, no matter what your age, colour, nationality or gender – we are all the same in Christ Jesus. Search your heart and leave no room for discrimination. Help and support anyone going through those problems and encourage them to know who they are in Christ.

To live free in Jesus is to live free of prejudice.

November 3

For by your words you will be justified and acquitted, and by your words you will be condemned and sentenced.
Matthew 12:37

Watch What You Say!

When you open your mouth, mind what comes out of it. Have you ever blurted out something and immediately knew it was the wrong thing to do and say?

There is awesome power in the words that we speak. We either edify or break down the people around us by our conversation.

Parents do not understand what damage they will do when they continually tear away at the character of their children by telling them they are useless, stupid and will never amount to anything in life. Eventually, when their children don't succeed in life, they get mad, while all along the way they prophesied doom over them.

You must control and be accountable for the words that you speak. You have no excuse! Train yourself to listen to what you are saying and before you answer anyone, check what you are going to say. Be slow to answer!

When tempted to answer quickly – perhaps you are in some kind of an argument – take a deep breath and wait until you have yourself under control before you answer.

It is part of learning how to discipline your flesh, and the Holy Spirit will help you while you are in training.

November 4

I have fought the good (worthy, honorable, and noble) fight, I have finished the race, I have kept (firmly held) the faith.
2 Timothy 4:7

Don't Quit!

Whatever you do, don't quit! God has given you a specific race to run, and it would be unfair if the race He set before you was too hard for you to finish, so finish it well. The particular race that you are to run may require serious endurance, so train hard, and get strong.

Life is full of challenging circumstances that can totally overwhelm and swamp you. You may be overcome by the files and papers heaped on your desk; you may be dealing with one crisis after the next; your home may be out of control; the washing, ironing, cooking, seeing to the children, homework and looking stunning for your darling husband.

Life's pressures can cause you to abandon the race and give up, and when you just get rid of one challenge the next one arrives. Welcome to the real world! Everything needs attention, some much more than others.

But, make up your mind that NOTHING is going to take you out of the race. God has equipped you well, and you can do it. Keep your running shoes on and your eyes on Jesus. Things will calm down again and then you can breathe. Thank the Lord for wisdom in each situation and keep smiling.

You are going to run your race and you are going to finish it – surely to win would be even nicer.

November 5

*Therefore a man shall leave his father and his mother
and shall become united and cleave to his wife,
and they shall become one flesh.*
Genesis 2:24

One Flesh!

A man should leave his mother and father and cleave (continually chase after) his wife. Most marriages suffer right there! The Mother and the Mother-In-Law get so involved that they almost move into the house with the newly weds!! But the man is to 'cleave' to his wife, NOT his mother, and the cleaving part is the best part for him. It's what God put inside of him!

Marriage is a wonderful institution if you are able to work through the things that get in the way. Taking two totally different lives and telling them to "live together until they die, and to be happy" is a miracle if it happens. In many cases the results are excellent, but through pressure and problems others do not last the fight of remaining together.

I personally believe in the miracle of one flesh. When marriage promises are made in the name of Jesus, there is far more power present to make that union successful than in any other case. Even so, a good marriage takes hard work on the part of BOTH parties as they adapt to one another. The woman by nature is submissive, but that will only be done willingly, if the man loves her with the love that Christ loved the church, and gave Himself for it. That kind of love NEVER fails!

Honor, respect and appreciation will build any marriage and make it stronger so that nothing will break it apart.

The most important key is to love, encourage and to build up the one that you are in covenant with.

November 6

By having the eyes of your heart flooded with light, so that you can know and understand the hope to which He has called you, and how rich is His glorious inheritance in the saints (His set-apart ones).
Ephesians 1:18

You Are A Gem

You are a precious jewel in the sight of the Lord. He has created and shaped you uniquely, with all the characteristics you have, your personality, your appearance, and your nationality.

Everything that you are today is the moulding and shaping hand of God on your life. The one thing to remember is that there are going to be a few rough edges that need working on.

Sometimes you may feel as though there is a sign that reads "to be continued" hung around your neck. Welcome to the club! He is at work inside of you. Stay pliable in His hands, and surrendered to whatever He wants for your life.

Just as a proud diamond cutter chips-off, polishes and shines the gem he is working with until it is brilliant with lustre, so you will shine with the glory of God. The work being done on you will be a little painful and uncomfortable at times, but God is getting rid of all the rough edges. He knows how to bring the brilliance out in you. You are going to be what He wants you to be.

Surrender all to the Lord, let Him cut, polish and shine your life until you glisten with His presence.

November 7

Learn to sense what is vital, and approve and prize what is excellent and of real value [recognizing the highest and the best, and distinguishing the moral differences], and that you may be untainted and pure and unerring and blameless [so that with hearts sincere and certain and unsullied, you may approach] the day of Christ [not stumbling nor causing others to stumble].
Philippians 1:10

A More Excellent Life

We need to be aware that there is a way of doing things, and then there is an excellent way of doing things! God has given us the means to be excellent in all that we do for Him. He has provided wisdom, understanding and knowledge, he also said that once we are born-again, we have the mind of Christ. When you live for God, you live for the best that there is; there is no other that can match His excellence.

When you show love to the unloved, overdo it. When you reach out to the hungry, go over the top and be a tremendous blessing. If God gave His prized possession, we can certainly do better than we do. With His unfailing love inside of us, we have the power to help others rise above their broken lives.

Make sure that you are not causing others to stumble but that you are the one helping to pick them up. Keep your life out of trouble and you will be a tremendous testimony to the world. Check your heart and your motives regularly and run from temptations. You have the power to walk free from them all.

To get more out of life, put your best into it.

November 8

I have strength for all things in Christ Who empowers me [I am ready for anything and equal to anything through Him Who infuses inner strength into me; I am self-sufficient in Christ's sufficiency].
Philippians 4:13

You Can Do It!

You have strength for anything that comes your way, even though you may not think so? You are empowered by the Spirit of God to accomplish His will for your life, and that you will do.

You are equal to and stronger than any opposition or challenge that arises. Not in your own strength and ability, but in the strength and ability that Christ is building inside of you.

You are more than capable (with His help) to complete everything you are supposed to do with Christ on the inside of you – the hope of glory and victory.

Hold fast to the God-given dreams and hopes that you have in your heart and do not let go of any one of them. You will see them come to pass as you serve the King even if there is persecution and rivalry against you. Opposition is part of life even as a Christian. Perhaps even more so, because you are a threat to the enemy, but keep pushing forward and never look back.

Have confidence that God will provide all that you need to accomplish His plans. He will empower you.

November 9

[Live] as free people, [yet] without employing your freedom as a pretext for wickedness; but [live at all times] as servants of God.
1 Peter 2:16

Free Indeed!

God has made you free. Only His opinion matters not your own opinion or the opinions of others. He also does not want you enslaved to yourself, being self-conscious and not having the courage to allow your personality and character to shine through. Or possibly, that you have to be the life of every party trying to be someone you are not.

Become God-conscious, place your focus on Him, practice living what His Word says about you.

We limit our lives with boundaries that we set up and they interfere with the plans that God has for us. He sees you accomplishing great things in His Kingdom; so don't imprison yourself with the past, and particularly with your low self-esteem and lack of confidence. Let God live in you and through you. Boldly step out in the ability that He has given you.

Make the tools that you have available for God to use aand become effective in the Body of Christ. Be free and purpose in your heart that nothing is going to stop you. Put your hand to the plough and don't turn back.

Whom the Son sets free, is free indeed.

In Christ Jesus there is no bondage, but glorious liberty.

November 10

For he was [waiting expectantly and confidently] looking forward to the city which has fixed and firm foundations, whose Architect and Builder is God.
Hebrews 11:10

Solidly Set

Put your feet on solid ground. That's where God wants you standing; on a fixed and firm foundation. He does not want you distracted by nonsense. Focus your attention on Him, and concentrate and be absorbed by the things of the Lord. They are life to your soul and healing to your flesh.

When I have so many things going on in my own life, I try my best to pray in the Spirit and meditate on the Word of God. It always amazes me how powerful just a few minutes in the Presence of the Lord is able to refresh my soul.

The Lord knows what just a few moments in His Presence will do for you. He continually invites you in to get your confidence and strength built up. He asks you to come. The temptations will come to entertain and amuse you, but that is why your faith in God has to be firmly rooted.

If you are starting a new venture, get confirmation and utter assurance from the Lord. Know in your heart that it is His desire for you, and then walk in that confidence. No matter how difficult the task – see it through to completion.

I pray that your life will be founded, grounded and rooted in the Lord Jesus Christ.

November 11

The Heavens declare the glory of God; and the firmament shows and proclaims His handiwork.
Psalm 19:1

Glorious Lord

God's glory is all around us. All that God is and all that He does, is revealed through the beauty of His Creation. His signature is on everything that He has made; it is the physical appearance of His Divine Presence. Manifestations of His glory causes man to reverently worship and respond to Him.

The Father is personally training, disciplining, moulding and turning you into His own handiwork. He waits for His glory to be seen in you and all the while wanting the best from you. He knows exactly what you are made of, more than what you realize. He placed it there and so He knows what it will take to get it out of you, too.

Where you are weak, God will be your strength. He takes the areas that are lacking, teaching you how to draw on His ability, making a difference in your life. He wants you totally dependent on Him and His strength, not relying on your own abilities.

You are His own handiwork, His moulding and His making. As a proud artist puts his artwork on show at a gallery that it may be viewed and appreciated by all, so the Lord boasts of you. He wants others to see His work and glorify His name.

The glory of the Lord will cause you to worship the Creator.

November 12

For you shall eat [the fruit] of the labor of your hands; happy (blessed, fortunate, enviable) shall you be, and it shall be well with you.
Psalm 128:2

Effective In Your Labor For The Lord

All the labor that you do on this earth is for you to enjoy. God wants it to be well with you, and for you to be happy. I have learnt to work hard for the Lord. At times I think that I am never going to make it through the day, but the Lord gives me the strength and the patience to wait for the fruit, and when it comes, He allows me to enjoy it.

Whatever you give to God, He multiplies it abundantly and lets you share in the blessings. Daily you see the changes that are happening, and you know that if it were not for the Lord's presence in your life, you would never be where you are right now.

You may even be in the middle of a huge struggle. Don't let up and don't give in. Let God reveal His love and support in your life, He will show you the best way out. Just make sure you are a good steward of what He has given you.

If you have a beautiful voice, then sing for God. Develop your gift, go for voice lessons, learn to read music and sing like a nightingale.

There is no joy like working for the Lord. Life is never dull.

November 13

*Now you [collectively] are Christ's body and [individually] you are
members of it, each part severally and distinct
[each with his own place and function].*
1 Corinthians 12:27

We Are Christ's Body

The Word of God calls believers the "Body of Christ"; we are also referred to as the "Bride of Christ". Whichever, we are all one in the Lord. Each one has their separate ministries, but together we make up a whole.

Just as there is order in an army, so is there divine order in God's army. There should not be any confusion, strife or jealousy in God's army. There is only one body, one voice with everyone working together in harmony, proclaiming the Good News of the Gospel.

We need to learn how to honor, respect and appreciate one another, to understand exactly how the body functions. We need to know that it is unacceptable to walk around as witnesses of the Lord, having bitterness, jealousy, hatred and anger in our hearts towards another member of the "Body".

To walk in this understanding, you need to have the Word of God as a priority in your personal life. You need to be ordered, disciplined and directed by the Lord to keep the harmony.

Change starts with you and I.

November 14

May the God of your hope so fill you with joy and peace in believing [through the experience of your faith] that by the power of the Holy Spirit you may abound and be overflowing (bubbling over) with hope.
Romans 15:13

Hook Into The Power Of God

You have the power of God at hand, what are you going to do with that power? Paul's prayer is for you to be filled from on high. Are you going to let it just lie dormant in your life, or are you going to be useful for God?

The more you are aware of God's Presence, the bolder you will become in God. Be sensitive to the power that is available for you to reach out to others. The Father wants you to do great things for Him and through Him.

Your confidence is overpowering to the enemy and destroys the fears that come your way. By standing and enjoying the results of your faith at work, your joy will begin to affect those who share your life.

The Holy Spirit gives you power; power to live right, power to know Him, power to obey the Word, power to be a witness, power to love, power to serve, power over the enemy and power to have joy and peace in your hope.

I pray that the power and anointing of God will distract you from worldly issues, that you will stay linked to your Source.

November 15

For it is God's will and intention that by doing right [your good and honest lives] should silence (muzzle, gag) the ignorant charges and ill-informed criticisms of foolish persons.
1 Peter 2:15

Shut Their Mouths

Your life should be above reproach so that no one can say an evil word about you, and if they do, they would have to lie to do it.

Not everyone is going to be thrilled about what you are doing and the way that you are conducting your life. After all, it was not too long ago, and perhaps you may have been the one who was leading everyone else astray. You cannot help these poor folks that cannot understand what you are doing? Keep your cool and continue to please God. The Word helps you to live right; it will help you to think godly thoughts and to stay on the things that will delight the Lord.

Don't sacrifice the things of God for a season of sin. Don't compromise your life with the Lord for an old friend or the lusts of the flesh. These bad decisions will only destroy your life down the road and keep you captive to its pleasures. The wages of sin are death!

If you know you are straying from God, read His Word, pray, trust and live according to His precepts. Pull yourself together. Keep a good strong eye on yourself and do what you know is best for your life.

Living for God will always get people talking, one way or another.

November 16

Come close to God and He will come close to you...
James 4:8

An Example In Word, Deed And Action

What example are you setting before your friends, family and co-workers? They are watching your every move so make sure you give them something good to see and talk about.

When it comes to finding out about someone's lifestyle just talk to their family. You will soon find out what their witness is like at home, where they feel totally relaxed and ready to be themselves. At times it is quite funny to hear the different comments when sport is on television and the wife wants the remote.

There are always going to be people watching your life and attitude – after all, you have found the answer.

Is your life a good example? Should those watching you be patterning their lives after yours? All you can do is to do your best. Live a life that lines up with the Word of God. Behave and act as though Jesus is standing right next to you.

We can all love, forgive and serve each other more. When you live a life of faith, it will spur and encourage other believers to stir up their faith. When you speak about the blessings of God, it will cause people to trust and believe God for more. Your life is to be an example of God's purity, in your spirit, your soul and your body.

You are a walking epistle, one to be read by all.

November 17

Let us therefore, receiving a kingdom that is firm and stable and cannot be shaken, offer to God pleasing service and acceptable worship, with modesty and pious care and godly fear and awe; For our God [is indeed] a consuming fire.
Hebrews 12:28-29

For His Good Pleasure

The kingdom that you are serving is set for eternity. You, as a worshipper, are being stirred in your heart by the Spirit to bring your acceptable worship to God Himself. He has given you the power to live for Him.

Every time you need Him, it brings Him great pleasure to be there for you as your Father. For you to desire and the will to work for His good pleasure and His delight is all that He is asking of you.

Daily, He creates in you the desire to seek Him and to know Him more intimately. He fuels up your hunger and zeal by His Spirit, enabling you to change into His image.

Do you honestly think that you can carry on with a casual attitude towards Him? No, He is your Father and He wants your love and affection too. Jesus first loved you so that you would come to Him – He sowed first into your life giving you something special to respond to. Praise the Lord that you did. Right now, He wants you to get closer to Him.

This is something to consider and take very, very seriously.

November 18

Exercise foresight and be on the watch to look [after one another], to see that no one falls back from and fails to secure God's grace (His unmerited favor and spiritual blessing), in order that no root of resentment (rancor, bitterness or hatred) shoots forth and causes trouble and bitter torment, and the many become contaminated and defiled by it...
Hebrews 12:15

Bitter Versus Better

Bitterness comes from years of practice. It first starts with a little offence, then it develops into resentment, animosity and anger until it is rooted deep in your heart. It stems from suffering that has not been properly dealt with.

We have all been wronged at some time in our lives, and we have all done wrong to someone else without even being fully aware of it at times. How do you handle this testing experience in a godly way?

Firstly, if you have wronged someone, you need to know about it, as you are unable to make it right without knowledge of the problem.

Secondly, if you have been wronged, the Bible encourages you to go to your brother (or sister) and try to make it right. If they hear you, you have gained a brother. If not, then release them and go on your way, having done all that you could.

Do not let the root of bitterness grip your heart –
it will defile you. Get better not bitter.

November 19

For I will [fully] satisfy the weary soul, and I will replenish every languishing and sorrowful person.
Jeremiah 31:25

Energised!

There are many weary and tired people in this world. Life is a constant rush: from one appointment to the next, taking children between school and sports, maintaining the home, balancing and juggling far too many things all at once.

Amidst this scurry, you get weary, fatigued and if you are not careful you run out of spiritual steam too. Even though life will never free you from seasons of fatigue, your spirit can always be awake and alive to God. He is the only One that can reinvigorate you, spirit, soul and body, with His resurrection power.

Lady, be sensitive about all the things that you commit yourself to. It is in order for you to say no occasionally, and then take the time to get your house in order. Business does not always mean fruitfulness.

Prioritize your responsibilities; slow down your frantic pace and follow the leading of the Holy Spirit. Take a break and don't feel condemned for doing so – you need to run a marathon, not the hundred-yard dash.

Set aside a little time for yourself, go ahead and smell the roses. Life is too short for you to let it rush by.

November 20

You are the salt of the earth, but if salt has lost its taste (its strength, its quality), how can its saltness be restored? It is not good for anything any longer but to be thrown out and trodden underfoot by men.
Matthew 5:13

Are You Salty?

hat happens when you use old salt and the flavour is gone? Today is the perfect time for you to do a salt check.

- When was the last time that you smiled widely at someone?
- What mood were you in when you left home today?
- When you thought about cooking dinner, did you sigh?
- Did you talk about the Lord to some dear heart this week?
- What about your love level – is it up or down?
- Can you speak to the dog without shouting?
- How did you answer the last time you picked up the phone?

All these little areas expose your salt level. You need to keep topping-up with the Word of God and sharpening your attitude.

When my levels are fairly low or rather high, I find that I cry quite easily – my heart is truly sensitive to the Lord. But when everything is just cool, I handle it in my stride, with the Lord of course.

When the day is a little tough, keep smiling, and add salt to the atmosphere by praise to the Lord.

November 21

And a sense of awe (reverential fear) came upon every soul, and many wonders and signs were performed through the apostles (the special messengers).
Acts 2:43

Unthinkable Things!

Today, you are going to see the hand of the Lord in your life. As you offer to do something unusual and out of the ordinary for someone else, God will lift you up and bless you with supernatural blessings.

I love waking up and saying to the Lord, "What's up today Father, is there anything You need me to do?" Then I get ready for the ride. He never does things the same old way. He is always surprising me with little things, and I know that they could only be stimulated by His plan.

Prepare your heart for an exciting event and when the opportunity arises – take the plunge. Stretch yourself. Telephone someone you have not spoken to for ages, send some flowers or a box of chocolates to an old friend, help someone with their overload of work, tell someone special that you love them, thank someone for their kindness to you. It all builds a better heart inside of you.

God is a miracle working God; His ways are higher than our ways and His plans are more than what we can imagine. Get out of your box and let God be God in your life.

November 22

But seek (aim at and strive after) first of all His kingdom and His righteousness (His way of doing and being right), and then all these things taken together will be given you besides.
Matthew 6:33

Seek God First!

You must put God first in the decisions you make for your life. Not to do this, would be crazy. He knows where you are headed and if it's the wrong way He will warn you. He knows your future better than you know your past.

Whenever God does something He does it right. He is a righteous God and all He does is in righteousness: if what you are planning is an unrighteous act, He will not bless it. You may have to take the longer and harder route, but it will be the right route. We like to take short cuts to get where we are headed, and often they are the wrong ones.

Get the Father's approval first and stop rushing. Talk to Him, talk to wise people of God, read your Bible to see if your plans are in order. When this has been done – go ahead. But always go to Him first.

God says He will add to you. What will He add? All that you need. But you will have to seek Him first.

As a child, I could not just do what I felt like doing; I had to get approval from my parents. When I had their blessing then I knew that I was going to be just fine.

First talk to the Father.

November 23

*See that none of you repays another with evil for evil, but always aim
to show kindness and seek to do good to
one another and to everybody.*
1 Thessalonians 5:15

Put Evil In Its Place

It is terrible what people will do to each other when they have been wronged. Thank goodness, with a brand new nature and the Spirit of God dwelling within us we do not have to act like the world, but we have to use our spiritual weapons.

Think about this, "Do not react, but respond." When you act in the heat of the moment, you want to fly off at a tangent with folks that have done evil to you.

Stop, think, and cool off a little; you must handle the situation properly. When you are ready, respond. You will behave in an entirely different manner than if you react in the heat of the moment.

Don't be like the others, behaving badly and exposing a bad attitude. Lift your level and behave like a child of God. That does not mean that you are weak and running away, but it proves your strengths and that you refuse to be a part of their strife and confusion.

You will have the victory and peace to go with it. Do good, no matter how much your flesh wants to let loose.

Love never fails, it always get the best results.
Respond in love and watch evil flee from you.

November 24

Behave yourselves wisely [living prudently and with discretion] in your relations with those of the outside world (the non-Christians), making the very most of the time and seizing (buying up) the opportunity.
Colossians 4:5-6

Wise Living And Gracious Speech

Let your speech at all times be gracious (pleasant and winsome), seasoned as it were with salt, (so that you may never be at a loss) to know how you ought to answer anyone (who puts a question to you).

It takes a lifetime to build a good name for your life, yet you can destroy it in just a matter of moments. Your life in the Lord is to speak of His kindness, goodness and mercy to those living in the outside world.

Since the day that you proclaimed that you belonged to Jesus (and that is the right thing to do) you became a goldfish in a bowl. Everyone is watching your lifestyle, attitude and behavior.

Now don't get into a panic. The Lord will help and keep you, but you will have to at least try and do your best to be a light to others.

People are often unnecessarily critical because their own lives are a mess. You can handle it, smile! Calm down, and let your light shine as brightly as possible. Persecution arises when you obey God's Word; think about it, it comes with the blessings!

I would rather live for God than have man's approval.

November 25

So be patient, brethren [as you wait] till the coming of the Lord. See how the farmer waits expectantly for the precious harvest from the land. [See how] he keeps up his patient [vigil] over it until it receives the early and late rains. So you also must be patient. Establish your hearts [strengthen and confirm them in the final certainty] for the coming of the Lord is near.
James 5:7

Jesus Is Coming Soon!

Jesus is coming back soon. What are you going to do until He shows up? He tells us to keep occupied until He comes. Use up the time effectively and do not waste it.

- Time to be stronger and draw closer to Him.
- Time to work for God.
- Time to touch broken lives with the love of God.
- Time to enjoy the victory in Him.

To establish your heart in the things of God is of the utmost importance. Reading and meditating on the Word of God will keep your heart and mind fixed on God. Worshipping will keep your spirit sensitive to His voice, serving God will keep your attitude and priorities in order.

There is no time like the present to expect the Lord to return.

Until He comes we must love the Lord with all of our hearts and minds and love one another as He commanded.

November 26

Clothe yourselves therefore, as God's own chosen ones (His own picked representatives), [who are] purified and holy and well-beloved [by God Himself, by putting on behavior marked by] tenderhearted pity and mercy, kind feeling, a lowly opinion of yourselves, gentle ways [and] patience [which is tireless and long suffering, and has the power to endure whatever comes, with good temper].
Colossians 3:12

Beloved Of God

From the moment you get out of your bed today, think about the One Who has done so much for you. He loves you more than you realise and has placed His divine favor upon your life.

You are chosen of God – His elect. Dress like His elect, with attitude and character; not in pride but in the knowledge of He Who died for you. Behave as one who is called of God and submitted to God. Be tenderhearted, kind, merciful, gentle and patient. Let Him teach you all these things and use the opportunity to learn and grow in Him. Search your heart and live a life that is pure.

You are a living, walking and breathing epistle; an open book for all to read. What story are they reading? Is it a wild novel or a true story of faith and love?

Being called "elect of God" and "chosen of God" is a very humbling thought, especially when you realise that without Him you are nothing and would be nothing.

November 27

And we earnestly beseech you, brethren, admonish (warn and seriously advise) those who are out of line [the loafers, the disorderly, and the unruly]; encourage the timid and fainthearted, help and give your support to the weak souls, [and] be very patient with everybody [always keeping your temper].
1 Thessalonians 5:14

Get In Line!

How long have you been waiting to do something for God? It was probably last year that you made those promises. The Scripture is very strong here and a good one to get you to line up. The sooner that you hook into the life that God has for you outside of your daily routine, the better. You will go forward and begin to prosper. Wishful thoughts and good intentions never bear any fruit.

If you are a mature Christian and just loafing away, I hope that this challenge will wake you up. You are not being fair to the rest of the Body and we are all sadly lacking without your gift. Notwithstanding you are not giving much to God and your seed is drying up and not bearing any fruit.

If you are a weak Christian then get hooked into God and His plans for your life, they will only strengthen you. You will begin to rise up stronger every day and the kingdom will be blessed for your obedience.

We should not be so busy that we have no time to sit at Jesus' feet – a good healthy balance of sitting and serving is the way to go.

November 28

Study and be eager and do your utmost to present yourself to God approved (tested by trial), a workman who has no cause to be ashamed, correctly analyzing and accurately dividing [rightly handling and skillfully teaching] the Word of Truth.
2 Timothy 2:15

Study God's Word

Life itself is an education without all the famous institutions. Waking up in the morning and facing a brand new day is awesome and builds character.

In Timothy we read how important it is for us to be taught and to study God's Word. It is the manual to life, and our greatest teacher.

Whatever you need to know about life, the Holy Spirit will teach you through the Word and help with your spirit, soul and body and every area. Whatever it is that you need, the Word of God has all the answers.

When you buy a new car you have to study the manual to know how everything works. We have feelings, attitudes, characteristics and behavior patterns, and need to know what is acceptable or not in our lives. The Word is our guideline to life.

A workman in the kingdom of God must not be ignorant of the things of God, but sharp, experienced and knowledgeable.

It only takes a couple of weeks to begin to really grow in God. You cannot grow with the television or the newspapers but you will grow in God when you study His Word.

Studying is a powerful tool. Begin today and put your heart into the Word – it will change your life forever.

November 29

But let it be the inward adorning and beauty of the hidden person of the heart, with the incorruptible and unfading charm of a gentle and peaceful spirit, which [is not anxious or wrought up, but] is very precious in the sight of God.
1 Peter 3:4

The Inner Man

You can spend as much money and time as you like trying to doll-up and change the outer man. This may bring you satisfaction for a while, but ultimately it's the inner man that needs the most attention.

Wearing designer clothing and having the best hairdos, body and facial treatments all help but if your heart is sick, the sickness will work its way to the outside making you look awful. If your heart is healthy and happy you will automatically look great.

Worries, strife and bitterness have no place in the life of a believer, but peace, tranquility, joy, contentment and love will only come from being close to God – something that money cannot buy. Let your love work from the inside to the outside of you.

Rich folks will do anything to have peace; take pills, move to the mountains, scuba dive in the ocean, buy an island. We just open our hearts to Jesus and get it without any cost because He already paid the highest price for our peace, and the quality is the best – peace that passes all human understanding.

If you want to be totally beautiful, He is the beautician, the Master of Peace and inner tranquility.

November 30

Do not, therefore, fling away your fearless confidence, for it carries a great and glorious compensation of reward.
Hebrews 10:35

Confidence In Him

*C*hrist is our confidence. Heaven is our reward.

As much as we may have trouble with our feelings, emotions and fears, we must never lose hold of what we have learned and experienced walking by faith. What God has planned and promised will come to pass in your life.

When I think of this determined confidence, I think of the times when my children Joshua and Kristen, at the earlier stages of their lives, never felt unwelcome in their dad's office, no matter what was going on inside. They would boldly open the door, walk straight to the fridge, grab a cool drink, say "hi, dad", kiss him on the cheek and walk right out again. President Mandela could have been visiting but they knew who their dad was. We have since taught them some wise etiquette.

When pressure and trouble come your way, do not throw away all that you have learned. Go into that secret place and go into it boldly because your Father is on the throne. Certainly do not let the devil intimidate you into a corner, rebuke him and kick him out of your life and confidently and loudly and boldly declare what you have and who you are in the name of Jesus.

Trusting, standing, knowing and relying on God's Word to come through will bring you a great reward.

December

Good Thoughts

December 1

Jesus answered him, I assure you, most solemnly I tell you, that unless a person is born again (anew, from above), he cannot ever see (know, be acquainted with, and experience) the kingdom of God.
John 3:3

Born Again

How long did you wait to come to the Father and to make Jesus the Lord of your life? Did you procrastinate? Perhaps you still have not yet come to that decision. Do not waste any more time, come to Him while you can.

Jesus spoke to one of the most dynamic religious leaders of the day and told him that he would have to take on a new life and be "born anew". Nicodemus hungered for God and he made the right choice. What are you going to do?

You cannot be born anew by any earthly manner, you have to come to the Father in the name of Jesus and be "born anew" from on high. It is the Presence of God living inside you that changes your heart. It is not positive thinking, or a hypnotic state, but it is a miracle from God that will change your life.

You cannot understand the things of God with your natural thinking. He is God! You cannot buy the experience or create this experience but you can come to God just as you are, in Jesus' name He will change your heart, and come and live inside of you.

Anyone who calls on the name of the Lord will be saved.

December 2

For sin shall not [any longer] exert dominion over you since now you are not under Law [as slaves], but under grace [as subjects of God's favor and mercy].
Romans 6:14

Sin... It's Over!

Don't tell me that you can't help yourself. Yes you can! In the name of Jesus you can do anything that you put your heart to.

You have authority and dominion over your flesh. You are in control of these desires that are not pleasing to God and to your own spirit. When you go ahead with these wrong desires and thoughts you will only make yourself depressed and unhappy. Your conscience will be grieved and your spirit discouraged.

Keep away from anything that you do not have power to control. Wait until you are strong in the Lord, and then you may display your strength openly.

It is not in your own strength that you stand against the desires of your flesh, but in the strength of the Lord who has already overcome all these temptations for you. God will make a way for you to escape the temptation, so look for it, take the gap and run. Do not let the devil get the better of you; you are not his servant.

When the enemy comes against you, get your eyes off the temptation and onto Jesus.

December 3

If we [freely] admit that we have sinned and confess our sins, He is faithful and just (true to His own nature and promises) and will forgive our sins [dismiss our lawlessness] and [continuously] cleanse us from all unrighteousness [everything not in conformity to His will in purpose, thought, and action].
1 John 1:9

Complete Forgiveness

It does not matter what you have done when you go to the Lord with a pure heart, and confess your sin, He is just and faithful to forgive you of that sin you committed.

It does not take away from the penalty of sin. For example, if you stole something and you were caught, you would still be responsible to pay whatever price is necessary to right your wrong with the law of the land. Just like the two thieves on the cross; they asked Jesus to forgive them, He did, but they did not get taken off the cross. It is the eternal wrong that you are righting when you acknowledge your sin before God.

Jesus already forgave you on the cross of your past, present and future sin. Repenting is acknowledging wrongdoing, receiving forgiveness and turning away from it.

The Heavenly Father does not only forgive you of the sin that you confess but also of all the other sins that you are not even aware of committing; like a proud look and mischievous feet.

Go to the Father... He loves you!

December 4

[God] disarmed the principalities and powers that were ranged against us and made a bold display and public example of them, in triumphing over them in Him and in it [the cross].
Colossians 2:15

A Public Display

It all came down to the Father having the final victory at the cross. Right through eternity Satan chanced his luck, he even thought he was greater than the Almighty God.

Jesus did it all for us, obtaining our liberty, peace and joy, giving us the pleasure of eternal life with God. It took everything that Jesus had to obey the Father right to the end. He was sinless, not guilty, and He took the debt and paid it in full.

They could not kill Jesus although they did try to on a number of occasions. He chose to give His life as a ransom for us. He knew that in the long term the wealth of winning us back to the Father was the ultimate victory. He laid down His life for us. When it was done He cried out, "It is finished!"

This brought total disrepute to the enemy's camp and since that hour Satan has continued to try and stop the children of God from gaining the upper hand. It's too late, we know who he is, and the Father has fully exposed his work. As the Scripture says "He made a bold display and a public example of them through the cross."

The enemy is under your feet, look down at him.

December 5

Little children, you are of God [you belong to Him] and have [already] defeated and overcome them [the agents of the antichrist], because He Who lives in you is greater (mightier) than he who is in the world.
1 John 4:4

The Greater One Inside

Coming to Christ does not make you weaker but stronger. For years I had the opinion that Christians were weak, sorry individuals. Only when I began to read the Word of God and discover the true nature of a Christian, did I discover the real truth. It shocked me!

The Father calls us overcomers, the head and not the tail, above and not beneath. He says that we have the mind of Christ and that we can do all things through Christ Jesus Who strengthens us. That is not the character of a weakling.

He mentions that we belong to God. I just love that – if you want to belong to someone, belong to God. He is the only one that will keep your life beautiful and give you the peace that you need. He will take you to higher heights in His love and teach you about true love.

Everything that the world tries to offer us is a counterfeit. We have a greater solution in Christ. We do not have to sacrifice the awesome life that we now live for some second rate life. Our life in Christ is the greatest life that one can live on earth.

You belong to the greater One who lives inside you.

December 6

Truly I tell you, whatever you forbid and declare to be improper and unlawful on earth must be what is already forbidden in heaven, and whatever you permit and declare proper and lawful on earth must be what is already permitted in heaven. Again I tell you, if two of you on earth agree (harmonize together, make a symphony together) about whatever [anything and everything] they may ask, it will come to pass and be done for them by My Father in heaven.
Matthew 18:18-19

Agreement And Binding And Loosing

That is the assurance we need to discover and to walk in. The fact that when we get together in unity and in agreement with the Word of God, there is nothing that can hinder or stop the Word of God from coming to pass in our lives.

Disharmony causes terrible problems, and is a major source of confusion and strife in the Body of Christ. However, if we get in agreement heaven will honor our prayers.

The Scripture says if you forbid to be improper on earth it is already forbidden in heaven.

If you permit, if you agree with the Word and with each other – just two of you, it shall come to pass.

Get a prayer partner and get into agreement with what the promises of God offer you, it is yours in Christ.

December 7

Jesus approached and, breaking the silence, said to them, All authority (all power of rule) in heaven and on earth has been given to Me. Go then and make disciples of all the nations, baptizing them into the name of the Father and of the Son and of the Holy Spirit. Teaching them to observe everything that I have commanded you and behold, I am with you all the days (perpetually, uniformly, and on every occasion), to the [very] close and consummation of the age.
Matthew 28:18-20

I Am With You Always

*J*esus will be with you no matter what happens, in your good or your bad times. You may feel as though He is not present but that is only because of your own feelings. If He promises you that He is there, then He IS there.

He was given every bit of authority and power on the earth and then He said, "Go ye." We are to go into the world and bring the Good News to anyone that will listen and we are backed-up with the same authority and power that backed-up Jesus. It takes effort to win people to Jesus, however it takes even greater responsibility on us to disciple (teach) them the Word of God. The wonderful thing is that we are not alone. The Holy Spirit works with us and we are ever in the heart of the Father.

We can boldly say that the Lord is with us; He promises He will never leave nor forsake us.

How can we ever be lonely or feel insufficient
when our lives are satisfied in God?

December 8

Now also we beseech you, brethren, get to know those who labor among you [recognize them for what they are, acknowledge and appreciate and respect them all] – your leaders who are over you in the Lord and those who warn and kindly reprove and exhort you. And hold them in very high and most affectionate esteem in [intelligent and sympathetic] appreciation of their work.
Be at peace among yourselves.
1 Thessalonians 5:12-13

Respect Your Leaders

You need to respect the one that is leading you in your spiritual life. He stands in a God-appointed office. If he is a true man of God, treat him with the respect and honor what God requires of you, otherwise you are showing disrespect to God.

The man of God is the one who has to set the example. Although he is a servant of God, he is not perfect. There may be some things about him that you do not like? That does not make him any less of a man of God. As long as he is not practising sin, you need to put your opinion in your pocket and respect him anyway.

What kind of sheep are you? How do you treat your leader? I would encourage you to love and respect your leader and his family, as he takes care of the most important part of your life. Pray for him; bless him continually, as that would make it more profitable for you in the long run.

Respect, love, honor and appreciate your spiritual leaders. You will bless God by doing this.

December 9

I have fought the good (worthy, honorable, and noble) fight, I have finished the race, I have kept (firmly held) the faith. [As to what remains] henceforth there is laid up for me the [victor's] crown of righteousness [for being right with God and doing right], which the Lord, the righteous Judge, will award to me and recompense me on that [great] day – and not to me only, but to all those who have loved and yearned for and welcomed His appearing (His return).
2 Timothy 4:7-8

Fight The Good Fight

What kind of battle are you in? Are you using all the available tools God has given you, enabling you to win the fight and come out on top for God?

Life is like a marathon, there are many hills to climb, valleys to pass through, and long stretches of highway to maintain. With full direction from the Lord, with your heart fixed on the vision for your life, you will say in the end, "I have fought a good fight, I have finished the race."

There are many rewards in heaven and many rewards to be gained here on earth. Having God's favor will take you further than you could go naturally. His hand on your life gives you the edge. You can live right and do right; that is what living for God is all about. Get on with the race. Overcome the challenges and fight till you win.

Nothing can stop you loving and serving God and looking forward to Jesus' return. He is coming soon.

December 10

How much more surely shall the blood of Christ, Who by virtue of [His] eternal Spirit [His own preexistent divine personality] has offered Himself as an unblemished sacrifice to God, purify our consciences from dead works and lifeless observances to serve the [ever] living God?
Hebrews 9:14

Christ Made You Free

Jesus is there all the time. Throughout the Old Testament the Presence of Jesus can be felt. He stepped out of Eternity, where He has always been with the Father God, to come down to earth to give His life for us. There is no fault in Him. He is the unblemished Lamb of God sacrificed for us. He redeemed us back to the Father God, through, and by His precious, Holy blood.

There is nothing in your life that this powerful, miracle-working blood cannot restore, repair and make brand new.

As you reach out to Him for your deliverance and healing, you are given the awesome opportunity of a miracle.

Jesus did not give up Eternity to come to earth for nothing. He came to open the doorway, enabling you and I to walk through, without a guilty conscience and a sin stained life.

Let the merciful love and compassion of the Lord build your confidence in His forgiveness. No matter what you have done, He is there waiting to forgive. He loves you.

December 11

Therefore do not worry and be anxious saying, What are we going to have to eat? or, What are we going to have to drink? or, What are we going to have to wear?
Matthew 6:31

Don't Confess It!

Do you know how you confirm your worries? By speaking them into existence. The Lord loves you and He will take care of you so when things are going crazy rather speak God's Word out of your mouth.

If you carefully read this Scripture you will note that the "saying" part is the critical part.

Our mouths are very powerful tools and can make or break our attitude, faith and confidence by saying the wrong thing. If you speak out your worries and hear yourself saying them, you will begin to build negative, doubting attitudes in your life.

We all know about positive thinking and how it works. Well, this is not positive thinking this is faith! When you get your words to agree with God's Word over your life then God's Word being far weightier, will bring it to pass.

Speaking negatively about your life couples your words with your doubts and fears and will work just as well for you as your faith filled words. Be careful what you say!

Speaking God's Word will build your faith and bring God's desires to manifest in your life.

December 12

The harvest is indeed plentiful, but the laborers are few. So pray to the Lord of the harvest to force out and thrust laborers into His harvest.
Matthew 9:37-38

Lord Of The Harvest

If you belong to God then you are a laborer. To work for God in the harvest fields is to share the wonderful Good News of the Gospel of Jesus Christ, with others. It really is not as frightening as it may seem, as people are so hungry for the Lord. He will help you to build your confidence as a laborer.

Here is a simple way to lead someone to Christ. All you have to do is ask the person if they would like to receive Jesus into their lives. If they say "yes", then pray a simple prayer of acceptance with them.

"Father God, I come to you in the Mighty name of Jesus. I realise that I need a Savior. Jesus, I welcome you into my heart make me brand-new and help me to live and honor God in my life. I repent of sin in my life and I now follow you. I am born-anew by the power of God that is working in me."

The first time someone prays with you, you will be beside yourself with joy and satisfaction. If they say "not right now" then smile, relax and encourage them to speak to the Lord from their hearts, whenever they desire.

Don't be afraid to bring people to Christ.

December 13

We love Him, because He first loved us.
1 John 4:19

He Loves You!

What would life be without the possibility of knowing and serving the Lord? I lived in that place for 19 years and knew that there was a greater life for me. My mom and dad took me to church on special occasions and that built in my heart an awesome reverence and fear of God.

The moment I heard the Good News preached, I responded to the Lord and I asked Jesus into my life. Only then, did I recognised that the Heavenly Father had been talking to my heart since the age of 13.

The Father has loved you all along. He has faithfully been knocking on the door of your heart using all kinds of opportunities to get you to respond to His love.

You will never be able to run away from Him no matter how hard you try. There will always be an individual, a song, a note, a friend – always something, reaching out with His love attached, just for you. You will know that the Father is involved because it is too well planned.

Because His love for us came first, is the reason that He will protect you. He is jealous and wants your affection and attention. Don't let anything take His place.

His love never runs out or dries up –
let Him enfold you with His love.

December 14

Then Jesus said to him, Begone, Satan! For it has been written, you shall worship the Lord your God and Him alone shall you serve. Then the devil departed from Him, and behold, angels came and ministered to Him.
Matthew 4:10-11

Bye, Bye, Satan!

You cannot fight Satan using your own strength and your own ability. People have tried that one, and come off second best.

Because Jesus already defeated him on the cross, all you have to do is enforce his defeat by; submitting to God and resisting the devil, speaking God's Word, walking in love, using the name of Jesus. These are just some of our powerful weapons.

Speaking the Word of God wisely is the one that Jesus used in the wilderness when Satan came to test Him. It was quite a battle but Jesus won it and Satan left Him for a season.

Maybe you think that the devil will only come once to test and tempt you, no – he leaves for a season. The only time he will never bother you, is when you go to heaven.

Simply, give him the treatment that God instructed you to give him, and he will run off in stark terror.

In Him you are stronger than you may think.

December 15

Therefore I always exercise and discipline myself [mortifying my body, deadening my carnal affections, bodily appetites, and worldly desires, endeavouring in all respects] to have a clear (unshaken, blameless) conscience, void of offence toward God and toward men.
Acts 24:16

Keep That Body Under

That's the kind of discipline it takes to get this little body sorted out and away from trouble. It has done its own thing for such a long time that it really does not like the discipline, but it is going to get it anyway.

The temptations that pass our sensory organs on a daily basis are getting worse as we press ahead in the 21st century. It's getting more difficult to do some things that were perfectly safe a number of years ago. The movies that had a 2-21 restriction now admit all ages. The advertising on television and in magazines is raunchy and leaves me blushing!

You need to be more diligent, keep yourself out of harm's way. Protect and guard your hearts and mind of invasive visuals that would steal your pure conscience and destroy the life that you have in God.

Build your life in God and you will never lack any good thing.

December 16

*So faith comes by hearing [what is told], and what is heard comes by
the preaching [of the message that came from the lips]
of Christ (the Messiah Himself).*
Romans 10:17

Develop Your Faith

Over the years I have heard faith described as many different things. One description was that when you were asked what faith you were you answered "Anglican".

Faith is not a denomination; it is not a type of Christianity or a part of your belief. Faith is what being a Christian is. It is what God calls us to live by; every moment of the day wherever we are, whatever we are doing.

How do you get your faith to grow? Certainly not only by being raised by lovely Christian parents, or singing Christians Hymns. Faith comes by hearing, and hearing the Word of God. Now, if your church preaches the Word of God, then you definitely will get enough food to help grow your faith.

Not all churches preach the Word of God. Some spend much time talking about politics; others criticise other denominations, then there are those who talk about poetry, flowers and rumbling skies and nobody can grow on that, and be strong enough to have victory over the devil.

"Desire the sincere milk of the Word that you may GROW thereby" - 1 Peter 1:2

Get into a church where you can feel your spirit growing. Where you
will be challenged to get your life in godly order and
where you can serve the Lord.

December 17

He did not weaken in faith when he considered the [utter] impotence of his own body, which was as good as dead because he was about a hundred years old, or [when he considered] the barrenness of Sarah's [deadened] womb.
Romans 4:19

Difficult Circumstances Make Us Stronger

Abraham's circumstances looked totally bleak. He was going to make Sarah pregnant and he was 100 years old! Now how would you have been under those circumstances?

Abraham used the circumstances for an even greater miracle for the Lord to perform in his life. He not only had to believe for a miracle in his life, but a mighty miracle in Sarah's life too as she was 90 years old and well passed the time of child-bearing.

This amazing miracle made Abraham a mighty man of God. It was the fight that made him strong and the victory that made him even stronger.

Don't run from an opportunity to believe God in the most impossible circumstances. Be like Abraham and take the promises of God and stand on them until they manifest in your life. As long as you are obedient and do your part of the covenant, God's promises belong to you.

Nothing moved Abraham and nothing should move you but the Word of God. Circumstances are subject to the Word of God.

December 18

Let your light so shine before men that they may see your moral excellence and your praiseworthy, noble, and good deeds and recognise and honor and praise and glorify your Father.
Matthew 5:16

Is Your Light Shining?

When I attended Sunday school, we used to sing "this little light of mine, I'm gonna let it shine!" I never knew until I was much older what that little song was all about. Even now, when I sing that song, tears run down my cheeks, as I remember the childlike faith with which I sang it. There is tremendous depth to the words.

It is in living and obeying the Word of God before others that causes your light to shine. When circumstances say:

- Be depressed, and you refuse – your light is shining;
- Fight and get into strife, and you refuse – your light is shining;
- You failed, and climb back up – your light is shining;

In every situation that you face it takes courage and determination for your light to shine. The best testimony is to the folks that know you best. They have seen your reactions and know how you normally behave, let your little light shine.

Just like a matchstick flame can be seen from a distance, so your light will drive back the darkness. And don't let anyone put it out.

Shine as brightly as you can.

December 19

For the rest, brethren, whatever is true, whatever is worthy of reverence and is honorable and seemly, whatever is just, whatever is pure, whatever is lovely and loveable, whatever is kind and winsome and gracious, if there is any virtue and excellence, if there is anything worthy of praise, think on and weigh and take account of these things [fix your minds on them].
Philippians 4:8

Good Thoughts

There are so many wonderful things that can occupy your mind instead of dwelling on the rotten things.

It will be a discipline for you to focus on the blessings that God has provided for you, and by developing this powerful tool you will change your outlook on life and create a grateful heart within you.

When I begin to meditate on the goodness of God in my life I am automatically blessed. The fact that He would call me into the ministry to share the Gospel to the world is a great honor.

His daily provision for my family is amazing. His immense love and mercy towards us passes my simple understanding. How great is my God. You have so much to thank God for. I know you may have had problems but that does not take away from His provision or love for you.

Count your blessing everyday.
Watch your heart and attitude change.

December 20

For [our earthly fathers] disciplined us for only a short period of time and chastised us as seemed proper and good to them; but He disciplines us for our certain good, that we may become sharers in His own holiness.
Hebrews 12:10

Hunger After Holiness

To be holy is to be like Jesus. It is the acknowledging of your place in Him and His role in your life. It is the degree of intimacy in your relationship with Him; it is knowing and fully trusting Him. Christians are called to live a life of holiness, a life "set apart" from the ways of the world.

Holiness does not mean isolation and loneliness. It is:
- Living close to God and not allowing the tarnish of the world to corrode your life
- A healthy heart before Him
- Experiencing His presence

Once you have chosen the things of God, it is the work of the Holy Spirit to make it possible for you to live a holy life before God. The Spirit will empower and work in you, cleansing, healing, leading and strengthening you against temptation and sin.

The more time you spend in the Father's Presence, the more your will takes on His Holy nature. You will get stronger and strong against sin and temptation until you become holy in your spirit, soul and body.

Live and embrace a consecrated life of holiness and purity.

December 21

The Lord is close to those who are of a broken heart and saves such as are crushed with sorrow for sin
Psalm 34:18

Healing The Broken-Hearted

Jesus will take your shattered life and make you whole. He will turn your hurtful experiences for your good.

It may not seem like anything positive can come out of your hurt, but when you surrender it to God and allow Him to heal you, you will marvel at what He will do for you.

You may be a victim of someone's hurtful actions whether they are deliberate or not – you are the one hurting. Many times devastation, rejection, fear and loneliness drive you closer or away from God. Don't lose sight of your future; God will empower you for even greater things. Jesus will heal your hurting heart and restore you beyond what you can see right now.

Trust God's plan and purpose for your life and don't let the devil steal your peace and victory. Stand against him and make this the very reason why you will continue to love the Lord and follow Him. God's love and loving-kindness will see you through and into a bright tomorrow.

There are occasions whereby we must set our faith and trust like flint. Let the power of God rise up inside of you and refuse to be moved. Stare evil right in the face and say, "I am not moving."

You belong to God; nothing can take that away from you.

December 22

So then, we may no longer be children, tossed [like ships] to and fro between chance gusts of teaching and wavering with every changing wind of doctrine, [the prey of] the cunning and cleverness of unscrupulous men, [gamblers engaged] in every shifting form of trickery in inventing errors to mislead.
Ephesians 4:14

Grow Up!

Children cannot keep their attention on one thing at a time. When they are busy doing a chore, something catches their eye and whoops... they are off!

I have had the wonderful pleasure of watching my two children grow up and, even though they are quite different in nature and character, they were both easily distracted.

You are not to be enticed or drawn away by some fad that comes to town in the disguise of Christianity. First, examine it according to the Word:

- Is it in agreement with the Word of God – not even a little bit off?
- How does your spirit feel? Ask yourself, "What do you think about this, do you witness with it?"
- Is your pastor supporting it? Ask him? He will give an account for you soul.

Once everything is in order, go ahead. If it is not, keep away. The Bible warns us of wolves that feast at our tables.

We are to grow out of the childhood stage of Christianity and become mature men and women of God.

December 23

And he replied: You must love the Lord your God with all your heart and with all your soul and with all your strength and with all your mind; and your neighbor as yourself.
Luke 10:27

Love The Lord, Love Your Neighbor

To summarise our Christian walk there are two major priorities that we need to do to walk in the wonderful blessed life that God has promised us.

Firstly, to love the Lord God with all of your heart, with all of your soul (your life) and with all of your mind and strength.

- Nothing should ever take His place in your life – put Him first.
- Worship Him only – get rid of any foreign gods.

Secondly, love your neighbor as yourself. Your neighbor can be anybody.

With the measure that you care and protect your own life, care for others – do not break down, destroy or abuse and misuse your neighbour.

Love yourself so that you can love others.

See the beauty of your own life: respect, honor and appreciate what God has put inside you.

Be determined to keep this treasure in mind. If you do, you will walk in everlasting favor with God.

December 24

And they were all filled (diffused throughout their souls) with the Holy Spirit and began to speak in other (different, foreign) languages (tongues), as the Spirit kept giving them clear and loud expression [in each tongue in appropriate words].
Acts 2:4

Power From On High

You have spiritual equipment to keep you in a place of strength and victory. You never need to feel that you cannot do what God has called you to do, just trust Him, step out on the water and walk.

Your prayer language is personal communication with the Heavenly Father shutting out distractions from your own understanding or the devil. You can talk and sing to Him and not feel at a loss for words.

Everyone in the upper room received a heavenly language, all of them. They were filled with power from on high. The Father wants all His children to have this special gift to equip them with power from on high.

Often I experience a stirring in my heart and I know it is time to pray in the Spirit, because my mind does not know what it is for, but my spirit does. I begin to pray in my Heavenly language and before too long I am released and at peace in my heart.

The other blessing is that when you pray in the Spirit you will build yourself up, in the Holy Spirit.

Pray in your known language and pray with your heavenly language, both are necessary and ordained of the Father.

December 25

In every prayer of mine I always make my entreaty and petition for you all with joy (delight).
Philippians 1:4

You Are In My Prayers!

My prayer for you is that you will grow in the Lord, daily become wiser, stronger and more like Jesus. Let His love under-gird you and carry you. Keep your eyes on Jesus. Do not be distracted by the troubles of the age, or by any subtleties of Satan. Keep him under your feet. Let Jesus rule and reign in your heart from this time forth and forever more, in Jesus' name.

Your vision is before you; the angels go ahead of you to prepare your way. Keep your feet on the right path and let your eyes look straight before you. The wonderful crowd of witnesses is backing and cheering you on. So do not be discouraged when you become a little weak, draw strength from your joy, which is in the Lord.

Be a witness, walk this amazing life and let others taste your salt. Shine with the love of Jesus. Bear healthy, stunning and wonderful fruit, allowing everyone to enjoy the Lord through you.

When the opportunity arises, tell someone about Jesus. You may be the only one that will ever have the opportunity to speak to them.

Lovingly pray the sinners' prayer with them.

December 26

To the pure [in heart and conscience] all things are pure, but to the defiled and corrupt and unbelieving nothing is pure; their very minds and consciences are defiled and polluted.
Titus 1:15

Pure In Heart

One thing I am constantly aware of is the fact that no matter how well I can hide something on the outside, the Lord sees my heart.

Harbouring bad feelings, bitterness, hurtful rumours and wrong intentions will make you sick. You have to continually keep your heart free from these pains if you want to be able to love others as God commanded.

I do my utmost to deal with these destructive emotions and feelings, the moment they try and grab hold of my attention. I "nip it in the bud"! It's far easier to pluck them out when they are budding rather than when they are in full bloom.

It's really up to the owner of the heart. If you choose to carry ill feelings around with you there is nothing anyone else can do about it, but pray, I encourage you to make the right choice.

As for me, I want my soul well and my heart strong. There is simply no place for futile feelings in my life.

When your heart is overloaded with bad thoughts and feelings, you cannot look through the eyes of love, and you will continually be judging others from your point of pain.

December 27

When Abram was ninety-nine years old, the Lord appeared to him and said, I am the Almighty God; walk and live habitually before Me and be perfect (blameless, wholehearted, complete). And I will make My covenant (solemn pledge) between Me and you and will multiply you exceedingly. And I will establish My covenant between Me and you and your descendants after you throughout their generations for an everlasting, solemn pledge, to be a God to you and to your posterity after you.
Genesis 17:1, 2, 7

Powerful Promise

God made this awesome promise to Abram when he was ripe with old age, and it all came to pass. How much more, through Jesus Christ, will the promises that God has made to us come to pass if we will honor and obey the Lord?

The Father will never let you down. He does not lie and He knows how to keep His end of the commitment. You and I are the ones that fail; we need to learn how to do our share.

When you stand on His Word and trust Him, and believe Him, you will be amazed at how faithful He is to see that His part of the promise comes to pass.

God did not only make His promise to Abram but to all his family after him. When you choose to live for God you will not only have the blessing of the Lord on your life, but that blessing is passed down to the generations that follow you.

December 28

And Jesus increased in wisdom (in broad and full understanding) and in stature and years, and in favor with God and man.
Luke 2:52

Jesus Grew

I used to think that Jesus was born with all the knowledge that He had. No, this Scripture explains that as He grew in years, He increased in wisdom and favor with God and man too.

So many people who express themselves as spiritual and mature in God are confused and receive no respect from anyone around them. Their lives are a mess and they do not often have a kind word to say about anyone.

Living close to God increases your level of wisdom and helps you make the right decisions. Knowing God makes you more pleasant to be around. Knowing God keeps your life in order.

Jesus was found in the temple daily listening to the teachers meditating and studying God's Word. He did not get more confused but more wise!

You may have a good idea, but after being in the Presence of the Lord your good idea will change to a God idea. It may be along the same lines but far more powerful and effective when He is finished with it.

Spending time in the Presence of God will cause your life to prosper and others to be drawn to you.

December 29

Do you not say, It is still four months until the harvest time comes? Look! I tell you, raise your eyes and observe the fields and see how they are already white for harvesting.
John 4:35

See, The Harvest Is Ripe!

We love to put things off into the future, "when the opportunity comes again, I will do it" or "when I have the time".

I do hope you have noticed how seldom that opportunity does come again. Stop procrastinating, get on with the things that need attention, do them now! You will make yourself miserable by not attending to them when the Spirit of God is dealing with you to do it.

Jesus says that the harvest is ripe now. Don't waste so much time waiting for things to come your way when actually they are waiting for you to go out and get them.

If someone asks you about the Lord, invite him or her to pray with you to receive Him into his or her heart, as you may never have the opportunity again. Do it then! You may have been thinking about someone and you know you need to give him or her a call – why are you waiting? The Lord will not waste your time.

Teach yourself to be prompt to obey the Lord. It could be urgent and you could certainly be saving someone from trouble.

Lift up your eyes and see the harvest is ripe. Do it now.

December 30

For in Him we live and move and have our being.
Acts 17:28

Living And Moving In Him

Many years ago I decided that I would never make a major decision, unless I knew deep down in my heart that it was the will of the Lord for me.

Before you make a decision – be careful, especially if the offer looks "rosy". You may be able to get more money, a house, a car and a promotion. If it is not the plan of God, you could be working for a company that is going out of business in just a few months' time. I have seen it happen over and over again.

Your priority is always to check it out deep down in your heart and not with your flesh. Your flesh always wants to be comfortable and have the easy way out. An excellent question to ask yourself is this: "What did God tell me to do, and am I doing it?"

When your flesh is the measure you will always land up in trouble – confused and desperate. If it is direction from the Lord the result will be a blessing and much fruit will be evident in your life for all to see.

I have been offered wonderful opportunities that my flesh would do anything to have. It's not worth it. Keep your life on track with God, as you will be amazed where His heart will lead you.

In Him you live, in Him you move – in Him you have your being.

December 31

Do not let yourself be overcome by evil, but overcome (master) evil with good.
Romans 12:21

Overcome Evil With Good

In Christ you are more than able to overcome any evil that comes against you. You may be a little nervous or afraid but the truth is, "you are victorious in Christ".

There are going to be mountains to climb and valleys to go through. Things are not going to drop into your hands without the effort.

What happens when things do not seem to go your way? What if the road gets very rough? Do you quit the journey? Do you blame God and get discouraged, depressed? I hope not!

Clearly we are told that when evil or opposition comes our way, if we dish out good instead of revenge, the evil is defeated.

The victory we have is not won by fighting the same fight that the devil uses. We have far stronger tactics and much greater weapons. Love overcomes hatred, kindness destroys nastiness and the peace in our lives makes unrest run away in terror. Your fight must be fought using Heaven's wisdom.

There is no way that you can understand this type of fight unless you trust the Lord. But I guarantee that you will always have the upper hand.

Salvation Prayer

Romans 10:9-13
That if you confess with your mouth the Lord Jesus and believe in your heart that God has raised Him from the dead, you will be saved. For with the heart one believes to righteousness, and with the mouth confession is made to salvation. For whoever calls upon the name of the Lord shall be saved.

Ask Jesus Into Your Life

While reading this book you may have felt the Lord speaking to your heart. If you have not yet invited Him in as you Lord and Saviour, then you can do that right now. With the sincerity of your heart pray this simple prayer:

Heavenly Father, I thank you for sending your son Jesus Christ to die on the cross and shed His blood for my salvation. I acknowledge that I am a sinner and need a Saviour, I repent of my sin and ask you Lord, to please forgive me.

Jesus, I believe that You are the Son of God and that You rose again from the dead on the third day. Come into my life and make me a brand new creature, wash me in Your blood so that I may be a child of the living God. I renounce the devil and all his works - hell has no place in my life and no power over me in Jesus name. Thank you Lord for saving me.

If you have prayed this prayer please connect with me and join me on social media.

@lyndiemccauley

For Women Only
by
Lyndie McCauley

I am thrilled to bring this series to you...
'**For Women Only**'!

Many secrets are revealed through these powerful teachings and you will be encouraged and stirred to RISE UP, and become an Uncommon Woman in all areas of your life!

Women Of Excellence
Am I Hot Or What?
Woman Be Strong
Men Of Excellence - (leave this one where is can be found!)

BONUS CD - Dr. Mike Murdock shares some deep secrets of 'The Uncommon Woman'.

Available from all good Christian Bookstores nationwide. For all other info, or to purchase please email: info@spiritledpublishing.co.za.

Product of Lyndie McCauley Ministries.
www.lyndiemccauleyministries.org

Made in the USA
Charleston, SC
14 February 2015